Natives and Strangers

NATIVES
AND STRANGERS

Blacks, Indians,
and Immigrants in America

SECOND EDITION

LEONARD DINNERSTEIN
University of Arizona

ROGER L. NICHOLS
University of Arizona

DAVID M. REIMERS
New York University

New York   Oxford
OXFORD UNIVERSITY PRESS
1990

Oxford University Press

Oxford   New York   Toronto
Delhi   Bombay   Calcutta   Madras   Karachi
Petaling Jaya   Singapore   Hong Kong   Tokyo
Nairobi   Dar es Salaam   Cape Town
Melbourne   Auckland

and associated companies in
Berlin   Ibadan

Copyright © 1979, 1990 by Oxford University Press, Inc.

Published by Oxford University Press, Inc.,
200 Madison Avenue, New York, New York 10016

Oxford is a registered trademark of Oxford University Press

Library of Congress Cataloging-in-Publication Data
Dinnerstein, Leonard.
Natives and strangers : Blacks, Indians, and Immigrants in America
Leonard Dinnerstein, Roger L. Nichols, David M. Reimers.—2nd ed.
p.   cm.   Bibliography: p.   Includes index.   ISBN 0-19-505722-8
1. Minorities—United States—History.
2. United States—Economic conditions.
3. United States—Social conditions.
I. Nichols, Roger L.
II. Reimers, David M.   III. Title.
E184.A1D49   1990   973′.04—dc 19   89-2857   CIP

4 6 8 9 7 5 3
Printed in the United States of America

To
Myra Dinnerstein
Marilyn Nichols
Cordelia Reimers

Preface

FOR GENERATIONS THE HISTORY of the United States has been celebrated as the triumph of free men, free political institutions, and free enterprise. During that time the nation's virtues were attributed chiefly to Anglo-Saxon "genius" and "enterprise." Scores of American histories emphasized these themes and thus encouraged Americans to accept such views as sacrosanct—almost, in fact, as if they had been delivered from on high to George Washington at Mount Vernon. This interpretation has been cogently challenged by scholars of ethnic and industrial America. Certainly the English colonists set the tone for the development of the United States, but to minimize the impact of other groups leads to a myopic vision of the past. America evolved from a colonial society into a modern industrial-urban nation not only because of its Anglo-Saxon enclaves but also because people of both sexes and differing backgrounds contributed ideas, skills, and especially labor to the building of the nation.

Our purpose in writing this book has been to emphasize—in a way that has not been done previously—the role of blacks, Indians, and immigrant minorities in the transformation of a colonial society into a behemoth of the 1990s. One could also describe the contributions of various ethnic groups to American art, music, and literature, or the roles ethnic groups played in American political history. But these, as well as other themes in American history, would require separate books. Though our book does not ignore culture and politics, it concentrates on economic growth and the development of social attitudes and how ethnic minorities were affected by and effected those developments.

Although an abundant supply of menial labor and natural resources, along with an inventive and entrepreneurial spirit, laid the foundations for success, until fairly recently most standard histories of the United States emphasized geographical advantages and technological and commercial innovations in explaining American progress. Menial immigrant laborers, many of whom aspired to a better life and whose descendants frequently achieved a more elevated status, have received far less attention. So, too, have Indians and blacks, whose place in modern American society is discussed somewhat differently here than in other narratives. Efforts to rectify that oversight resulted in a plethora of works about virtually all the groups that had hitherto received little scholarly attention.

Historians, like other people, are often attracted by the successful, unusual, dramatic, and glamorous aspects of the past. The so-called masses and deprived groups possess few of those attributes and hence have received little attention. Since the 1960s, however, their plight has been of increasing concern to American historians, and much of the new social history emphasizes how millions of nameless, faceless peoples of yesteryear adjusted to their lot, contributed to the economy, and strove to gain acceptance and equal treatment. This book is intended to deepen and enrich the current exploration of various aspects of social and minority group history.

The new social history focuses on how well ordinary people adapted to their surroundings, but ethnic exploitation, strife, and brutality cannot be ignored. Minorities were desired for their labor, and old-stock Americans, as well as peoples who themselves had been victimized, were not loath to exploit and abuse them. Yet we have also tried to describe the impact America had on minority cultures and how those who were thought to be of lesser value dealt with their personal experiences. Obviously in a book of this size we have not been able to emphasize all groups to the extent that we would have liked. We have discussed some peoples not only because of their importance but also because their experiences illustrate common themes.

The dates we use in the chapter headings are merely rough approximations and not rigid guidelines. In a book of this nature many themes overlap chronological barriers, and in several chapters ideas and movements of other periods seemed to fit best in a given narrative context. Hence the dates we indicate in the chapter headings should be interpreted loosely.

We have used the expression "ethnic group" to mean a people with a shared or common culture and/or a sense of identity based on religion, race, or nationality. Hence although Jews, blacks, and Italian Americans are alike in certain respects, each possesses a distinctive background. We have tried to be specific in identifying those peoples we are discussing.

As in the first edition of this book, our survey has attempted to integrate the experience of racial, religious, and national minorities and to explain how their histories intertwined with the emergence of modern America. We have focused on those aspects of ethnic groups that illuminate major themes or trends in the growth of the United States in order to inform college students about an important but relatively neglected dimension of the American past.

For this second edition we set ourselves several goals. One was to incorporate some of the findings of the scholarship published in the 1980s. The second was to bring the story of ethnic groups in the United States up to date. A third was to put more emphasis on what each group added to the society and how it strove to retain its cultural identity.

Immigration and minority group experiences have dominated many of the news stories of the past decade. Indian tribes long thought to have been extinct—like the Narragansett of Rhode Island and the Grand Traverse Ottawa and Chippewa of Michigan—have recently been acknowledged to have been reconstituted, and one, the Passamaquoddy, filed suit claiming 60 percent of the land in the state of Maine. The Reverend Jesse Jackson has emerged as a major political figure in the nation, and immigrants (mostly Latin Americans and Asians) have once again become a topic for serious national consideration. In fact, approximately six million newcomers (not including undocumented aliens), the largest number since the first decade of the century, arrived in the United States in the 1980s. The *New York Times* noted the upsurge in immigration in August 1988, pointing out that "for the first time since the 1920s, the tide of immigration is at flood stage in New York City, with millions of Asian, Carribbean, and European newcomers in search of a better life." As a result of these events, as well as the continued success of our first edition, a revised version of our text seemed particularly timely.

All three of us participated in the writing and editing of each chapter, and the book is a result of our joint efforts. Original responsibility in the first edition for the preparation of material on blacks and contemporary events was assumed by David M. Reimers; on Indians and American society to the 1840s, Roger L. Nichols; and on European, Latin American, and Asian immigrants, Leonard Dinnerstein. David Reimers assumed the major task of rewriting the last two chapters for this second edition, while Roger Nichols rewrote all sections on Indians.

Tucson, Ariz.   L. D., R. L. N.
New York   D. M. R.
January 1989

Acknowledgments

A NUMBER OF PEOPLE helped with revisions for this edition. Mary Sue Passe typed and Donna Watson and Karen Mostyn photocopied endless changes. Bibliographical suggestions for updating were made by Karen Anderson, John Campbell, Colette Hyman, and Jack Marietta, while Ruth Dickstein eliminated at least a week's work when she provided us with a bibliography on ethnic women. The staff at Oxford University Press has always proved helpful, and our editor, Nancy Lane, is invariably there when we need her.

Contents

Natives and Strangers

1

Colonial Foundations
(1600–1780s)

EUROPEAN DISCOVERY OF THE NEW WORLD at the end of the fifteenth century launched powerful economic and social currents that first created and then shaped the United States. Within a few generations of the early explorations knowledgeable Europeans realized the potential of North and South America. Moreover, the continents of the Western Hemisphere fit nicely into the evolving mercantilist economic theory of that day. According to this view each government tried to organize and regulate its national economic activities to strengthen itself. Thus during the sixteenth and seventeenth centuries Spain, Portugal, France, Sweden, Russia, the Netherlands, and Great Britain established trading posts and colonies around the world. Those that flourished provided riches such as gold, silver, and precious gems, which the rapidly growing national governments needed to pay their debts. If no precious metals could be extracted from a colony, the mother country gained profits from selling manufactured goods there while getting inexpensive raw materials in exchange. In some cases colonists received bonuses for producing items needed by the mother country so that it did not have to spend its wealth buying such things from foreign competitors.

COMING OF THE ENGLISH

Among the major powers Britain proved most successful in North America and eventually gained control over most of the continent. Unlike the Spanish colonies in South and Central America, which quickly yielded immense treasure in gold and silver as well as raw materials needed in Europe, the British North American colonies failed to bring instant wealth. Instead they developed agricultural and commercial enterprises that often rivaled, instead of supplementing, economic activities in the mother country. Lacking resources that could be exploited rapidly for large profit, the English colonies needed increasing numbers of people to serve as a market for English goods as well as to provide laborers for their own agricultural, chiefly rural societies. Their attempts to enslave large numbers of Indians, as the Spanish had done elsewhere, failed and they had to look elsewhere for workers. Within only twelve years of the first successful Virginia settlement in 1607 the colonists began importing blacks to increase their labor force, but at first this effort also proved inadequate and they called for continuing numbers of immigrants—at first from Great Britain, but later from the rest of Europe as well.

When the first Virginia colonists stepped ashore from the decks of the *Susan Constant*, the *Godspeed*, and the *Discovery* in 1607 they not only began the task of building a colony that was supposed to strengthen England in its international competition with its European neighbors; they and the settlers who followed also brought ideas and customs that laid the foundations for continuing ethnic practices in American society.

First, they brought along a sense of English racial and cultural superiority. Many would have agreed with the cleric who in 1558 told his flock "God is English." They considered Protestantism the true expression of Christian faith, and at least in the Massachusetts Bay Colony, believed that only the Puritans practiced it appropriately. Whether in New England or farther to the south the colonists felt that in the new country they could make money—get ahead—and thereby improve their personal economic and social status. From the beginnings of settlement this drive for economic gains motivated most Englishmen in the New World. The attitudes associated with commercial capitalism and economic expansion therefore became one of the dominant forces in early American development.

The English, as did other peoples, tended to regard those who were different as inferior. Toward the native American Indians they held two contradictory views. On the one hand Englishmen hoped to meet friendly tribesmen who would be eager to help, guide, and trade with them. At the same time they feared these "savage and backward" people. Black Africans, because of their color and customs, were both feared and scorned. Toward Europeans from the continent, whose ways varied only slightly from their own, Englishmen felt a certain kinship, but they regarded their own practices as superior. In the New World these attitudes would prevail and leave their own mark on the development of American society.

The modernization process, which gradually transformed a few isolated settlements along the Atlantic coast into the United States, included several developments initiated during the seventeenth and eighteenth centuries. Transplanting English culture to North America occurred first. It took several generations, and its speed varied widely depending on time, place, and source of immigration. In colonies such as New York and Pennsylvania large numbers of non-English people originally established a society that for a time was more European than English, but even the most cosmopolitan towns and regions bore distinctive English markings in language, laws, social customs, and economic patterns.

INDIANS AND ANGLO-AMERICANS

When the English landed in North America, they found much of the coastal region heavily populated. Estimates of Indian population in the United States vary, but many scholars now

accept the figure of four million to eight million people prior
to colonization. Sharing elements of Eastern Woodland and
Southeast cultures, the tribes had begun to emerge from their
New Stone Age development, as evidenced by their use of copper for jewelry. Otherwise they still fashioned their tools, weapons, and household utensils from wood, reed, clay, stone, or
bone. They had no domesticated animals except dogs, no wheeled
vehicles, no written languages, but they lived in well laid out
villages of comfortable wigwams. Skilled in farming, gathering, hunting, and fishing, they had mastered their environment, their technology permitting them to live in modest comfort.

The degree of social organization within individual tribes
varied widely from the tightly structured Natchez and Iroquois
to much smaller and less firmly connected groups. Nevertheless,
all were organized by family relationships into clans or kinship
bands. Several clans formed a tribe—often mistakenly called a
nation by the English. In some areas several tribes might be part
of still larger confederacies. In New York the five nations of the
Iroquois Confederacy faced the Dutch, French, and English with
a well-organized political and military force, and in Virginia a
group of thirty tribes was directed by Powhatan. By 1607, when
the English arrived, the Virginia Indians had encountered Europeans for decades. Thus Powhatan considered the newcomers as
just one more element in his already complex relationships with
the nearby Indian groups. By manipulating the English, he
hoped to strengthen his power over the other tribes in his confederacy. After a few months of observation the Virginia tribal
leader clearly felt little awe of the Europeans or most of their
technology, and his people made few basic changes in their lives
because of the whites. However, the early experiences had a
more profound impact on the colonists. Once the English realized that the nearby tribes had neither gold and silver nor interest in an extensive trade, their early dreams of wealth faded.
This meant that the Virginia authorities had to change their
goals. What was to have been a trading post now became an

Indian Tribes, 1492

agricultural settlement, based on the cultivation of tobacco, needing large amounts of land, which could be obtained only from the Indians. Under these circumstances the tribal people held the upper hand, at least temporarily, but it was dangerous to have what the whites wanted. As would-be trading partners the Indians were necessary, even valuable to the English, but once farming became the economic base for the colony the Indians became an obstacle, and repeated clashes occurred.

After five years of sporadic fighting the Indians accepted a peace settlement in 1614. The resulting calm lasted only a few years: as the Virginia Company sent hundreds of new colonists to America, pressures for more land increased. At Powhatan's death in 1619 his successor and brother, Opechancanough, assumed leadership. Three years later he directed an all-out war against the colonists. His 1622 attack caught the Virginians totally unprepared and nearly a third of the whites died in the fighting. The English retaliated with crushing force and for ten years they burned villages, killed people, and seized good cropland. Having failed to annihilate the English in 1622, the Indians lost what little chance they had to destroy the colony or even to halt its further growth. Although the warriors of the Powhatan Confederacy fought a second war in 1644, this too failed and the Virginians forced the survivors west beyond the frontier.

Events in New England differed for a time. A series of European diseases carried by early settlers swept through the coastal tribes in 1616–17, killing thousands and causing the survivors to flee. As a result, when the Pilgrims landed in eastern Massachusetts in 1620 cleared fields stood unused, villages lay in ruins, and few people remained nearby to contest English settlement. In fact individual Indians such as Squanto and Samoset helped the struggling Europeans for a time. Despite this favorable start, within a decade the situation changed drastically as growing competition with Dutch traders and rapidly increasing numbers of pioneer farmers strained relations between the tribes and the English. The whites' efforts to dominate the fertile Connecticut Valley farther west led to intrigue and war. Efforts by the resident Pequots to block Puritan expansion failed and a bitter war in 1637 nearly destroyed the tribe. One group of Pequots, led by Chief Uncas, joined the whites against their relatives, and with additional help from the Narragansetts the New Englanders won. They sold some of the survivors into slavery, scattered the rest among other nearby tribes, and then began moving into Pequot territory.

Even those Indians who chose accommodation and negotiation rather than retreat or war fared badly. The Puritans segregated individuals who became Christians into the so-called Praying Towns and remained suspicious of Native Americans living there. During Metacom's War (also called King Philip's War), in the mid-1670s, these peaceful Christian converts barely survived efforts to destroy them as a subversive and dangerous element within the colonies. The war signaled the Indian realization that conciliation and negotiation with the whites had failed; for the Puritans this desperate struggle proved the need to remove or destroy the tribesmen whenever they thwarted English economic development or territorial expansion.

The patterns of events in Virginia and New England occurred elsewhere, but other patterns emerged as well. For example, in South Carolina within a single generation the Indians provided a source of both wealth and power through furs and slaves. When the English arrived in the 1670s they found the coastal tribes caught up in bitter warfare. The whites capitalized on these conflicts and within a few years they had been drawn into an ever-widening circle of trade and warfare, which brought destruction to the nearby tribes.

Thousands of deerskins provided the major staple for trade between Indians and whites for years. In addition, however, Carolina leaders aggressively sought Indian slaves by encouraging the coastal tribes to make war on their enemies. By rewarding their tribal allies with guns and other goods in exchange for Indian prisoners the Charleston traders stimulated intertribal warfare and hurried the depopulation process in the coastal region. Wars of virtual extermination against the Westo (1680–83), Savannah (1707–08), Tuscarora (1712–13), and Yamasee (1715–16) provided thousands of slaves. Not only did these wars open vast regions for settlement and trade; they strengthened the English while weakening the nearby tribes. These conflicts resulted in large part from the almost total adaptation of the Carolina tribes to the English trading system. The Indians' eagerness to acquire trade goods sometimes blinded them to the results of their competition with the whites. At the same time, some tribes gloried in their newly acquired firearms and the destruction they could heap on their enemies.

The bitter warfare in Carolina produced an active slave trade as hundreds of captives arrived in Charleston annually as potential slaves. By 1708 the colony included 1,400 Indian and 2,900 black slaves. The authorities shipped thousands more Indian captives to the West Indies and the port cities in other North American colonies. For example, as late as 1730 Kingston, Rhode Island, included 223 Indian slaves in its modest population. Despite the continued enslavement of tribal people, they proved dangerous prizes as many sought to escape or otherwise cause trouble for their owners. Within a couple of decades after the trade began, major objections arose to this labor supply. Citing the Indians' "conspiracys, insurrections, rapes, thefts, and other execrable crimes," in 1715 several New England colonies prohibited the importation of any more such slaves. These events and the continuing destruction of the tribes by European epidemic diseases ended most efforts to enslave Indians in eastern North America.

Throughout the first century of English–Indian contact the tribal situation shifted drastically. In 1607 the Indians were politically independent, economically self-sufficient, and equal or even superior to the whites in terms of using the natural environment. However, continuing relations with the English brought a downward spiral of major population loss, the erosion of tribal autonomy, and economic collapse, which left the tribes heavily dependent on the invading whites. At the same time, the English and the Indians developed ideas about each other that led to continuing trouble. The whites considered the tribal people to be hostile, untrustworthy, and dangerous. Meanwhile, the tribesmen came to view the Europeans as dangerous and insatiable invaders who killed their people and stole their land. True, the whites' trade goods made their lives easier, but the expanding English settlements brought frequent land surrenders and increasing cultural breakdown among the Indians. In addition, sporadic raids by pioneers and warriors and the four colonial wars between Britain and France all created suspicion and hatred between the races. The toast "Civilization or death to all American savages," given during a campaign against the Iroquois, illustrates these feelings.

ATTRACTING SETTLERS

Since attempts to enslave the tribesmen were only partially successful, English colonial promoters soon realized that other sources of labor were required. To meet growing demands for laborers, colonial officials needed to get whites over to the colonies. The Virginia Company, and later the British government, promised free land to colonists who brought other settlers to the New World. To attract those unable to pay their own way across the Atlantic the Company offered to pay the cost of passage. Thus in exchange for their labor for a period of years, often four to seven, poor whites secured passage to America. At the end of their service these indentured servants, as they were called, sometimes were given land. Such promises lured many lower-class Englishmen who sought to become independent landowners in the New World. During the seventeenth and eighteenth centuries the opportunities in English colonial societies encouraged people to leave Europe and settle in America. The need for labor was constant; skilled and unskilled alike usually were welcomed. At the fringes of settlement newcomers would help counter the potential Indian menace, for as the population increased in newly settled communities, attacks from Indian warriors diminished. A third need for population growth arose out of the evolving colonial economy: immigrants helped expand the market for farmers and businessmen. At the same time the British government viewed prosperous colonies as national assets, and therefore encouraged colonial economic development. The Crown also believed that England was overpopulated and that emigration would benefit the mother country.

Indentured servitude became the prime way of bringing poor people from the Old World to the New. It allowed those indigents who wished to seek opportunities in America to do so, while at the same time providing additional workers to the labor-short colonies. The policy proved beneficial to the immigrants in the long run, but during the first few years the laborers' lot was little better than that of slaves. Planters drove them hard, and indentured servants were supervised by overseers who, as one historian wrote, "were not apt to be men notable for Christian charity." An observer recalled, "I have seen an Overseer beat a Servant with a cane about the head, till the blood has flowed, for a fault that is not worth the speaking of; and yet he must have patience, or worse will follow." There are also tales of a Virginia master who had his servant's ears nailed to a pillory and left him standing there for four days and of a Massachusetts master who punished a servant by "hanging him by the heels as butchers do beasts for the slaughter." American colonists, one scholar tells us, succeeded

> in treating their indentured servants as private property. They bought and sold them, sued each other for possession of them, and set up engines of law for the protection of their rights in them. Though on occasion the state took a servant away from a cruel master without providing due compensation, this was certainly avoided as often as possible, and many cruel masters, though losing their servants, received the sum procured by selling them elsewhere. To be sure, the servant had rights, but while he was in servitude these rarely conflicted with the conception of him as property.

If working and living conditions were harsh, so too were the general health conditions of early America, and many servants did not survive their terms. In spite of these hardships, inden- tured servants willingly provided the main source of labor for the Southern colonies in the seventeenth century. Economic op- portunities and possibilities for social advancement for these people were practically nonexistent in England, whereas in the colonies, once the period of servitude had ended, one's origin presented no insurmountable stigma. There was a real chance for betterment in the New World. It has been estimated that at least half, and perhaps two thirds, of all the white laborers in the colonies before the American Revolution arrived there as in- dentured servants.

In addition to the volunteer white labor force, the English occasionally kidnaped laborers and sent them to America. They also used the colonies as a dumping ground for convicts, and between 1718 and 1775 the courts banished at least 50,000 peo- ple to the colonies. Clearly England believed that this practice was a good way to get rid of undesirable prisoners. Some of the colonists thought otherwise. In 1751 the *Virginia Gazette* com- plained that these people were "Serpents" and declared, "In what can Britain show a more Sovereign contempt for us than by emptying their jails into our settlements?" Several colonies passed laws attempting to halt the shipment of convicts to Amer- ica, but England disallowed them. Not all colonists opposed the incoming convicts; some planters welcomed persons of "Evil fame" as cheap labor.

DEVELOPMENT OF SLAVERY AND RACISM

The desire for cheap labor and economic gain would dominate American society for centuries. Almost every major movement or recruitment of peoples from outside the colonies or the United States would be rationalized on the grounds of adding needed laborers, who would work at wages so low that extraordinary profits could be achieved. During the colonial era changes in

British government policies dictated the need for even cheaper labor, and this in turn resulted in the importation of African slaves on a grand scale.

Before the 1650s Virginia tobacco growers had been selling their produce to the mother country as well as to other nations. But in 1650 and 1651 the British government passed the first of the Navigation Acts, which regulated trade within the empire. Seeking to strengthen the English economy and to weaken competing Dutch shippers, the laws limited colonial exports to English ships. The acts also restricted the sale of colonial tobacco to Britain, Holland, and other parts of Europe, and ultimately led to lower tobacco prices. The Dutch had often purchased inferior grades of colonial tobacco, but after the Navigation Acts not only were they eliminated from the trade but the British demanded only the first-quality leaves. During the 1650s and early 1660s overproduction also contributed to lower prices and reduced profits. Moreover, the fixed terms of English indentured servants necessitated a continual turnover in workers and a period of time to train new ones. This in itself would not have been a major burden, but upon the restoration of the monarchy in England in 1660 Charles II and his ministers concluded that the country was no longer overpopulated and it would be unwise to continue to allow members of the work force to leave. A policy to discourage emigration was inaugurated.

These factors—the Navigation Acts, lower tobacco prices, and difficulties in obtaining additional indentured servants from England—combined to make the colonists, especially the owners of large Southern plantations, favor importation of African workers. In 1662 the British government granted a monopoly in the slave trade to the Royal African Slave Company, thus initiating a major new policy of bringing in blacks to help lower the costs of producing tobacco, rice, indigo, and other colonial staple crops. Slaves would not terminate their servitude, as did indentured servants; they would increase and multiply, thereby guaranteeing a permanent work force, and their purchase price and maintenance costs would detract only minutely from the ultimate wealth they would contribute to their masters. With such obvious economic advantages, moral concerns, if any, were quickly submerged. Entrepreneurs, in the sixteenth century or later, have rarely allowed moral scruples to affect the way they utilize people for economic profit. More often than not some heretofore unfamiliar minority group has appeared on the scene to provide the needed brawn. As a nation, the United States has always been fortunate that at the time of its greatest needs conditions in other countries, or other sections of the nation, have been conducive to migration.

According to a number of scholars, some of the first Africans who were brought to Virginia in 1619 were treated not as slaves but as indentured servants. The colony had not grown sufficiently to envision the need for many blacks, and while white Englishmen were still coming large numbers of black Africans were not sought. Although well entrenched in South America and the West Indies, the practice of slavery was not common in the British colonies of North America in the 1620s and 1630s but evolved as the decades passed. Neither Virginia nor Maryland, the original Southern colonies, formally recognized slavery until the 1660s. Prior to the enactment of Virginia's first slave codes in that decade the status of blacks had not been consistent, although court documents and other written records indicate that they stood apart from white servants. Thus social and economic practice and a growing number of legal restrictions preceded the first slave codes.

The Southern governments expanded their codes throughout the remainder of the colonial period by placing a tight system of control over black slaves. The colonists decided that conversion to Christianity did not bring freedom, and they made the status of the child follow that of the mother—a decision prompted by the fact that most interracial sexual unions were of white males and black females. In the eighteenth century new laws made the manumission of slaves by individual owners more diffi-

The cargo of a slave ship. The slave deck of the *Wildfire* brought into Key West in 1860. From *Harper's Weekly*, 1860. (*Library of Congress*)

cult. African slaves also lost their right to hold property and to testify in court and were increasingly considered property, not persons.

As white men enslaved blacks, they also regarded them with suspicion, fear, and contempt. We know little of how blacks viewed whites during the colonial period, but we have much evidence of the growing racism among whites. Even before the European explorations of Africa, Europeans, especially the English, believed that black connoted evil, and white, purity. The *Oxford English Dictionary* indicated that before the sixteenth century black meant "soil, dirty, foul . . . atrocious, horrible, wicked." To the first Europeans who explored Africa and encountered blacks the difference of color made a profound impression, and, in the long run, skin color defined the relationships between blacks and whites.

Europeans also noted other differences. Africans were not Christians, and whites gradually began to consider blacks, as they considered Indians, savage and uncivilized. They started describing Africans as beasts and were fascinated by the resemblance they saw between them and the chimpanzees discovered in the African explorations. White men also viewed blacks as lustful, sexual beings. These ideas eventually led to the ethnocentric conclusion that their darker pigmentation symbolized the innate inferiority of blacks.

At first slavery grew slowly. In 1650 blacks comprised less than 5 percent of England's North American colonies, and by 1671 Virginia counted only 2,000 slaves in a population of 40,000. During the eighteenth century the number of slaves increased rapidly and on the eve of the American Revolution they constituted 22 percent of the colonial population. Most of these slaves lived in the Southern colonies, particularly Maryland, Virginia, and South Carolina, where in 1770 they accounted for 40 percent of the total population. Virginia alone had 188,000 slaves, or about half of the slave population of the United States. South Carolina also had large numbers of slaves, especially in the counties surrounding Charleston. Blacks outnumbered whites by two or three to one in some regions, and throughout the eighteenth century the black population outnumbered the white in South Carolina. This was also true of other areas in the tidewater regions of the Chesapeake Bay colonies.

Colonial slaves labored in nearly all occupations. Blacks had been imported for the cultivation of rice, indigo, sugar, and tobacco, but the slaves were not simply field hands. They worked as carpenters, coopers, tailors, cooks, blacksmiths, personal servants—indeed they labored in most of the South's occupations. For those few who lived in the towns such as Williamsburg,

Charleston, and Baltimore, a variety of skilled trades might be learned. In Charleston, for example, urban craftsmen sometimes trained slave apprentices, who then could be sold to the plantations for higher prices than common laborers. In the same city some blacks were fishermen, a skill they may have brought with them from Africa.

Colonial slavery was harsh. This is hardly surprising, for life could be cruel for the white servant or offender as well as the enslaved black in colonial America. Branding and public whipping were common punishments for violators of the law, and for the slave punishments were even more severe. One observer noted of an especially brutal planter in the 1730s, "Colonel Lynch cut off the legs of a poor negro, and he kills several of them every year by his barbarities." Colonial documents record cases of maiming of slaves through castration, nose-slitting, and the chopping off of hands and ears. Such brutalities became less common in the eighteenth century, but rebellious slaves might expect the worst. Slaves also worked long and hard and might have their families destroyed by sales. During periods of great tension, particularly when fears of slave insurrections were high, the laws and their execution could be especially fierce.

If physical labor extracted from slaves was harsh and if the codes regulated blacks to an inferior status, the attempt to impose English culture on the Africans was also part of the story of slavery. Historians know little about how much African culture slaves retained in colonial America, but judging from the more abundant sources of the nineteenth century and scattered earlier records, blacks managed to hang on to many of their ways and blend their heritage with that of the English to form an Afro-American culture. For example, part of the "seasoning" process involved teaching English to the slaves; most learned the language but many flavored the new tongue with African words. In the Sea Islands along the South Carolina coast, the blend produced Gullah speech, which still survives. The slaves also withstood many of the early efforts to Christianize them, for they brought with them complex religious ideas that resisted destruction. Eventually, especially after the Great Awakening of the 1740s, Christianity made inroads on African religions and customs concerning life, death, and belief, but by the time of the Civil War black religion was a blend of African religions and white Christianity, not a carbon copy of the latter.

White men were fearful of the newly arrived Africans, who seemed to resist slavery more than those who had been born in the United States. One South Carolina planter remarked, "The Negroes that most commonly rebel, are those brought from Guinea, and who have been inured to War and hardship all their lives; few born here, or in the other Provinces, have been guilty of these vile Practices." Planters were eager to exploit black labor, but too many blacks in their area, possibly out of their direct control, posed a threat. Runaway and rebellious blacks were not only a labor loss but a threat to white supremacy.

The most menacing form of resistance was open rebellion and some blacks did foment rebellions. Insurrections were not common in the American South, but a number did occur during the colonial era. Among the most famous was the Stono Rebellion in South Carolina. This uprising in 1739 took the lives of approximately twenty-five whites and twenty-five blacks, damaged property, and frightened the colony. Whites took up arms to crush the revolt; afterward they attempted to bring the slaves under a tighter rein. Yet even more controls and greater imposition of English culture on blacks were no guarantees of security. Some of the most assimilated slaves, the artisans, led one of the most famous rebellions in Virginia in 1800.

Other slaves disrupted the system by refusing to work hard, breaking tools, stealing, feigning illness, or running away. But the chance of successfully escaping was slight, and most blacks had to cope with bondage as best they could. If their master was well off, or kinder than most, there would be leisure time, better food, clothing, and housing, and concern for their welfare. They also found comfort in their religion, music, and, above all, their families. Slave families had no legal standing but nonetheless provided the close human relationships necessary for survival.

The Northern colonies also developed slave societies, but slavery was not important to the economy of the North. Forty percent of the Southern population consisted of black slaves compared to only 5 percent in the North. About 10 percent of Rhode Island's mid-eighteenth-century residents, and a slightly higher proportion of New York's inhabitants, were slaves. Northern regulations, and slavery generally, were less harsh than in the South. In New England slaves were considered property but were given more protection as persons than were Southern slaves. As property they resembled Southern slaves—they could be bought, sold, and inherited and they faced restrictions, such as curfews. Still, as persons they were entitled to a jury trial, could testify against whites in some cases, and were able to acquire property. In the North, New York and New Jersey were most oppressive. The slave codes there resembled those in the South. New Yorkers also shared the fear of rebellion, especially after an uprising in 1712, and like Southern whites, they retaliated with severe repression. Whether in the North or South, however, slavery provided cheap labor and often significant profits for the growing colonial society.

Except in South Carolina, where the whites remained a small minority among large numbers of Indians, and blacks, colonial Americans seem to have paid little attention to contacts between the two non-European peoples. In Carolina, however, the colonists feared that Indians and slaves might combine forces and destroy them, or that the tribesmen would offer a haven for runaways. To prevent these occurrences, whites spread tales of Indian torture and atrocities among blacks, and at the same time paid the nearby Indian tribes to return escaped slaves. At other times colonial officials, lacking sufficient white manpower, reluctantly armed some blacks for campaigns against the Indians. This policy also made future cooperation between the two groups even more difficult. Whether or not the possibility of Indians and blacks launching a race war against whites actually existed, Carolinians thought it did. Their policies offer yet another example of how the Anglo-Europeans dominated and used the other two races to their own benefit.

EUROPEAN MINORITIES

Blacks and Indians were not the only minorities to be exploited in colonial America. Europeans, although welcomed for their wealth or potential labor, also suffered from English domination. Nevertheless, both the Scotch-Irish and the Germans played significant roles in the development of colonial society, especially during the eighteenth century, when nearly a half million of them arrived in America. In 1683 Francis D. Pastorius led the first German families to Philadelphia, responding to William Penn's advertising campaign and the promises of religious toleration and personal freedom. For the next century Germans poured into the English colonies, the largest number settling in Pennsylvania. By the 1760s they comprised a third of that colony's population. From there some migrated slowly to the south and west, settling in Virginia, the Carolinas, and Georgia. To the north, Germans moved into New York, particularly along the Hudson Valley.

This flood of non-English immigrants eventually caused friction and difficulties. Some of this resulted from long-held bitterness toward people from competing European nations, but many of the problems grew from local issues in the American colonies. Although it is not possible to consider all the nationalities and scattered settlements, the situation in Pennsylvania shows how negative feelings toward non-English peoples developed. There the Germans—incorrectly called Pennsylvania Dutch—were divided into several groups. Those who attracted the most attention were the so-called sect Germans: Amish, Mennonites, Moravians, and Dunkers. These people were pacifists and sided with the Quakers in matters of military service and defense.

Most Germans, aside from wanting to maintain their own language and customs, agreed with other pioneers about the need for strong action against the Indians but they mainly wanted to be left alone. When the Quaker-dominated legislature refused to pass laws committing the colony to fighting in King George's War during the 1740s, Benjamin Franklin and other non-Quaker leaders tried to organize an unofficial militia for defense against the French and the Indians. They appealed unsuccessfully to the Germans for cooperation. This aloofness in the war between Britain and France convinced some Pennsylvanians that the Germans were a potential danger to the colony.

The pacifist Germans in particular encountered hostility from other settlers as well as from colonial officials. The Moravians, or Brethren as they called themselves, had been forced out of Georgia during the 1730s for refusing to bear arms. A few years later New York authorities suspected their missionaries of persuading the Indians to join the French against the English and forced the Moravian mission in Dutchess County to close. Then in 1747 Governor William Gooch of Virginia denounced the Brethren for their pacifism. As a result of these difficulties the Moravians received a promise from Parliament that they would not have to bear arms or take oaths in legal matters. After that they fared slightly better. By the 1770s the pacifist groups included no more than 10 percent of the German population in Pennsylvania, and they aroused less antagonism from the rest of the colonists.

Pennsylvania leaders suspected and feared the Germans not only because some refused to fight but also because they rejected Anglo-American customs and the English language. German immigrants separated themselves from the English-speaking population whenever possible during the middle decades of the eighteenth century, causing suspicion and some bitterness. Benjamin Franklin denounced them as "Palatine Boors" and in a fit of exasperation asked, "Why should *Pennsylvania*, founded by the *English*, become a Colony of *Aliens*, who will shortly be so numerous as to Germanize us instead of our Anglifying them?"

To break down the language and cultural barriers in the colony, English-speaking leaders organized a "Society for the

Propagating of Christian Knowledge among the Germans." This association proposed a system of twenty-five English "charity" or free schools for the German communities. These institutions could then "Americanize" the students. Leaders among the German community recognized why the schools had been offered and objected immediately. One wrote that the school supporters "care little about religion; nor do they care for the cultivation of the minds of the Germans, except that they should form the militia and defend their English-American properties." As a result, only about half of the schools got started, and by 1763 the last one had been closed.

The largest number of non-English Europeans coming to the colonies during the eighteenth century were Scotch-Irish. By the time of independence, these people comprised between 7 and 10 percent of the white population. Beginning in 1717 descendants of the Scots, who had gone to Ulster in northern Ireland a century earlier, started migrating by the tens of thousands. By 1776 nearly a quarter of a million Scotch-Irish had entered the colonies. Although not English, these people spoke the same language as the English colonists and usually had little trouble adjusting to American society. They might well not have been considered as a distinct ethnic group except for their large numbers, their habit of settling together, which resulted in their domination of many frontier regions, and their open dislike for the English.

The flood of Scotch-Irish pioneers landed in Philadelphia and moved west into central Pennsylvania and then either north or south following the mountain valleys into western New York, Pennsylvania, Virginia, and the Carolinas. Often within a few months, or a year or two, they established communities in the West. There they quarreled with both their non–Scotch-Irish neighbors and with government officials, but not because of ethnic differences. As Presbyterians, they encountered some religious persecution in those colonies where the Anglicans received official recognition and tax support. The Scotch-Irish objected not only to Anglican doctrines and practices but to the prohibitions against having their own clergymen perform marriages. Nevertheless, such difficulties proved minor.

The major problems that the Scotch-Irish immigrants faced resulted from their position as pioneers. They often asked for defensive measures against the Indians or expensive road-building programs. Such demands brought them into conflict with eastern-dominated legislatures that either would not, or could not, support these requests. In Pennsylvania, for example, riots during the winter of 1763–64 and the frontiersmen's march on the colonial capital at Philadelphia show the depth of Scotch-Irish anger with the government. Inadequate defensive measures during the recent French and Indian War, the ensuing horrors of Indian raids during Pontiac's Rebellion in the summer of 1763, and the refusal of the Philadelphia-controlled government to offer protection produced the riots.

During the eighteenth century the Germans and Scotch-Irish were the two largest groups to enter the colonies. They both pushed to the newly opened frontier regions and peopled extensive areas. They provided substantial markets for American and English manufactured goods and brought immediate economic development just as a result of their numbers. They were, however, by no means the only European immigrants to British North America. The Dutch had preceded the English to New Netherlands—later New York—where they remained for generations. In the Hudson Valley land grants to Patroons, or large landowners, established enormous semifeudal manors. At what became Albany, Dutch fur traders opened a successful trade, which the English later inherited, with the tribes of the Iroquois Confederacy. In New Amsterdam, the principal Dutch settlement, farmers and shopkeepers mixed freely with the people from other nations. When the British seized their colony in 1664 perhaps ten thousand people lived in New Netherland and half of those were English. Dutch influence in New York thereafter declined rapidly except for the language, family and place names, and local architecture.

Refugees from religious persecution such as the Jews and

Huguenots (French Protestants) contributed to colonial economic development despite their small numbers. Jews settled first in New Netherland and in Rhode Island. Other colonies prohibited atheists and even non-Christians from becoming permanent residents—rules that slowed Jewish entry. By the middle of the eighteenth century Jewish merchants and shippers engaged in considerable trade between Rhode Island and the British West Indian colonies. In that same century Jews moved to Philadelphia, Charleston, and several other towns, but their population and influence remained small.

The Huguenots also enriched the colonial society and economy. Fleeing their homeland because of religious persecution during the late 1680s, they began arriving in the colonies in small numbers. These first French immigrants reached New England on the eve of an eighty-year series of wars between the British and French in Canada and received less than an enthusiastic welcome. French immigrants to South Carolina made more positive contributions—if only because they avoided the suspicion so prevalent in New England. They entered Carolina hoping to raise silkworms, olives, and grapes, but these ventures failed. Instead the French moved into Charleston, learned English, and became well-established merchants and businessmen. Others, Roman Catholics who had originally settled in Nova Scotia, were expelled and ventured further south and located in and around present-day New Orleans.

Immigrants from Scotland, especially the Lowland Scots, who arrived in fairly large numbers between 1763 and 1776, also prospered as merchants. While the Highland Scots were clannish and remained aloof from other colonists, much like the Germans, a minority of Lowland Scots played a vital role in colonial ports, acting as factors, or agents, for Great Britain's merchants. Because of their economic ties to England, these Scots frequently became Tories during the Revolution and some returned to England or migrated to Canada during the Revolutionary era.

COLONIAL SOCIAL STRUCTURE

By the time of the American Revolution the colonies had grown to a population of about two and one-half million, with much of the growth coming after 1720. Most of the people settled along the Atlantic seaboard, east of the Appalachian Mountains. Manufacturing remained chiefly a home industry and most colonists made their living from the soil. Less than 10 percent of the population lived in towns. America needed profits from shipping or the exports of its farms and plantations for survival and growth. This placed the colonists in competition with English shippers, farmers, and merchants, severely straining relations between the colonists and the mother country. During the eighteenth century British efforts to strengthen their mercantile controls over the colonies caused much resentment there, and if adequately enforced, they would have caused much hardship.

By the end of the colonial era the patterns of future social and economic growth had emerged. In the Southern colonies the elite planters invested their capital in land and slaves in order to grow and export tobacco, rice, and indigo. They depended on merchants in the cities and in England for their shipping and trade. The commitment to land and slaves and a plantation society would dominate the American South through the Civil War; the major difference was that by the middle of the nineteenth century cotton would replace tobacco as the chief export.

If the economic pattern was set, so too was the racial structure. The South did not attract large numbers of diverse European groups in colonial America and would not do so through most of the nineteenth century. White Southerners looked to blacks for their labor supply, which they obtained either through the slave trade or the natural growth of the black population. Black slaves and white masters were the unique way of the South and remained so until the Civil War. Black servitude promoted the belief in white supremacy, a view that continues to haunt contemporary America.

Table 1.1
POPULATION OF COLONIAL CITIES, 1760–1775

		1760	1775
1.	Philadelphia	23,750	40,000
2.	New York	18,000	25,000
3.	Boston	15,631	16,000
4.	Charleston	8,000	12,000
5.	Newport	7,500	11,000
	Total	72,881	104,000

Whereas staple crops and slavery characterized the Southern states, the North had few slaves. Most of the blacks found in the North, however, were slaves. All blacks were treated as inferiors and did not figure prominently in the regional economy. Northern, and especially middle colonies depended on the Germans and Scotch-Irish for their new settlers and farmers. Northern colonies also had a more diverse economy and depended on their farms and shipping for prosperity. Cities were more important in the North and four of the nation's urban centers, Philadelphia, New York, Boston, and Newport, Rhode Island, were located there (see Table 1.1). Charleston was the only Southern colonial city whose population exceeded five thousand in 1776.

Although not particularly big, the urban centers held the key elements for modernization. The business skills of the commercial class, risk capital obtained from business and local industry, and opportunities for larger economic profits than those offered by agriculture pointed toward the future. The modest colonial towns and cities attracted both the people and the capital needed to stimulate the burst of industrial and urban development that took place during the early decades of the nineteenth century. Thus these towns would lead the transformation from agriculture to the large-scale industrial activities that characterize modern American life.

An aspect of colonial urban life that received notice from contemporaries, and increased as cities grew larger, was the inordinate number of poor people. Although outside of New York City most of the residents were of English descent, it was commonly and unfairly assumed that "foreigners" received disproportionate assistance. Some of those receiving poor relief from local governments were newly arrived immigrants but most of the poor were in bad health, elderly and incapacitated, or widows and orphans unable to provide for themselves. Many ethnic groups established societies to help keep new immigrants from joining the ranks of the dependent. The first such immigrant aid society in colonial America, the Scots Charity Box, was founded in Boston in 1657. Most of the others began between the 1760s and 1790s and included Die Deutsche Gesellschaft, the Friendlly Sons of St. Patrick, and La Société Française de Bienfaisance de Philadelphie. The immigrant aid societies or benevolent groups, which would expand considerably in later centuries, were begun to improve conditions on emigrant ships, to provide food, clothing, shelter, and employment for newcomers of their nationality, and to give fellow countrymen opportunities for meeting one another. These organizations came to fill a central role in immigrant lives and would appear wherever large numbers of foreigners settled in the nineteenth and twentieth centuries.

The ethnic mixture of the Northern colonies led to conflicts as English Protestants distrusted other nationalities, Jews, and Catholics. Yet the non-English brought labor and skills and were generally loyal to the Patriot cause during the Revolution. As long as their numbers were low and they seemed to accept American values they were welcome; but the tension remained and would cause further clashes with the beginning of large-scale immigration in the nineteenth century.

Socially the South differed from the North. The planters dominated Southern society. They held the best land, large numbers of slaves, and controlled the political assemblies. The middle-class farmers usually showed both social and political deference to them. Southerners, even more than Northerners, were of English descent; hence the planters' model was the English country gentleman.

In the North society's orientation was more urban, educated, and middle class. The Puritan influence, in the form of Congregationalism, was strong in New England and helped to mold the institutions and attitudes there. Northerners and some travelers to the New World thought the North was more fluid than Europe and the Southern colonies with their large numbers of slaves. One observer declared there was "scarcely any part of the world" in which the "lower classes" of people were better off than in New England. There the "ease of gaining a farm renders the lower class of people very industrious; which, with the high price of labour, banishes everything that has the least appearance of begging, or that wandering, destitute state of poverty, which we see so common in England."

Yet the North had its elites too, especially the wealthy merchants in the major ports, who dominated urban society. In places like Long Island, the Hudson Valley, and the Connecticut Valley powerful landowners controlled local society. One traveler remarked of New England on the eve of the American Revolution that "gentlemen's houses appear everywhere" and on the landed estates the "owners live much in the style of country gentlemen in England." In the eighteenth century these elites had grown rich and the gulf between the rich and poor had widened as it had in the South, creating a propertyless lower class in Northern cities. In 1687 the wealthiest tenth of Boston's population owned slightly less than half of the taxable property and in the 1770s about 63 percent, while the bottom third had practically nothing. In rural Chester County, near Philadelphia, the richest tenth of the farmers also increased its share of the wealth in the eighteenth century. But because of the lack of large concentrations of slaves, the North was less stratified than the South and offered modest opportunities for social and economic advancement.

MINORITIES AND THE AMERICAN REVOLUTION

Throughout the Revolutionary era minority rights remained a major issue for policy and debate in both North and South. During the War for Independence Loyalists, who opposed the Revolution and supported England, proved a major threat to the Patriot cause. Strongest in the middle colonies of New York, New Jersey, and Pennsylvania as well as in Georgia, these people soon were known as Tories. According to one popular definition, a Tory was "a thing whose head is in England, and its body in America, and its neck ought to be stretched." England drew support from perhaps a third of the colonists, although the exact number of Loyalists was never known. The Patriots had good cause to fear Loyalists in their midst. Some Tories served as spies or guides for the British, while about fifty thousand of them actually fought alongside the Redcoats. At least two of the colonies, New York and Georgia, provided more men for the armies of the king than they did for General Washington.

Among colonial immigrants, at least three ethnic groups heavily supported the British. Although most of the Scotch-Irish seem to have favored the Patriot cause, those near Philadelphia joined a Loyalist regiment known as the Volunteers of Ireland. In North Carolina bitterness caused by the earlier quarrels within the colony kept many Scotch-Irish from joining the move for independence. Some Germans also became Loyalists. In the South they feared losing British protection from the Indians, but in Pennsylvania religious factors remained important. Britain had given them freedom from persecution less than thirty years earlier, and Revolutionary authorities still frequently fined them for refusing to swear support for the government, despite their plea that taking oaths violated their religious beliefs. The Highland Scots were almost the only people who wholeheartedly became Loyalists, and the British organized units of these men to fight in both New York and North Carolina. Because the fighting lasted eight years much bitterness toward British supporters resulted. Often the persecution of Loyalists had little direct impact on immigrant or ethnic minorities as groups in the colonies, but the use of violence and coercion to achieve conformity remained a threat to them.

For both Indians and blacks the War for Independence brought changes, but for the tribal people these proved mostly negative. During the years just preceding the war British authorities had tried to satisfy colonial land hunger by concluding treaties with the Iroquois Confederacy of New York for land cessions just beyond Pittsburgh and in Kentucky. This brought outraged denunciations from Shawnee and Delaware bands that lived in the ceded areas, and violence spread along the frontier. When intruding whites killed the family of a tribal leader named Logan, who had worked for peace, retaliation was swift, and in 1774 Lord Dunmore's War occurred. Although isolated diplomatically by the British, the Shawnee launched a series of devastating raids on pioneer settlements, hoping to drive the whites east of the mountains, but these failed. Instead, the colonial troops forced Chief Cornstalk and his warriors to accept peace and American penetration of at least part of their homeland. In the South, too, similar incursions into Cherokee country kept the frontier tense.

With this background of white–Indian violence and suspicion it is not surprising that the Second Continental Congress quickly turned its attention to Indian affairs. In July 1775 that body declared that "securing and preserving the friendship of Indian nations" is "of the utmost importance to these colonys." Thus the Congress, hoping to satisfy Indian demands, sent to the frontiers negotiators, who had little but talk to offer. As a result, when war with the British began, violence and ill will existed all along the frontier.

Certain that the British would enlist Indians to raid the frontiers, the authors of the Declaration of Independence denounced King George III for using "the merciless Indian Savages, whose known rule of warfare is an undistinguished destruction af all ages, sexes, and conditions," as allies. Bitter fighting between Indians and whites flared across New York, Pennsylvania, and the Carolinas as Mohawk leader Joseph Brant and Cherokee chief Dragging Canoe led their followers down the war path on the side of Britain. Although most of the tribes remained neutral, and a few small groups sided with the colonists, when peace came in 1783 many white Americans considered Indian Americans to be savages who had no place in the new country. George Washington stated this idea clearly when he wrote that "the gradual extention of our Settlements will as certainly cause the Savage and the Wolf to retire; both being beasts of prey tho' they differ in shape." Because of such attitudes, when control of eastern North America shifted from Britain to the United States, tribal people found themselves being treated like defeated enemies.

Military demands for manpower enabled thousands of black slaves to obtain their freedom, while free blacks also improved their social status through wartime service. Except in the Deep South, militia authorities welcomed both slaves and free blacks into army and naval units. A recent study estimates that some five thousand blacks served in American military units and perhaps another one thousand fought for the British. Many of these blacks got their freedom in return for their service while others slipped away to freedom during the war-caused turmoil. In either case, whether serving in the military or running away, blacks used the War for Independence for their own benefit.

By the 1780s both white Northerners and Southerners agreed on one thing. They had obtained their independence from England and had won a large land mass reaching to the Mississippi River as part of the peace settlement. They meant to expand to the west and exploit the land. Farmers, planters, and land speculators sought new economic opportunities as worn-out soil or overpopulation of the eastern lands forced them to look west. An eager, restless people, Amercians at the end of the Revolution were already pushing over the mountains and seeking new worlds to conquer.

2

Forging a New Nation
The South
(1776–1840s)

EARLY ISSUES

IN JULY 1776 the Declaration of Independence affirmed as self-evident "that all men are created equal, that they are endowed by their Creator with certain unalienable Rights, that among these are Life, Liberty, and the pursuit of Happiness." Theoretically this document put the new nation on record as supporting freedom for all people. Noble as these pronouncements were, they could not obscure the attitudes that individual Americans held or the actions their society took in relation to the ethnic minorities within the nation. As a result, the question of how to deal with the Indians, black slaves, and immigrants in a society that wanted their labor or, in the case of the Indians, their land plagued the new nation for many decades.

The American Revolution uprooted thousands of people, disrupted trade and commerce, discouraged immigration, and damaged farms, homes, and cities. Yet the former colonists soon resumed their economic activities, united behind a new government, and bound themselves into a nation. The process of nation building proved difficult at first, but important compromises by all groups enabled the thirteen states to discard the Articles of Confederation and ratify the federal constitution. Even this new frame of government, however, could not overcome the sectional differences or solve existing problems to the satisfaction of all. As a result, during the pre–Civil War decades two conflicting threads run through the pattern of American history. On the one hand, a deepening sense of nationalism and a growing optimism in the future of America are clearly evident. Most pronounced in the 1776–1820 era, these feelings remained significant factors in national life. At the same time, however, differences in social patterns and economic development continued to exist. Increasingly the North developed towns and cities with expanded commercial enterprise and growing industries. Although some commerce and industry emerged in the South after 1820, these economic developments lagged far behind similar ones in the North. Instead, Southerners chose to invest their capital in land and slaves, concentrating most of their economic effort in staple-crop agriculture. These diverging economic patterns both reflected and shaped the differing needs in North and South. By the 1830s there was an unmistakable trend toward sectionalism. The two sections had gradually drifted away from their earlier feelings of nationalism and now looked on each other as competitors with dissimilar economic and social needs.

In the 1780s few Americans believed that the differences between the North and South were of long-range significance. Cotton had not yet become the mainstay of Southern agriculture, and slavery seemed to be dying out everywhere. Few could have predicted that the North would develop major urban centers and the industrial economy that emerged prior to the Civil War. Nevertheless, the gap between the two regions over slavery and economic development would grow and divide America into two nations, one slave and the other free.

WESTWARD EXPANSION

Despite the small but growing strains between North and South many Americans continued moving west. They looked in that direction for national expansion and coveted the foreign-owned and Indian territory that lay in their path. Beginning with the 1803 Louisiana Purchase American leaders and citizens confidently predicted that settlement would eventually reach to the Pacific Ocean. The famous Lewis and Clark Expedition that crossed the northern Plains, Rocky Mountains, and Pacific Northwest in 1804–6 was planned before the United States had acquired any of the region traversed by the explorers. New technological developments such as steamboats made settling the frontier easier than it had been during the early decades after independence. National pride, fear of European powers taking parts of North America, and the pressures of a growing population and economy impelled the federal government to gain new territory. In 1818 negotiators for Great Britain and the United States agreed on a boundary settlement between Canada and America in the region west of the Great Lakes. The next year Secretary of State John Quincy Adams concluded the Adams–Onís Treaty with Spain, which gave Florida as well as the Spanish-claimed portion of Oregon to the Americans while defining the boundary between the United States and the Spanish territory in the Southwest.

For the next two decades pioneers moved west and in the last half of the 1840s the nation experienced renewed territorial growth. In 1822 Mexico opened its northeast province of Texas to foreign settlers, offering some free and some cheap land. As a result of this inducement Americans by the mid 1830s outnumbered Mexicans in Texas by a ratio of nearly nine to one. This frightened the Mexican government. As Protestants the Americans had no desire to assimilate into Mexican society, yet Mexican law required that all immigrants be Catholic; as slaveholders the Americans were aghast when Mexico outlawed slavery. After 1830 Mexico tried to prohibit further immigration of Americans into Texas. Obviously a clash between the Texans and the Mexicans was coming. In 1835 a series of minor disturbances culminated in revolution and within a year the Texans declared their independence and sought annexation to the United States. Domestic political wrangling prevented the fed-

eral government from immediate action; not until 1845 did
Texas join the Union. The next year the United States and Great
Britain settled their differences over the Pacific Northwest and
the Americans acquired the region between the 42nd and 49th
parallel from the Rockies west to the Pacific coast. Then in
1848, as a result of the war with Mexico, the United States annexed practically all of what is now California, Nevada, Arizona, New Mexico, and parts of Wyoming and Colorado. Five
years later, through the Gadsden Purchase, American negotiators rounded out the southwestern border between the United
States and Mexico.

INDIAN RELATIONS

Before, during, and immediately after the American Revolution
Indians in the South faced heavy pressures to surrender their
lands to the advancing pioneers. Although most of the tribes
had remained neutral during the war, there was plenty of
Indian–white violence along the frontiers. Responding to continuing demands for land during the 1780s, Cherokee, Choctaw,
and Chickasaw leaders signed several treaties bringing peace,
recognition of American control over the region, and specific
tribal boundaries. The chiefs hoped that the treaties would sta-
bilize relations with whites and limit state encroachments into
their country, but in this they failed. Southern frontiersmen
continued to seize Indian lands, so tribal leaders next turned to
the Spanish in Florida and along the Gulf coast for help. The
mixed-blood Creek leader Alexander McGillivray, who had
been on the British army payroll a few years earlier, now became a paid Spanish agent among the tribes of the Southeast.
McGillivray and other chiefs met Spanish officials repeatedly in
their effort to forge an Indian confederacy, but their work failed
to produce any solidarity in opposing the United States. Instead,
American negotiators persuaded the Indian leaders to travel to
New York for negotiations. There, McGillivray accepted a gen-
eralship in the United States Army and so lost at least some of

his earlier enthusiasm for anti-American plotting. Yet other reasons proved more important in the collapse of the Indian confederacy. Certainly the defection of both the Cherokee and Chickasaw tribes during the 1790s hurt. In addition, when Spain and the United States signed the 1795 Treaty of San Lorenzo, the Spanish agents left their Indian allies to face the American pioneers on their own.

Although isolated bands of warriors and pioneers clashed repeatedly, the major Southern tribes remained at peace with the whites. Nevertheless, they faced continuing pressure to sell their land and experienced repeated incursions by the frontiersmen. Such provocations convinced many tribal leaders that war against the United States was futile, and when the War of 1812 broke out most Indians in the South remained at peace, a stark contrast with their fellow tribesmen in the North. The Red Stick faction among the Creeks of Alabama proved to be the only major exception. Led by William Weatherford (Red Eagle), in 1813 Red Stick warriors attacked pioneer settlements and destroyed Fort Mims in Alabama. Countering the Red Sticks, however, a majority of Creek warriors under William McIntosh as well as companies of Cherokee and Choctaw warriors joined General Andrew Jackson's forces. Unfortunately for the Southern tribes, their cooperation with Jackson's army brought no relief from the repeated demands that they sell their land to the United States. Even before the war with Britain had ended, the Treaty of Fort Jackson had stripped them of most of their territory in Alabama and Georgia. Thus at the end of the War of 1812, the Indians once again found that they had either been on the wrong and losing side or, when they helped the Americans, it did them little if any good.

With peace in 1815 the federal government shifted its emphasis from forced land cessions to several related but different programs. Working with Protestant church groups, it encouraged missionary and educational activities among the villagers, hoping to interest the Indians in European-style agriculutre so that the tribes would need less land to support themselves. At

the same time the government began encouraging groups of
Eastern Indians to sell or trade their lands for territory beyond
the Mississippi River, which would also open more land for pioneer settlement. Clearly the programs worked at direct cross-
purposes with each other, but then consistency was never a hall-
mark of federal Indian policy. Even if it had been, the tribes
presented the government with a stark dilemma. Responsible
officials wanted to maintain peace, but they had to satisfy the
pioneers, too. Usually what met frontier whites' demands angered the tribes. The problem became acute after the War of
1812 when settlers demanded that the government get the Indians out of their way. Technically the tribes had two alternatives: they could remain on a reduced portion of their land and
farm as the whites did or they could move west. But few Indians had a real choice as greedy farmers, lumbermen, and
miners swept onto their tribal territory with little hinderance
from the federal government.

In the face of increasing white pressure, Cherokee leaders
sought to preserve both their culture and their land in several
ways. They encouraged the acceptance of missionary-sponsored
schools, thus benefiting from the education. They employed a
newly developed Cherokee syllabary that enabled many villagers to read their own language for the first time, thus foster-
ing a deep sense of unity and nationalism that swept through
the villages. While the Indians did that, as early as 1790 Congress authorized spending up to $20,000 a year to buy seed,
livestock, and tools for tribal farmers. The villagers accepted
this help and some modified their farming methods somewhat,
but in the long run what they wanted most was to be left alone.

This wish was denied. Rather, in 1819 Congress increased its
pressure on the tribes when it established an Indian Civilization
Fund of $10,000. Through this legislation the government now
paid churches and other benevolent groups that agreed to build
and run schools for the tribes, whereas earlier it had only encouraged their efforts at acculturation of the Indians. This program received widespread public support despite inadequate

funding. By the 1840s the federal government still provided the same $10,000 each year, but private mission groups and even some of the tribes themselves were spending a total of $150,000 a year to "civilize the savages and christianize the heathen." In addition to building schools and churches, missionaries established model farms to teach the Indians the latest agricultural techniques. Between 1783 and 1815 some of the tribesmen responded to these efforts by learning English, or weaving, or use of the white man's farm implements. Others acquired skills as mechanics and blacksmiths. Many, however, clung to their tribal cultures, taking only those things in American society that made their lives easier or more comfortable while rejecting other aspects of white "civilization." In particular the tribesmen spurned or ignored efforts to make them individuals. They retained their allegiance to family and clan, which characterized Indian society, and thus retained an outlook different from that of other Americans in the nineteenth century. By repudiating the popular goals of private property and economic advancement Indians only proved their innate "inferiority" and "savagery" as far as most other Americans were concerned.

This was not an accurate view of all Southern tribes. In particular among the Cherokee, located mainly in North Carolina, Tennessee, and north Georgia, tribal leaders had been fully bicultural for several generations. Literate, articulate, bilingual men directed tribal affairs in ways to increase Indian strength and wealth. By the mid-1820s the Cherokee owned at least 22,000 cattle, some 1,300 slaves, 31 grist mills, 10 saw mills, and 8 cotton gins. In addition, the tribe operated 18 schools and published the *Cherokee Phoenix*, a bilingual Cherokee–English newspaper. With imposing brick plantation homes and successful slave-operated staple-crop agriculture, these tribal leaders presented a major challenge to Southern whites. Such men could hardly be classed as shiftless savages or inferior vagabonds. Despite the obvious evidence of Cherokee achievement, some whites concluded that assimilation would take far longer than they had originally assumed, while others decided that assimilation might never work or that it might not even be a worthy goal. As a result, in the years immediately following the War of 1812, pressure grew to find other answers to the Indian question. This led the federal government, while pursuing a policy of assimilation, to embark on another program, known as Indian removal. By removal whites meant that Indians would be moved from their home east of the Mississippi and sent to lands west of the river. Officially announced by President James Monroe just before he left office in 1825, this program merely made formal what had been happening piecemeal for several decades. Working in direct conflict with the civilization approach, it was nevertheless seen as a better way to end the continuing difficulties with the Indians. Also, once the Indians had left, new areas for settlement by immigrants and pioneers would open more quickly.

This removal policy had many supporters. Those who favored gradual assimilation of the tribesmen hoped to speed the process by isolating the Indians from the frontiersmen. Then they might learn from just and concerned whites. Monroe's secretary of war, John C. Calhoun, estimated that within thirty years after moving west the tribes might be "civilized" enough to join the white majority. Some federal officers actually envisioned Indian territories and states in the West. Apparently no one in the 1820s anticipated the incredible speed with which white Americans would spread west beyond the Mississippi, and it was the rapidly advancing frontier that destroyed any chance of achieving the goals of the removal program.

Not all whites favored pushing the Indians aside, and, particularly in the Northeast, public leaders spoke out against forced removal. John Quincy Adams, who followed Monroe as president, was among those who questioned American tactics toward the Indians. Expressing the unpopular view that the nation should deal fairly with the Indians, he hesitated to force them west.

His successor, Andrew Jackson, had no qualms about removing the tribes. A popular frontier leader and famous Indian fighter, "Old Hickory" announced in his first inaugural address his intention to push the Indians beyond the Mississippi. In May 1830, less than a year later, Congress passed the Indian Removal Act, which provided funds to buy tribal holdings and to pay the costs of relocation. The new law also gave the president authority to use force if needed. The pattern had been set; the Indians had to move or be destroyed.

The removal efforts applied to tribes in the North and Midwest as well as those in the South, and during the 1830s about 73,800 Indians moved west under this policy. Usually the federal government appointed a special agent to gather, organize, supply, and lead the braves. Civilians supervised the moving of cooperative Indians, and army officers superintended the recalcitrants. Local businessmen provided food, clothing, and transportation, an arrangement that caused needless suffering among the uprooted Indians. Frequently the contractors' greed overcame their scruples, and they bought condemned meat and spoiled flour to feed their charges. For transportation, the contractors rented cheap, untrustworthy boats to get the Indians across major streams, sometimes with disastrous results. One steamboat, jammed to the rails with Creeks, sank in the Mississippi River and 311 Indians drowned. The Cherokee suffered similar difficulties, and some scholars estimate that nearly 4,000 of the 15,000 tribesmen who started west at gunpoint died either on what the Indians called the "Trail of Tears" or during their first months in what is now Oklahoma.

Not all of the Indians accepted removal as inevitable. The Cherokee, among the most acculturated of the Eastern tribes, sought to use their acceptance of the white man's ways as the basis for retaining ancestral lands. Hoping to present a unified front to the Georgia legislature, the tribal leaders met during the summer of 1827, drafted a constitution, and formed the Cherokee Republic. Then they elected John Ross as president and prepared to defend themselves. Unfortunately, the act of creating their republic made forced removal inevitable. The United States Constitution prohibits the creation of a new state within any existing state without its permission—something Georgia refused to give. Georgia officials demanded that the federal government force the Indians to vacate their lands. After the passage of the Indian Removal Act in May 1830, the tribal leaders appealed to the United States Supreme Court. In *The Cherokee Nation* vs. *Georgia* (1831), and the later *Worcester* vs. *Georgia* (1832), the Court ruled in the Indians' favor, but it proved unable to help them. President Andrew Jackson allegedly remarked after the latter ruling, "John Marshall has made his decision. Now let him enforce it."

In addition to showing the Court's inability to stop removal, these decisions had a second long-range impact on the status of Indians. In *The Cherokee Nation* vs. *Georgia* Chief Justice John Marshall described Indian tribes as "domestic dependent nations." This position meant that they must look to the United States "for protection; rely upon its kindness and its power; appeal to it for relief for their wants." A year later, Marshall reiterated this idea in his decision for *Worcester* vs. *Georgia*. His rulings in these two cases strengthened the position that individual tribes were not independent nations. The Marshall views became the basis for the later opinions that Indians were wards of Washington, that Indians had to be looked after, and that they could not manage for themselves. These ideas became an important influence on Bureau of Indian Affairs policies in the decades following the Civil War.

The Seminole tribe in Florida also refused to be moved and in 1835 started a guerrilla war that cost the United States thousands of casualties and at least $50 million. The army even imported bloodhounds from Cuba to track down its elusive foe, but with little success. Sporadic fighting dragged on until the mid-1840s when the army captured Indian leaders by treachery. When the Seminole War ended and the defeated tribesmen had been shipped west to Indian Territory, the last major group of Indians was gone from the eastern third of the nation. By the Mexican War only a few scattered remnants of the once numerous and powerful tribes remained. Removal had succeeded.

Unwillingly the tribesmen moved west ahead of the rising tide of settlement. Industrialization, agricultural expansion, and mechanization called for land and resources that only the Indians had. Unlike the immigrants and black slaves who helped build the American economy with their hands, backs, and minds, the tribesmen contributed their property to the process. Modernization received a major boost from the involuntary Indian contribution while at the same time nearly destroying the tribes.

While white Americans evolved a policy toward the Indians they also questioned their attitude toward black slavery. The Quakers, particularly in New England and Pennsylvania, acted first, but even those in the South began to manumit blacks wherever the law permitted it.

FAILURE OF SOUTHERN ANTISLAVERY

The ideology of the Revolutionary era buttressed the cause of those who opposed slavery. Emancipationists frequently used the ideas of the Declaration of Independence, and state constitutions and laws included sentiments about the rights of man. Critics noted that equality and slavery were incompatible. One Massachusetts judge observed, "The idea of slavery is inconsistent with our own conduct and our constitution. . . . There can be no such thing as perpetual servitude of a rational creature." The military support given by blacks to the Revolutionary cause also encouraged the colonies to emancipate a few slaves who had served in the army. Lord Dunmore, the British governor of Virginia, had promised freedom for those blacks who had fought with the Loyalists, but the English did little. Some Northern states granted freedom to black soldiers, but the South rejected such proposals.

In the South many planters, like Thomas Jefferson, held slavery to be morally wrong. Yet Jefferson owned numerous slaves and depended on black plantation labor. He was not sure that whites and blacks could live together in freedom, and when he thought of emancipation he hoped for colonization of blacks outside of America. In the end Jefferson, like so many of the South's leading planters, made few concrete proposals to end slavery. He freed Sally Hemings and her children, who were probably his also, and took his ambivalent feelings about blacks and slavery to his grave.

Many other Southern planters who reaped the benefits of the slave system also considered freeing their bondsmen. In the upper regions of the South, Maryland and Delaware enacted laws making it easy for planters to manumit their slaves and many did so. As a result the number of free blacks increased significantly in those states. Virginia and North Carolina passed laws to make manumission easier and a few planters like George Washington freed their slaves in their wills while others freed them outright. But in South Carolina and Georgia there was no antislavery movement to speak of.

Economic factors largely account for the failure of antislavery in the Southern states. The slaveholders depended on their chattels for labor and were unwilling to make a large financial sacrifice in the cause of human freedom. After the Revolution planters hoped that with English control and restrictions gone the West would be open for expansion and foreign trade in tobacco would be more profitable. Yet it was cotton that formed the base for Southern expansion and became the cornerstone of the region's economy. Eli Whitney's invention of the cotton gin in 1793 made it economically profitable to grow short staple cotton in much of the South. Americans produced only 13,000 bales of cotton before its invention, but by 1860 output had increased to about 4,500,000 bales annually. As the nineteenth century wore on English and Northern mills became ready consumers of American-grown cotton.

Not all Southerners raised cotton. In the older states, diversified farming and other staple crops remained important. Substantial production of rice in South Carolina, sugar in Louisiana, and tobacco and hemp in North Carolina, Tennessee, and Kentucky indicates Southern dependence on cash-crop agriculture. In addition, Southern farmers also raised cattle, hogs, corn, and other foodstuffs to feed their people.

Some white Southerners urged moving to a more diversified economy, especially manufacturing, and the South did witness the spread of cotton mills, iron works, and other industries before the Civil War. The mining of gold and lead also grew, as did timber and turpentine production. To serve these industries and to help move people and goods more easily, some Southerners earned their living building or operating canals and railroads. Nevertheless, in both industry and viable transportation facilities the South lagged behind the rest of the nation because it devoted most of its capital to land and slaves for agriculture.

As a result, the South had few major cities before the Civil War. Some towns grew into small cities in the early nineteenth century, but the region could boast of few urban centers when compared to the free states. Of the cities in the future Confederacy, only New Orleans had a population of over 100,000 people and it was the only Southern community large enough to rank among the nation's ten largest cities in 1861. Although a few Southern towns served as important regional centers of trade, banking, and even some manufacturing, the region remained overwhelmingly rural throughout most of the nineteenth century. The technological breakthrough of the cotton gin, coupled with growing demands of British and Northern mills for fiber, helped encourage the spread of cotton agriculture across the South. There good farm land and a favorable climate contributed to its growth.

SOUTHERN FREE BLACKS

With improved prospects for expansion of cotton-growing areas many white Southerners became more firm in their beliefs about the necessity of maintaining slaves. At the same time, however, they felt uncomfortable with free blacks in their midst and sought ways of removing them. One popular notion espoused by many whites, including Abraham Lincoln, had an organization to support it: the American Colonization Society, formed in 1817. Originally some proponents of colonization saw it as a way to eradicate slavery; they reasoned that white Americans might be willing to abolish slavery if all blacks were deported to Haiti or Liberia in Africa. Others were unconcerned about slavery and wanted to rid the nation of free blacks. Even the antislavery Republican party, founded in 1854, had its share of colonizers. Senator James Doolittle of Wisconsin said it would keep "our Anglo-Saxon institutions as well as our Anglo-Saxon blood pure and uncontaminated," while others said it "would relieve us from the curse of free blacks."

Because few free blacks favored it, the colonization movement had little success, and whites instead enacted laws aimed at excluding blacks. Several states barred the entrance of free blacks; others required them to post bonds guaranteeing good behavior. Fearing their states would become "an asylum for all the old and decrepit and broken down negroes that may emigrate or be sent to it," or "the Liberia of the North," voters approved these measures by large majorities. Angry whites sometimes decided that laws were insufficient and resorted to violence. Periodic rioting erupted between blacks and whites in the antebellum period. Perhaps the worst episode occurred in Cincinnati in 1829 when mobs of whites assaulted blacks, burned their homes, and drove about half the black population out of town, most fleeing to Canada.

Attempts to deport blacks or keep them from settling in communities were only part of the hostility confronting the free black population in the pre–Civil War period. The ending of slavery in the North, and the freeing of some slaves in the South, did not bring equality for the newly freed and their descendants. Blacks remained second-class citizens and hostility toward them sometimes intensified as the Civil War approached.

In the South free blacks lived on the margin of society; they were virtually "slaves without masters." The 250,000 free blacks living in the slave states in 1860 found themselves with few legal and social rights. They could not vote, except in Tennessee, North Carolina, and parts of Louisiana, and in the 1830s Tennessee and North Carolina disfranchised them. Through custom and by law the white South heaped restrictions on them, especially after the 1830s. By the Civil War free blacks were banned from the schools, the militia, public places, and some types of employment and were subject to curfews, registration systems, and verbal and physical abuse. They could make contracts, be married, sue, and hold property, but they generally could not testify against whites in the courts or sit on juries. They also faced harsh penalties if convicted of crimes.

It is not surprising that Southern blacks lived on the edge of the economy and that most existed in or near poverty. Only a few free blacks managed to become successful planters. Those in rural areas barely scratched out a living, and if they owned land, it was usually a small amount. The landless frequently became hired hands or casual laborers. In the cities there were more opportunities, but here too the former slaves faced discrimination and often found jobs only as unskilled laborers or as domestics. In 1831 Savannah banned blacks from becoming apprentices in the trades of "Carpenter, Mason, Bricklayer, Barber, or any other Mechanical Art or Mystery," and later extended the list. In spite of such discrimination some free blacks did become skilled workers. The Deep South's most prosperous blacks lived in New Orleans. There, proportionately more of them than Irish or German immigrants were skilled workers, and some even became successful businessmen and professionals.

Southern free blacks formed their own social institutions. Especially important was the church, although whites were suspicious of, and passed laws to restrict, black religious life. Blacks also organized schools, clubs, and cultural groups and sought to improve and educate themselves, while a few of the more prosperous sent their children north or abroad for their education.

SLAVERY IN THE OLD SOUTH

White Americans tried to ship free blacks back to Africa, but they could not end slavery. Antislavery agitation failed nationally, although the Northern states did abolish the institution. In 1787 the Northwest Ordinance outlawed slavery in what became Ohio, Indiana, Illinois, Michigan, and Wisconsin, but at the same time slave owners could bring their human property into the region south of the Ohio River. The Constitution prevented the banning of the international slave trade for twenty years. Thus until 1808 Americans continued to import blacks legally from Africa or the West Indies. Even after Congress prohibited the trade, smuggling continued for several more decades. These latter-day importations had less effect than the natural increase in the domestic population. By 1860 four million slaves lived and worked in the South.

One of the most repulsive aspects of slavery was the interstate sales of human beings. Planters who occupied the best lands of the Gulf states on the heels of Indian removal, and who wanted to purchase slaves, did so from dealers in the Eastern seaboard states or the Upper South. Estimates of the interstate slave trade are not precise, but Virginia, the largest seller, provided roughly 300,000 slaves to the Gulf states between 1830 and 1860, and hundreds of thousands more were sent south from more northern slave states such as Maryland and Kentucky. Even defenders of slavery considered public auctions of slaves a necessary evil and sometimes looked down on the dealers. The buyers usually wanted "prime fields" (young healthy males), but women and children were also sold in the marketplace. Occasionally slave traders made some effort to keep marriages intact, but the South did not have legal safeguards to prevent the separation of husbands and wives. Families, as opposed to marriages, were even more vulnerable to the slave trade. Most sellers did try to keep children and their mothers together, but once the children became young adults, at about age thirteen, they were often sold separately and without regard

One of the most horrible aspects of slavery was the slave trade itself. This painting, done in 1853, is of slaves going south after the sale. By Eyre Crowe. (*Chicago Historical Society*)

for their parents and kin. The traumatic experience of being bought and sold like cattle has been immortalized in black folklore with songs like "No More Auction Block for Me."

Even if the planter did not purchase slaves but brought them with him to the new cotton lands of the Deep South, he was apt to destroy slave families. Frequently husbands and wives lived on different plantations, and if a planter migrated and took his male slave along, the slave's wife and children on another plantation would be left behind. Such occurrences were common in the antebellum South as planters seeking new opportunities took hundreds of thousands of slaves with them to the Deep South. Thus whether by sale or migration the massive movement of slaves between 1820 and 1860 was especially hard on the slave family.

Slaves working the cotton fields. From *Harper's Weekly*, 1875. (*Library of Congress*)

Whether slaves were sold, carried by the owners, or simply born in the newer regions of the South, slavery expanded rapidly in the Gulf states. At the time of the American Revolution over half the slave population lived in Maryland and Virginia; by 1860, although Virginia still had the largest number of slaves, these two states accounted for only 15 percent of the bond servants. Alabama and Mississippi, two states that did not come into the Union until after the War of 1812, ranked closely behind Virginia. Of the nearly four million slaves in 1860, about half dwelled in the cotton kingdom.

At the time of the Civil War only about one quarter of the South's white families owned slaves and most of these owned only a few. Twelve percent of the owners had more than 20 slaves, and a small minority owned large numbers: 3,000 families had more than 100 slaves and a few families more than 500. Some of these large owners held several plantations, using overseers to run them. Most bondsmen lived on plantations

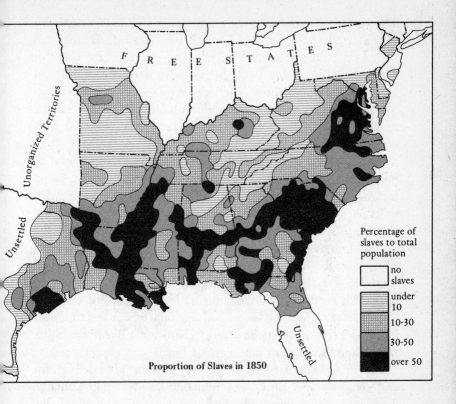

Proportion of Slaves in 1850

Percentage of
slaves to total
population

| no slaves |
| under 10 |
| 10-30 |
| 30-50 |
| over 50 |

having 20 or more slaves. These were usually the large cotton plantations in Alabama, Mississippi, and other cotton-growing regions (where according to the 1850 census, more than two thirds of the South's 2.5 million slaves worked), rice plantations in South Carolina, and sugar plantations in Louisiana. In the cities concentration was less than in the countryside and only a few owners had large numbers of slaves.

Although most slaves were found on cotton plantations, not all toiled in the fields. A minority became skilled workers such as carpenters and blacksmiths. Some cooked food; others cared for children or were servants in the master's house. Overseers were usually white, but the bulk of the drivers, who supervised the slaves in the fields, were black. Plantations usually grew their own food and raised their own cattle and hogs, and slaves cared for the food crops and raised the livestock. During the off season even the hands who usually worked in the tobacco, rice, sugar, and cotton fields helped with domestic chores and the maintenance of the plantation, including such jobs as construction and repair of fences and buildings. Of course, on the smaller farms having only a few slaves, blacks engaged in a variety of tasks.

Slaves also toiled in the Old South's industries. They could be found in iron foundries and tobacco plants in Virginia, hemp factories in Kentucky, sugar mills in Texas and Louisiana, rice mills in Georgia and South Carolina, and even in the fledgling cotton mills, the coal, iron, salt, gold, and lead mines, and the timber and transportation industries. In Charleston about one quarter of the adult male slaves were skilled laborers and in some cities of the Old South slaves outnumbered the whites in important crafts. It was not unusual for these skilled slaves to hire themselves out for wages and live apart from their masters in quasi-freedom, although many urban slaves lived in a building behind the master's house.

For many Southerners, obviously, slavery provided profits and comforts that they were reluctant to abandon. Although during the 1780s slave codes and laws restricting manumission were moderated, the invention of the cotton gin in 1793, and the profits that it promised, lessened the talk about freeing slaves. By the nineteenth century Southerners again tightened their grip over their "peculiar institution." After 1830 fear of slave revolts, such as Nat Turner's in Virginia in 1831, and the rise of abolitionism in the North hardened white attitudes. The South became more militant in defending slavery, increasingly viewing the system as a benefit to both white and black, a blessing sanctioned by God. Southern voices of criticism against slavery became fewer and fainter, while the belief in black inferiority reinforced the white man's view that servitude was an appropriate condition for blacks. "He the negro is but a grown up child, and must be governed as a child," wrote George Fitz-hugh, one of the better-known defenders of the institution. "The negro race is inferior to the white race and living in their midst," he continued, "they would be far outstripped or out-witted in the chaos of free competition. . . . The negro slaves of the South are the happiest, and in some senses, the freest people in the world."

In the antebellum South the slave codes became increasingly more repressive to make the slave stand in fear of the white man. As one judge said, "The power of the master must be absolute, to render the submission of the slave perfect." Slaves could not possess firearms or leave the plantation without per-mission. It was illegal to teach them to read and write, and they could not hold meetings without a white person present. They could not insult or strike whites or testify against them in courts. Separate laws and courts dealt with slave offenses and for certain crimes blacks sometimes received more severe sen-tences than white people did. Whipping was the most common form of public punishment for slaves, though South Carolina permitted branding until 1833, and there were cases after that of slaves having their ears chopped off. Alabama permitted up to one hundred lashes on the bare back of a slave for forging a pass. For some offenses death was permissible.

The harshness of the law was somewhat mitigated by the profit motive, by planter paternalism, and in some cases by the slaves' legal status as persons. Slaves were defined as prop-erty but considered persons too. For example, the malicious killing of a slave was considered murder, and some codes regu-lated the hours of labor and told masters to provide a proper diet. These provisions were partly motivated by self-interest and partly by the fact that white Southerners recognized blacks as human beings. The killing of a slave was both the taking of a life and the destruction of a valuable piece of property. When a slave was executed for a capital crime the state generally compensated the owner for his loss. Occasionally masters discharged overseers who were too brutal; some masters even sued overseers for injuring their slave property; and on occasion the state prosecuted overseers for killing or maiming slaves.

In practice the slaveholders controlled the legal process, and the courts offered meager protection for people in bondage. If the owners' power made for only a slight legal protection as persons, however, it also enabled masters to disregard such features of the codes as the ban on teaching slaves to read and write. The practice of hiring out and living away, although frowned on and illegal in many places, was nonetheless common in the cities. A Savannah grand jury maintained that the practice of slaves being able "to hire their own time or labor for themselves" was "an evile" that "is striking directly at the existence of our institutions." But that same city had slaves who hired out, including one who "hired his time of his master at two hundred and fifty dollars a year, which he paid in monthly installments. He did what he called job work, which consisted of undertaking jobs, and hiring men to work under him," and he had seven or eight other blacks, "all hired to help remove the cotton in wheelbarrows."

The practice continued because masters found it profitable to hire out their bondsmen and employers needed skilled or even unskilled blacks for short periods. The skills blacks possessed made them valuable enough for many Southern whites to overcome their fears about the lack of controls under the hiring-out system. City governments rented slaves for municipal projects, such as building the streets and removing the garbage. Some cities, however, owned their slaves. One historian has noted that the city of Savannah even used its slaves as firemen and they were reported to be the pride of the town. "We suppose that there are no more efficient or well managed companies in the United States," boasted the local newspaper.

Evidence exists that urban slaves had better shelter than those living on the plantations in run-down cabins, but usually slave housing was crowded, drafty, dirty, and lacked adequate furniture. Some visitors found the slave quarters "in the most decayed and deplorable condition," and "built of logs, with no windows—no opening at all, except the doorway, with a chimney of sticks and mud." Kind and prosperous planters provided their slaves with sturdy whitewashed log cabins and privacy.

Diet, medical care, and clothing varied, but they were frequently inadequate. Frederick Douglass said that as a child in slavery he was "kept almost in a state of nudity; no shoes, no stockings, no jacket, no trousers; nothing but coarse sack cloth or town-linen, made into a sort of shirt, reaching down to my knees." Adult slaves were usually better clothed and many had special attire for holidays. In the cities one could find well-dressed slaves, the household bondsmen of rich townfolk and planters. Masters tried to provide a healthy diet, but some relied on cornmeal, salt pork, hominy, and fatback. More fortunate slaves had their own gardens and hence ate better food. Because the black population grew rapidly through natural increase in the antebellum South there must have been a certain minimum standard of living; but life expectancy of slaves was less than that for whites.

Most slaves worked long hours, often from sunup to sunset. During the harvest season they were driven especially hard; in the off season blacks had less to do, but plantation repair and maintenance chores kept them busy. Slaves working in industries and mining had few seasonal adjustments and seldom got relief. Usually owners allowed their slaves to rest on special occasions, like Christmas and after the harvest, and some gave Sundays and occasional Saturdays as holidays. Pregnant women received time off just before and after the birth of a child, but the young mother was expected to be back in the fields, or at the "Big House," within days after the delivery.

How masters extracted labor and disciplined their bondsmen was crucial to the daily life of the individual slave. Stories abound about physical cruelty. Some historians believe that brutality was more common on the large plantations of the Deep South, but it could be found everywhere. In the narratives of ex-slaves, many blacks remembered frequent beatings and it appears that force characterized the system. One slave recalled, "I have seen slaves whipped and I was whipped myself. I was whipped particularly about a saddle I left in the night after using it during the day. My flesh was cut so bad that the scars are on me to this day." Cruel masters also stingily rationed food and shelter, did not allow slaves to leave the plantations, and used dogs to hunt runaways. A few even maintained jails for the slaves and took care to give public whippings as an example for the others.

Yet many masters tried to avoid brutality, and ex-slaves recalled those who did not use force. An Alabama bondsman related, "Us lucky, 'cause Massa Cole don't whip us." Even some who used the lash urged caution. A Louisiana planter observed, "I object to having the skin cut, or my negroes marked in any way by the lash. . . . I will most certainly discharge any overseer for striking any of my negroes with a club or the butt of his whip." Others avoided the whip either because they found such brutality repugnant ("The overseer whose constant and only resort is to the lash . . . is a brute, and deserves the penitentiary") or because they favored different methods of control. Instead of punishment they offered inducements—better housing, food, and clothing. They allowed slaves to grow and even sell their own food.

Owners and overseers sometimes used their power to take sexual advantage of slave women. At one extreme the sexual bond was accompanied by deep feelings; some men kept mistresses to whom they were strongly attached. In New Orleans the practice was quite open; elsewhere it was done quietly. The mixed offspring of these unions were sometimes educated and freed. One wealthy Virginia planter made his paramour head of the household. He tutored and freed their four children. When his daughter married a slave he purchased the husband's freedom and gave them land, and at his death willed his property to his three sons. This planter was uncommon but it was not unusual to see free blacks of mixed blood; a large proportion of the free black population had some white ancestors.

At the other extreme masters could force themselves on un-willing slaves, and some looked on blacks as fair game, for, as Frederick Douglass said, the "slave woman is at the mercy of the father, sons or brothers of her master." Nor could the male slave protect his wife or sister or mother without risking severe punishment. Most interracial sexual unions were of white males and black females. White females and black males some-times became attached, but such unions were considered taboo in the Old South.

Miscegenation and the lack of legal status of the family did not mean that all slaves lived without a family life. To be sure, some masters cared little about morality or stable families. In fact, they realized that promiscuous behavior often resulted in children, which increased the plantation labor force. But most owners wanted reliable workers and if they thought that mo-nogamy encouraged stability, they promoted such relationships. If they thought that loose arrangements did not upset the routine of the plantation, however, they ignored the slaves' sexual practices. Some whites, of course, were deeply religious and paternalistic, and assumed responsibility for slave conduct and morality. These masters insisted on sexual purity, family stability, and monogamy. But, as we shall see, slaves themselves had their own ideas on these subjects.

Control over family life was part of the general power owners possessed. Masters ruled and ultimately slaves had to come to grips with that fact. Many appeared cooperative, even passive and docile. Southern whites liked to think that their charges were happy, faithful, and loyal. They frequently saw this "Sambo" type as the typical plantation "darkie." In his extreme form "Sambo" had no thoughts of freedom and was willing to sacrifice his life for the beloved master and mistress and their family. There were passive slaves, but many hid their true feel-ings about their hatred of slavery and whites and only appeared to be loyal and contented. When their chance came, many of these supposedly contented slaves fled; or in the case of the Civil War, they joined the Union army. Even the house servants, supposedly favored and more trustworthy, sometimes left their masters when they had the opportunity. Thus slaves could exhibit both a willingness to accept slavery and the will to resist. At the other end were the rebels, the Nat Turners, who resisted violently. Turner's revolt sent a chill throughout the South. Literate and skilled, Turner was convinced that "I was ordained for some great things in the hands of the Almighty." In 1831 he led a revolt that massacred several white families before armed whites crushed it. Turner and 40 blacks were either executed or murdered because of the rebellion.

Still other slaves were neither Sambos nor rebels. They were sullen and resentful or were alternatively sullen and cooperative. They broke tools, worked slowly and inefficiently, killed livestock, and sometimes made life difficult for their owners. Slaves even sued, sometimes successfully, for their freedom on the grounds that they were illegally being held in bondage. Most slaves were efficient workers, however, even though they might have yearned for independence. Of course, if slaves resisted openly they risked punishment, but it was a chance many took. When life was especially unbearable they ran away, and the more resourceful and fortunate were able to escape. But it was not easy. Slave patrols and the long distance to the free states hindered the flight of the fugitives. Another obstacle to running away was the loss of loved ones, for slaves had strong familial ties and fleeing the plantation meant probably never seeing one's close relatives again. Yet, although the numbers are not known exactly, thousands did manage to break away. Until the United States took Florida that area was a haven, especially among the Indians there, but fugitives usually headed north and followed the north star to either the free states or Canada.

Despite their intense desire for liberty, most slaves obeyed their masters and accommodated themselves to the "peculiar institution." Some even developed close ties with their owners. There were slaves who, when given the chance, did not flee. Some were too old with no place to go; others had relatively kind masters for whom they had feelings of affection. Whites later exaggerated the loyalty of slaves, especially that of the black "mammies" who raised the masters' children, but close bonds often did exist between such black women and those whom they nursed and raised. Then, too, they were sometimes treated much better than the field hands. Moreover, some of the privileged slaves identified with their oppressors. The black drivers, for example, gained power and status while household servants received fancy clothes. One slave recalled when he got new clothes: "I had known no comforts, and had been so cowered and broken in spirits by cruel lashings that I really felt lighthearted at this improvement in my personal appearance, although it was merely for the gratification of my master's pride; and I thought I would do all I could to please my Boss." Others received money, gifts, better food, and fewer restrictions.

There were even slaves who informed on their brethren. They turned fugitives in, or reported plots or revolts to the master. Perhaps it was a personal conflict that motivated some to turn on others, or perhaps they were seeking special privileges or rewards. Angry slaves called these bondsmen "white folks' servants" because "they are just the same as white men." Having such trusted help, masters were known to leave the plantations under their care and reward them for work well done when they returned. Yet even such privileged slaves, or those with close ties to the Big House, longed for emancipation. The white South feared this desire but dared not admit it existed.

The slaves did not organize their lives solely according to white peoples' dictates. They possessed a rich culture from their African background, and from the combination of this culture and New World experiences an Afro-American way of life developed, centering on God and religion. Although white masters imbued their charges with a Christianity of work and obedience, the slaves harmonized aspects of African religions with these teachings into a faith more suitable to their needs. Black spirituals envisioned ultimate redemption and recognition

of personal worth. Old Testament themes of the release of the
Hebrew children from bondage, of David's triumph over Go-
liath, and of Daniel's deliverance from the Lion's Den dominated their prayers:

>He delivered Daniel from de lion's den
>Jonah from de belly ob de whale,
>And de Hebrew children from de fiery furnace,
>And why not every man?

In other cases African culture resisted any fusion with Christianity or the white world. African beliefs in magic, voodoo, and
conjurers survived into the nineteenth century and through
these some slaves tried to retaliate against oppressive whites.
Owners could control the legal status and much of the physical
life of the slave, but not necessarily his mind or culture. A con-
jurer who allegedly could affect whites as well as blacks was a
powerful person, a supernatural defense against the harshness
of slavery. One slave recalled that "I was led to believe that I
could do almost as I pleased without being flogged." When
threatened by his master with a beating, "I did not believe that
he could do it, while I had this root and dust, and as he approached me, I commenced talking saucy to him."

Folk tales also played an important part in slave culture.
Some of the oral traditions told of the African past and tribal
religion, but most were secular, taught a moral, and emphasized
survival. The most famous of the narratives concern Br'er Rabbit, the shrewd bunny who managed to outwit his foes. Scholars
have traced these animal trickster stories to Africa, but they
were well suited to a slave society. Faced with white power the
blacks, like Br'er Rabbit, had to be cunning to endure. "De
rabbit is de slickest o' all de animals de Lawd ever made. He
ain't de biggest, an' he ain't de loudest but he sho' am de slickest." Clearly the folk tale and other forms of slave culture
pointed to ways of dealing with a harsh world. As one scholar
observed,

In their religious songs and sermons slaves sought certainty in a world filled with confusion and anarchy; in their supernatural folk beliefs they sought power and control in a world filled with arbitrary forces greater than themselves; and in their tales they sought understanding of a world in which, for better or worse, they were forced to live. All forms of slave folk culture offered their creators psychic relief and a sense of mastery.

If religion, magic, music, and stories gave slaves a sense of themselves, so did the most important institution of slavery, the family. The power of the master to make and break families should not lead us to minimize their importance. While some masters stressed family life, the bondsmen had their own reasons for doing so and managed to establish rules for courtship, sex, and marriage. Slaves, for example, did not marry their blood cousins. The sexual code among slaves accepted prenuptial sex along with fidelity in marriage.

Most slaves lived in two-parent households. Of course the master and overseer supervised slave families, but the slaves themselves could and did socialize their children. If the father lived on another plantation, relatives played a more significant role in the life of the mother and her children. Aware of the importance of their family and kin, slaves used family names for their children's first names. But unlike whites they never named children after their mothers. Some slaves even used surnames that differed from those of their masters. The choice of names shows how the bondsmen regarded their families.

SOUTHERN WHITES

Blacks were not the only poor people in the antebellum South. Many white farmers had neither slaves nor decent land and lived in wretched poverty in the piney-wooded or swampy areas. So did the unskilled urban workers and those in the industries of the Old South. Industrial workers labored long hours for low wages, faced occupational hazards, and lived in crowded housing. The Irish who toiled on canals and railroads, as well as other white laborers in the mines, were among the lowest paid workers in America.

The vast bulk of this white population descended from colonial stock, as few immigrants came to the Old South. In 1860 the slave states possessed about 500,000 immigrants, who barely accounted for 13 percent of the nation's foreign-born. The South's major ports, Baltimore and New Orleans, attracted many of these foreigners, while the states of Maryland, Missouri, Louisiana, and Texas contained the majority of them. The Germans, who were concentrated in Maryland, Missouri, and Texas, and the Irish, in Louisiana and Georgia, constituted most of the foreign-born population, although ethnic enclaves could be found in Alabama and Mississippi as well. About 30,000 central European Jews also found their way to the South and many of the rural hamlets received visits from Jewish peddlers, who later became small shopkeepers in many a Southern town. Louisiana, with about 8,000, contained the largest number of Jews in the antebellum period.

Most immigrants chose to settle outside the South because the shipping routes generally took them from Europe to Northern ports like Boston and New York, and because they believed there were more opportunities in the free states. The newcomers did not want to compete with the plantation system and slave labor. Furthermore, by the time of the mass immigration after 1845, they were aware that most of the best cotton land of the Old South had been gobbled up by the old-stock whites. Of course, there were still opportunities in the South. Germans settled in Texas, for example, because land was available there; both the Irish and Germans worked in the cities; and the Irish also found jobs building canals and railroads.

The nativism (hostility to foreigners) of pre–Civil War America, most pronounced in the free states, might have discouraged foreigners from settling there, but the slave states also had their share of bigotry. In some areas of the South the Irish were detested because of their Catholicism, and both

the Germans and the Irish were scorned for their clannishness. Some Southerners blamed the massive immigration to the
North after 1840 with tipping the population balance in favor
of the free states, to the detriment of Southern interests, and
many were apprehensive about the views toward slavery of
the immigrants in their own region. In particular, the antislavery sentiments of German settlers alarmed white Southerners and caused them to suspect the newcomers. In the 1850s
German radicals in Louisville denounced slavery, while in San
Antonio another group called the institution "an evil, the removal of which is absolutely essential according to the principles of democracy." Most Southern Germans, however, accepted the region's views and denounced the Republicans, and
Irish and Germans were generally known to dislike both blacks
and abolitionists. If Southern Germans did not own many
slaves it was not because they abhorred the institution but
rather because they settled in areas unsuitable for cotton production, or were urban dwellers.

Whether foreign-born or native-born, rich or poor, white
Southerners had one thing in common—the color of their skin.
Some poor whites did not wish to fight for slavery and refused
to do so during the Civil War. Yet Caucasians in the South generally agreed that the region belonged to white men and they
enthusiastically supported Indian removal and black slavery.

The differences between the North and South became more
pronounced after 1830 with the rise of antislavery sentiment
above the Mason–Dixon line and the growing divergence of the
economies of the two sections. It was the struggle over slavery,
however, and especially slavery in the territories, that would
eventually split the nation.

3

Forging a New Nation
The North
(1776–1840s)

WHILE PLANTATION AGRICULTURE SPREAD WEST across much of the Lower South the Northern economy followed a different path. Although agriculture remained important in almost all regions of the country, in the North commerce and industry developed at a more rapid pace. Commercial and industrial ventures depended on more urban markets and improved transportation facilities, so the Northern economy and society became more diversified than the basically rural and agricultural South. As the two sections drifted apart economically they developed different needs, and they often competed with each other rather than cooperating. Whereas both sections faced similar problems in regard to the Indians, the South had a much greater interest in the slave system while the North had to consider ways of accommodating its increasing number of free blacks and, later on, a continuing flood of European immigrants.

INDIAN RELATIONS

The creation of an independent United States gave the Northern Indian tribes few reasons to celebrate. They had fought alongside the British, but the Treaty of Paris, which granted independence to the United States, ignored the tribes' contributions as English allies and gave them no consideration as owners of land in North America. After signing the treaty, the British did not withdraw completely from the region but kept troops stationed at Detroit and other frontier outposts, which were used as bases for a lively trade and propaganda effort among the tribes. Under these circumstances and in response to American claims of sovereignty and efforts to extract land from them, tribal leaders resolved to oppose the "Long Knives" and to drive the pioneers out of their country. During the 1776–1815 era they tried diplomacy, trade alliances, cultural and religious movements, intertribal confederacies, and warfare. Despite their eventual defeat, the tribes demonstrated that they recognized the threat posed by the advancing pioneers, and they used every means at their disposal to thwart and defeat their white enemies while working to retain their tribal identities.

During the mid-1780s American negotiators concluded treaties with tribes in the Upper Ohio Valley and New York. Not satisfied with these agreements, representatives of individual states and spokesmen for the trans-Appalachian frontier settlers often ignored the treaties and tried to seize the tribes' ancestral lands. Seeing that their efforts to reach a peaceful agreement with the United States had failed, Indian leaders such as Blue Jacket (Shawnee), Joseph Brant (Mohawk), and Little Turtle (Miami) worked to organize a northwestern confederacy, and in 1786 they rejected the earlier treaties as fraudulent. Instead, they announced that the Ohio River was the boundary, and that all land north or west of that stream belonged to the Indians.

This brought the tribes into direct confrontation with the United States, for one year later, in 1787, the Congress claimed the same land, calling it the Northwest Territory. Pioneers from Kentucky raided north into Ohio and Indian war parties retaliated to destroy frontier settlements. Despite an estimated 1,500 pioneer deaths, the Indian raids failed to keep the whites out of Ohio. In 1790 and 1791, after President Washington called for troops to pacify the area, frontier militia armies marched north into Ohio building forts and destroying Indian villages, but each time large Indian forces under Little Turtle and Blue Jacket crushed the invading white armies and drove them back south of the Ohio River. Finally, in 1794 General Anthony Wayne led a well-trained army of regulars north and defeated the tribes at the Battle of Fallen Timbers. This quieted the northern frontier for the next decade.

Having lost the initiative to the advancing Americans, the tribes turned inward and began to place increasing dependence on their own cultural traditions. Choosing to focus on spiritual values, several Indian prophets offered tribal alternatives to either warfare or surrender. Among the Seneca of New York, Handsome Lake began a native revival movement. By 1800 he was calling on his people to forsake alcohol, to place more reliance on agriculture, and to combine some Christian and some traditional religious ideas if they hoped to survive. His teachings offered renewed hope for immediate survival and future well-being to some Seneca, and his followers proved almost completely resistant to later American demands for tribal land cessions in New York state.

While Handsome Lake preached his code to the Seneca, another medicine man, the Shawnee Tenskwatawa, experienced several life-changing visions in 1805. These transformed him from a village drunk to a sober, earnest teacher, so that his example and powerful denunciations of the white man's weapons, food, and alcohol appealed to many Shawnee, Delaware, and Miami people. Urging the tribes to accept his new ideas and ceremonies, he preached that all tribes were a part of a greater Indian nation and that none should cede any more land to the advancing Americans. He promised that if the converts followed his teachings, they would be spared at some future time when a great catastrophe would destroy the whites and unbelieving Indians. Hundreds of villagers accepted Tenskwatawa's teachings, and many flocked to Prophetstown, a village newly formed in northwestern Indiana.

By 1809–10 Tecumseh, the Prophet's brother, assumed at least joint leadership of the movement. A warrior rather than a religious leader, Tecumseh saw the resurgence of tribal pride as yet another chance to forge an Indian confederacy with the British against the Americans south of the Great Lakes. A dynamic and clever speaker and a forceful leader, he stressed that the tribes all had to agree not to sell more land as he strove to turn the Indian cultural and religious movement into a political and military alliance. After the 1809 Fort Wayne treaty talks Tecumseh and the chief American negotiator, Governor William Henry Harrison of the Indiana Territory, had several angry debates over land cessions. Not only did the Indian leader reject the validity of treaties concluded earlier by any single tribe, but he also demanded that the Americans return lands taken in the recent past. At one point in a meeting between the two men they sat next to each other on a long bench, and Tecumseh crowded Harrison so that he had to move to the end of the bench. When the governor objected, Tecumseh replied that he was just showing Harrison how the whites had pushed the Indians off their land. Despite the inspirational leadership and organizational skills of the Shawnee brothers, the tide of settlement continued. In late 1811, during Tecumseh's visit to the Southeast seeking new recruits for the alliance, Governor Harrison defeated the Indians and destroyed Prophetstown.

Having tried diplomacy, warfare, religious revival, and political confederacies to little avail, the Indians readily joined the British against the United States during the War of 1812. That conflict provided the tribes with their last real chance to halt American expansion, and then only if the British won. In the North Tecumseh rallied the tribes of the Great Lakes region, joined the British forces in Canada, and engaged in heavy fighting in Ontario. He died in late 1813 during the American victory at the Battle of the Thames. With his death Indian efforts to stem the flood of pioneers into the region ended.

During the next two decades the Northern tribes had neither the strength nor the organization to resist the continuing American demands for more land. When the removal program began in earnest, during the late 1820s, they lacked the power still available to the Southern tribes. Certainly the tribes objected to being forced off their ancestral homelands, and they tried every available tactic to delay the exodus. For example, they hurriedly planted corn each spring and then insisted on remaining to harvest it—thus making their westward trek more difficult because they were forced to move during the autumn or winter. Despite the delays, removal continued and the tribes crossed the Mississippi, no matter how reluctantly. Only one group, a splinter of the Sac and Fox tribes, objected enough to cause bloodshed, and that resulted more from misunderstanding than from any conscious decision to fight.

What became known as the Black Hawk War resulted from a longstanding dispute that began in 1804 when Governor Harrison had tricked a few warriors into signing a treaty ceding their lands in Illinois. The tribesmen ignored the agreement because their regular leaders had not participated in the negotiations. Then, because the treaty allowed them to live on the ceded land until it was needed, most of the tribe forgot about the arrangement. In 1831, however, frontier settlers in Illinois forced the Sac and Fox to cross the Mississippi at gunpoint. The villagers spent a miserable winter in Iowa and in early 1832, led by the aged warrior Black Hawk, about 1,000 men, women, and children returned to western Illinois to plant corn in their old fields. This "invasion" caused Illinois Governor John Reynolds to muster the state militia and demand federal troops. The Indians, frightened by the show of force, tried to surrender, but undisciplined Illinois militiamen fired at envoys carrying a white parley flag, causing the rest to retreat. During the summer of 1832, regular troops and militiamen chased the fleeing Indians across northern Illinois and southern Wisconsin before catching them on the east bank of the Mississippi. There, in the so-called Battle of Bad Axe, the soldiers destroyed all but 150 of the 1,000 people who had dared to migrate east instead of farther west.

ANTISLAVERY IN THE NORTH

In contrast to the unaltered relations with the Indians, American treatment of blacks in the Northern states underwent a fundamental change. The assault on slavery predated the Revolutionary era. In the eighteenth century a few religious groups worried about their connection to slavery, and the Quakers took the first steps away from it by withdrawing from the slave trade and freeing their individual slaves. This proved relatively easy to do in the Northern colonies where antislavery sentiments encountered a relatively weak bondage system. Quakers in New England and Pennsylvania acted first, but even those in the South began to manumit blacks wherever the law permitted.

Quaker opposition to slavery received strong support during the Revolutionary era. Spokesmen demanding liberty and equality realized that slavery was incompatible with such concepts. Blacks served in the armies fielded by some Northern states, often gaining their freedom as a result. Thus a combination of pressures to end bondage reached its peak in the Northern colonies where by court decisions, individual emancipations, and state constitutions and law, slavery was gradually abolished. Between 1780, when Pennsylvania passed the first manumission law, and 1804, Rhode Island, Connecticut, New York, and New Jersey provided for the gradual ending of black bondage. In Massachusetts court cases and individual manumissions by owners terminated slavery, and in Vermont the state constitution of 1777 banned it. What happened in New Hampshire is not known precisely, but apparently some owners freed their slaves in return for military service while other blacks simply ran away. In any event New Hampshire had only 674 slaves in 1773 and none by 1810.

Despite the gradual phasing out of slavery in the North and efforts to end or at least limit it in the South, national antislavery agitation failed. The Northwest Ordinance of 1787 outlawed slavery in the area that eventually became Ohio, Illinois, Indiana, Michigan, and Wisconsin, but there was still ample room for its expansion in the southwestern region, which reached to the Mississippi River, and, after the Louisiana Purchase, farther westward. Though not mentioned by name, slavery was recognized and sanctioned by the United States Constitution in the provision of the fugitive slave clause and in the three-fifths compromise, which allowed the South to count each slave as three-fifths of a white person for purposes of taxation and allocation of seats in the United States House of Representatives. The Constitution also specifically prevented Congress from banning the slave trade until 1808. For the most part, Southern blacks would have to wait for the Civil War for their deliverance.

IMMIGRATION AND ASSIMILATION

The years immediately following national independence witnessed a gradual renewal of immigration from Europe, but at a volume much smaller than in earlier decades. Although no official records show the number of people who entered the United States, scholars estimate that about 250,000 newcomers arrived between 1783 and 1815. Usually the new settlers came from those European nations that had supplied the largest number of emigrants during the late colonial period. Scotch-Irish immigrants continued to arrive by the boatload, and the British consul in Philadelphia estimated that perhaps 20,000 of them had left Britain during the 1780s. Fewer people left the German states, either because conditions there had improved or because it had become increasingly difficult to get away.

A renewed influx of French-speaking people entered the country during the era of the French Revolution in the 1790s. In 1791 the black, largely slave population of Santo Domingo in the Caribbean revolted, forcing between 10,000 and 20,000 white French-speaking islanders to flee. Many of these refugees migrated to the United States where the public welcomed them and Congress appropriated funds for their aid. The French

Revolution and wars resulting from it drove thousands of French from their homeland at about the same time. By 1792 royalists and aristocrats fleeing their enemies reached America, but these groups remained small. Most of the incoming French settled in Eastern cities or towns and remained there as urban workers, entertainers, or professional people. In Philadelphia, at least one hundred French or bilingual publications appeared in the 1790s, which was seven times as many as had originated only a decade earlier. As a group, the upper-middle-class French-speaking immigrants melted into the general population rapidly and with little difficulty.

The relatively small number of immigrants between the 1780s and 1815 meant that there was little to interrupt the ongoing process of assimilation. By the time the Revolutionary War ended many former immigrants proudly considered themselves Americans, and even had that not been the case, the small stream of newcomers from their homelands was not enough to sustain feelings of national or ethnic identity in those who had arrived earlier. In particular, the steady decline in the use of languages other than English provided the most obvious measure of assimilation. Dutch and German—the two most widely used foreign languages—both became second languages, local curiosities, and even died out in some areas. Without a renewed supply of native-speaking clergymen churches grudgingly shifted their services to English. In 1794 the General Synod of the Dutch Reformed church accepted English as its official language. Dutch preaching lingered on in parts of New Jersey and New York, but often as a special service "to gratify the aged, who love to hear the Word in their mother tongue." Much the same story can be told of the German churches. By the turn of the century American-born ministers were replacing those from abroad and were introducing English instead of German. Congregation after congregation adopted English in their services, although some of the Pennsylvania German churches resisted the trend for a long time.

As churches Americanized, so did the foreign language press.

During the late eighteenth and early nineteenth centuries the number of German newspapers declined and many that tried to keep the language alive lasted only a few years. By the end of the Napoleonic Wars, the German press survived only in Pennsylvania.

FEAR OF FOREIGNERS

Many Americans in the new republic thought of their society as a haven for those escaping from oppression and expected the nation to gain strength from the immigrants attracted to its shores. Others feared that the United States might be overrun by the malcontents and dregs of other societies. In the First Congress, Representative James Jackson of Georgia went beyond the prevalent anxieties to call for the exclusion of "the common class of vagrants, paupers and other outcasts of Europe." This and similar statements show the continuing fear of national groups whose ways differed from Anglo-American traditions. Debate on the problem continued sporadically, but the Naturalization Act of 1790 called for only a two-year waiting period before aliens could apply for citizenship. An influx of people during the French Revolution kept the issue alive and in 1795 Congress increased the waiting time from two to five years.

The nation's two political parties, the Federalists and the Jeffersonian Republicans, agreed that too many foreigners might endanger American institutions but split over which people posed the greatest threat. Conservative Federalists believed that French Jacobins and Irish radicals were most dangerous, whereas the Jeffersonians welcomed these people while criticizing French royalists and other aristocratically oriented groups. The growing numbers of Irish in the major cities hated the British and supported the Republican party because of its pro-French and anti-British stand. Many New England Federalists were traditionally suspicious of foreigners and especially those of Republican leanings. Harrison Gray Otis of

Massachusetts wanted no foreigners to come, above all no "hordes of wild Irishmen, nor the turbulent and disorderly of all parts of the world, to come here with a view to disturb our tranquility, after having succeeded in the overthrow of their own Governments."

Not content with verbal outbursts, in 1798 the Federalist-controlled Congress passed a series of laws clearly aimed at cutting Jeffersonian strength by reducing the personal liberties of aliens and other dissenters. A new naturalization law extended the residence period needed for citizenship from five to fourteen years, and an Alien Enemies Act and an Alien Friends Act gave the president authority to arrest and deport resident aliens suspected of subversion. These laws, which were based on the assumption that the United States and France were on the brink of war, got little use. Nevertheless, they achieved at least part of their goal because during the year hundreds of French men, women, and children fled the United States.

Still unsatisfied, the Federalists pushed the Sedition Act through Congress. This measure was meant to stifle most domestic criticism of the Adams administration, and although not designed exclusively to attack recent immigrants, it was particularly applied to Irish and French newspapermen. Through this law the Federalists attempted to silence what they called the "pack of imported scribblers." Although the government imprisoned some journalists, the presses continued to attack the Federalists and contributed directly to the Jeffersonian victory in the 1800 presidential election. Jefferson's supporters were less suspicious of aliens and his administration returned to the earlier five-year residency requirement for citizenship.

THE MOVEMENT WEST

While Easterners coped with suspected radicals, other Americans streamed across the Appalachians into the Ohio Valley and the Great Lakes area. This flood of settlement had begun just prior to independence and continued with only slight interruption until 1820. In the area south of the Ohio River, Kentucky became a state in 1792 and Tennessee just four years later. To the north, Ohio entered the Union in 1803. Economic difficulties related to the War of 1812 slowed Western development, but by 1820 all of the territory east of the Mississippi River had been carved into states except for Florida, Michigan, and Wisconsin.

Most of the new Westerners were farmers or small business-men and professional people whose jobs depended on agriculture. Millers, tanners, meat packers, blacksmiths, wagon makers, store operators, and bankers all owed their livelihoods to the farmers. With the exception of a few efforts at large-scale farming or livestock raising in Illinois, the Northern settlements had nothing to compare with the plantation agriculture of the South. Northerners invested in large amounts of land more for speculation than for farming.

The Western regions, however, did not remain agricultural and rural for long. In fact, towns such as Pittsburgh, Cincinnati, and St. Louis existed before many farmers had arrived in the area. In any case, the early Midwestern settlers needed urban centers nearby, for although they did not resort to plantation agriculture, they were still commercial farmers, and they looked to the towns as markets or at least trading centers for disposal of their crops. Thus the most expensive land usually lay near the avenues of transportation such as rivers, canals, or roads, and near the market towns. Even a casual glance at a current map of the Midwest indicates that many of these urban centers remain today.

The rush of Western settlement forced Americans to look for better means of transportation. During the colonial era waterways offered the best transportation and communication, and although the mountains separated East from West, rivers continued to be the best way of moving people and goods. At first pioneer families moved down the Ohio River, its tributaries, and the Mississippi on rafts, barges, arks, and keelboats, but the voyage of Robert Fulton's steamboat *New Orleans* from Pittsburgh to New Orleans in 1811 inaugurated a new mode of travel. By 1820 steamboat navigation on many Western streams had reduced the costs of transportation by 60 to 80 percent and noticeably speeded travel. It also tied the agricultural Midwest to the port of New Orleans until the 1830s, when the major Eastern cities developed better facilities for trade with the West.

Because rivers often flowed in the wrong direction, or were simply too far away for easy use, many Americans depended on the existing roads. These, however, could be as frustrating and difficult to use as the streams, for only a few were actually wide enough for large freight wagons or carts, and they often contained stumps and boulders. Unpaved, most roads became muddy tracks in spring and fall, and frozen ruts in winter. Governments at all levels tried to improve the roads, but with only modest success. In 1806 Congress chartered the Cumberland, or National, Road to connect the Chesapeake region with the Ohio Valley. Unfortunately, work on the road did not start until 1811 and then halted during the war that began the next year. It took until 1818 for the builders to reach Wheeling, where work again came to a stop. In 1825 Congress provided more money and the workers inched their way west to Illinois over the next several decades. Private road or turnpike companies built more than ten thousand miles of improved roads, mostly in New England and the middle states. Most of these ventures cost so much that the companies went broke or gave their roads to the individual states.

Clearly something more than roads and rivers was needed, and during the 1820s Americans turned to canals with the hope that they would solve the nation's transportation woes. Canals cost more to build and maintain than roads, and so most had to be constructed with public rather than private funds. In 1817 only a handful of canals, with an aggregate total of about a hundred miles in length, existed in the United States. That year New York Governor De Witt Clinton convinced the state legislature to authorize a project to connect the Hudson River with Lake Erie by canal. In 1825 this project, known as the Erie

Canal, was completed, linking New York City by water with the Great Lakes and offering Midwestern farmers an alternative to trading with merchants in New Orleans.

Equally important, the Erie's instant financial success stimulated the other major Eastern cities to try similar ventures. Boston considered a canal, but the terrain prohibited this, so the city fathers began to build railroads. In 1826 Philadelphia got legislative support for a scheme using canals, railroads, and rivers to tie that city to Pittsburgh beyond the mountains. Baltimore decided to build the Chesapeake and Ohio Canal in its efforts to tap Western trade opportunities, but this canal never got past the mountains. In 1828 Baltimore, too, turned to the railroads and the Baltimore and Ohio Railroad was begun. Ohio, Michigan, Indiana, and Illinois all tried building canals with state funds, but with little success. By 1840 some 3,326 miles of canals stretched across the country, but despite their immense cost these could be used only part of the year, and thus failed to offer cheap, dependable transportation on a regular basis. By the 1840s, public interest had shifted to railroads as the best means of transportation for both goods and people.

INDUSTRIAL GROWTH

As better transportation facilitated movement to the West, the region became an increasingly important market for American goods. This in turn stimulated the growth of Eastern business and manufacturing. The process of industrialization proceeded slowly during the early decades of national independence, and before the South and West opened as large markets manufacturing remained local and small scale. In 1791 Secretary of the Treasury Alexander Hamilton wrote that "the expediency of encouraging manufactures in the United States . . . appears at this time to be pretty generally admitted." Yet several more decades would pass before the nation had either surplus labor or capital, and until an adequate transportation system emerged industrial production remained a minor element in the economy.

Nevertheless, some manufacturing had existed in America since well before independence. Many towns had local forges, flour or saw mills, paper factories, tanneries, and even small textile shops, although most of these remained only part-time ventures or lasted but a few years. The first factory of significance was a New England cotton mill directed by Samuel Slater. Begun in Pawtucket, Rhode Island, in 1791, the mill employed children at wages of 12¢ to 25¢ a day, and it remained a small operation until the Napoleonic Wars limited the supply of European goods available in America. Then in 1808 Congress, at President Jefferson's urging, passed the Embargo Act, which severely curtailed foreign trade. Thereafter the New England cotton textile mills grew at a fantastic pace. In 1808 there were only 15 mills in the United States; 87 more had been built by 1809. The number of spindles in the nation increased from 8,000 in 1808 to 31,000 in 1809 and to 80,000 in 1811. Between 1815 and 1831 the number of spindles in New England alone had tripled, and by 1860 it had tripled again. On the eve of the Civil War the average cotton textile mill in New England had 7,000 spindles compared to an average of 2,000 spindles for the mills in the South and West. At the Boston Manufacturing Company in Waltham, Massachusetts, which built the first integrated cotton mill in the world in 1813, factory workers did everything from unbaling cotton to dyeing the cloth before it was sold. The Lowell Mills, as they came to be called, abandoned child labor and chose instead to hire young farm women, aged 18 to 22; by the middle of the century immigrants started replacing the young women. The operation at the Lowell Mills was both an immediate and a long-run success, stimulating other groups of investors to imitate its methods.

Industrial progress was not limited to the textile mills. The iron industry grew steadily, producing consumer products like stoves and, later, rails for the railroads and a variety of iron and steel products. The boot and shoe industry, concentrated in New England, lagged behind textiles, but the invention of the sewing machine in 1846 revolutionized the manufacture of boots and shoes.

Economic expansion was by no means even. The nation suffered from an agricultural depression between 1828 and 1831, a recession from 1833 to 1835, and a near-disastrous economic collapse between 1837 and 1843. These slumps in the economy temporarily retarded economic growth and contributed to social conflict. President Jackson's veto of a bill recharting the Bank of the United States in 1832 and the subsequent withdrawal of federal government funds from that bank precipitated retaliatory action from Nicholas Biddle, director of the Bank of the United States, who called in loans and contracted credit. This action in turn triggered a near panic as economic conditions worsened in 1834 and 1835. Coincidentally the number of riots and labor disturbances increased at the very time of the downturn. More than a thousand young women walked off their jobs in Lowell, Massachusetts, in February 1834 to protest a 15 percent cut in wages. The National Trades Union conducted at least 175 strikes between 1834 and its ultimate demise in 1837, when the business collapse crushed the trade movements.

As factories grew, the continuing demand for laborers attracted many to the towns and cities. Young people from rural areas as well as foreign immigrants sought employment in the burgeoning industrial concerns. This growth of manufacturing and the increasing urbanization in the Northeast and Midwest set those areas apart from the more rural South. As Table 3.1 shows, by the 1830s Eastern and Northern cities had far outpaced all of their counterparts in the future Confederacy except New Orleans.

The Northern seaport cities outdistanced all others as centers of commerce, industry, and population. Of these New York, the nation's largest city, clearly stood out. It benefited from a large hinterland market whose residents transported their produce to, and purchased manufactured goods from, the city via the Erie Canal and/or the Hudson and Mohawk rivers. New York's prosperity also rested on its prime location between New En-

Table 3.1

POPULATION OF MAJOR CITIES, 1830–1860*

	1830	1840	1850	1860
New York	202,589	312,700	515,547	813,669
Philadelphia	80,462	93,665	121,376	565,529
Brooklyn	20,535	47,613	138,882	279,122
Baltimore	80,620	102,313	169,054	212,418
Boston	61,392	93,383	136,881	177,840
New Orleans	46,082	102,190	116,375	168,675
Cincinnati	24,831	46,338	115,436	161,044
St. Louis	4,977	16,469	77,860	160,773
Chicago	—	4,470	29,963	112,172
Charleston	30,289	29,261	42,985	40,522
Richmond	16,060	20,153	27,570	37,910

* Some increases are due to changes in city boundaries.

gland and the middle states; its excellent port; the keenness of its businessmen who, among other things, had the foresight to build the best warehousing facilities for the transatlantic trade; and the boldness of the Black Ball clipper ship line, which scheduled regular transatlantic crossings regardless of the amount of cargo on board or the nature of the weather. The New York City merchants were also extremely ambitious. Not satisfied with the volume of wheat, flour, fish, and other commodities that they received from the Northeast, they also inaugurated a triangular trade that took their ships to New Orleans, Mobile, and Savannah to pick up cargoes of cotton on their way to Europe. On their return trip to the United States they carried both immigrants and a variety of manufactured goods. Thus the shrewdness of its citizens, combined with a favorable location, thrust New York into the forefront of American urban industrial development. Philadelphia, Boston, Pittsburgh, Cincinnati, and Chicago also progressed industrially and benefited from their locations, which made them centers for trade and commerce. But while Northern cities celebrated commercial and industrial expansion the South remained wedded to agriculture and slavery.

National economic and diplomatic policies favored commerce and industry over agriculture, thus bolstering the North and West at the expense of the South. George Washington's administration undertook a policy of encouraging industry through tariffs and a national banking system, and although the Jeffersonians looked askance at such actions, they failed to repeal them once in office themselves. During Jefferson's presidency the nation acquired the territory of Louisiana, which more than doubled the nation's size. This step secured the use of the Mississippi River for Americans and spurred thousands to move west. In 1816 Congress chartered the Second Bank of the United States and adopted the first really protective tariff. In 1819 the federal government moved to recognize the newly independent republics of South and Central America, partly motivated by the desire to obtain trading rights in those countries. The Monroe Doctrine of 1823, Andrew Jackson's efforts to purchase Texas and the San Francisco region in the 1830s, and the later annexation of Texas and the Oregon Country in the 1840s were all part of American economic and territorial expansion during the first half of the nineteenth century.

FREE BLACKS IN THE NORTH

As the nation spread west to the Pacific, developed industry, and established growing cities, attitudes toward minorities changed little if at all. Although slavery had been ended in the North, people there had no love for the blacks and many supported the work of the American Colonization Society, established in 1817, to return free blacks to Africa. As did Southerners, Northern whites thought that blacks were inferior and wanted them segregated or removed like the Indians. Some states enacted codes to deny blacks the ballot, to segregate them in schools and public accommodations, and to prohibit them from testifying against whites in the courts. Even in New England and New York, where blacks could vote and where they found some degree of legal and social acceptance, they nevertheless encountered considerable hostility and segregation. They were usually expected to attend separate churches and schools, and when black and white abolitionists attempted to desegregate Boston's schools in the 1850s, the Primary School Committee refused and declared that racial distinctions were made by the "All-Wise Creator" and that "a promiscuous intermingling in the public schools" was harmful to both races. Massachusetts eventually desegregated Boston's public schools but not without heated political battles in the courts and the legislature.

Not all such attempts were successful. In the Connecticut village of Canterbury, Prudence Crandall, a Quaker, announced her intention of admitting a black girl to her boarding school. Protests from the white parents and many withdrawals of white students led her to open the school exclusively to black girls. Whites in the community protested bitterly; one town official vowed that no "nigger school shall ever be allowed in Canterbury, nor in any town in this State." He was certainly right about Canterbury; angry mobs and legal harassments forced Crandall to leave town.

Despised as they were, blacks did not have an easy time economically. One scholar has estimated that about 87 percent of them toiled as servants, dock workers, or common laborers. In 1838 the Pennsylvania Abolition Society said that nearly a quarter of Philadelphia's free black artisans did not practice their crafts because of "prejudice against them," and by the 1850s the percentage of those skilled blacks in Philadelphia not working in their trades rose to 38 percent. The causes and effects of such discrimination were often reversed in the minds of observers. One Pennsylvanian, unable to find blacks in high-status positions, commented, "We see them engaged in no business that requires even ordinary capacity, [and] in no enterprizes requiring talents to conduct them. The mass [of blacks] are improvident, and seek the lowest avocations, and most menial stations." An English traveler to the United States noted that most white men "would rather starve than accept a menial office under a black." Many black women in the North earned their keep by washing white people's clothes. Despite the existing prejudices, however, some blacks became skilled workers, and a few achieved success as teachers, ministers, and businessmen. The coming of large-scale immigration made life difficult for Northern black workers. After the 1840s many lost their jobs—especially to the poor Irish—in service positions, along the docks, and in canal and railroad construction. In 1849 one observer in Philadelphia noted about stevedores and hod-carriers that while "a few years ago we saw none but blacks, we now see nothing but Irish." Nor were the new factories of the North willing to hire free blacks. In 1847 less than 0.05 percent of Philadelphia's black males were employed in the city's factories.

Northern, like Southern, free blacks formed their own organizations, and these groups had more freedom than in the South. The first of the all-black groups appeared in the Northern states shortly after the American Revolution. Mutual aid and fraternal societies appeared as early as the 1780s to provide funds for burials and schools for blacks. Black churches were more important than the societies and their ministers emerged as leaders in the urban communities. When Richard Allen and his fellow black worshipers were made unwelcome in Philadelphia's predominantly white St. George's Methodist Church in the 1780s they established an all-black congregation that evolved into the African Methodist Episcopal Church. Similar incidents led to the creation of other black churches and eventually black denominations, either Methodist or Baptist.

Northern blacks also published their own newspapers, like Frederick Douglass's *North Star*, and became active in the underground railroad, which assisted fleeing slaves. Blacks also organized groups to agitate for the end of slavery and racial discrimination in the North. Some worked with white abolitionists but others formed all-black groups. Yet, although the emergence of the white abolitionist movement and antislavery parties in the 1830s gave hope that bondage might end and racism be eradicated, many Northern whites greeted abolition-ism with fear, hate, and even violence.

Northern blacks created their own world because they had little choice; they were excluded from the white community. The black organizations protested against separation and gen-erally accepted the values of white America. They urged self-help among blacks, stressed education and mobility, pushed for equal rights, and rejected schemes to send them back to Africa. In 1831 one black gathering argued that "the time must come when the Declaration of Independence will be felt in the heart, as well as uttered from the mouth, and when the rights of all shall be properly acknowledged and appreciated. . . . This is our home, and this is our country."

Yet not all blacks accepted white society's values and desired assimilation. Some said that blacks would never find equality in the United States and that they must emigrate to Africa or the West Indies. Although emigrationist sentiment stemmed largely from despair of winning freedom and equality in white America, a few blacks even began to view Africa and their heritage in a positive light; they rejected the view that Africa was a back-ward continent. These glimmerings of black nationalism would become stronger in the post–Civil War era as blacks developed their own institutions and culture and sought their own heritage. Pre–Civil War free blacks were facing the issue that all black Americans would face. Black leader W. E. B. Du Bois later put it. "One ever feels his two-ness—an American, a Negro; two souls. . . . He simply wishes to make it possible for a man to be both a Negro and an American, without being cursed and spit upon by his fellows, without having the doors of opportu-nity closed roughly in his face."

RENEWAL OF IMMIGRATION

Although Americans seemed preoccupied with the fate of the black people, they also were aware of the overall needs of their developing industrial society. They needed labor and many Europeans were eager to furnish it. Between 1819, when Congress mandated the inauguration of a system to keep statistics on the immigrants, and 1840 approximately 743,000 foreigners reached the United States. Of these more than 80 percent came from Ireland (335,000), the German states (155,000), and England, Scotland, and Wales (103,000). Only smatterings arrived from other places in Europe. Though some of these people left their homes for political and religious reasons, the majority, like immigrants before and since, did so to improve their economic status. While the number who would come after 1840 totaled in the millions, this stream of population in the 1820s and 1830s may be regarded as the first wave of the high tide that followed.

These newcomers entered a nation fresh from two victories over the world's strongest power, Great Britain, in the War for Independence and the War of 1812. Self-conscious nationalism ran wild in the years following the latter conflict. General Andrew Jackson's crushing victory over the British in the Battle of New Orleans in 1815 created a new national hero, whose popularity rivaled that enjoyed by George Washington only a few decades earlier. Efforts to establish American science, American art, and an American literature all received widespread public attention at the time. So, too, did a new wave of religious ferment that stirred a good many New Englanders and New Yorkers.

JOSEPH SMITH AND THE MORMONS

At the same time that the majority was becoming more self-consciously "American," a number of different, and sometimes home-grown religious groups came under increasing public disfavor. Among these were the Roman Catholics, who will be discussed in the next chapter, and the Mormons, or members of the Church of Jesus Christ of Latter-day Saints. Founded by Joseph Smith, a western New York farm boy, the Mormons rapidly became one of the most despised peoples in America. In 1820 Smith had the first of a series of visions and visits from the Angel Moroni, from whom he learned of a hidden set of golden plates on which God's revelations were written in hieroglyphics. According to Smith's testimony in 1826, he received permission from the angel to remove and translate the plates. The task took two years. In 1830 Smith published the completed translation of the Book of Mormon. Together with his family and friends, he then organized the Church of Jesus Christ of Latter-day Saints. Smith claimed that the Book of Mormon was a direct revelation from the Almighty, and equal to the Bible. As a result of these beliefs the Mormon soon became objects of suspicion and derision.

By moving west to the small community of Kirtland, Ohio, in 1831, Smith and his followers hoped to avoid further conflict. For a few years they attracted new converts, established farms and businesses, and even started a bank. Then the Panic of 1837 struck, ruining their efforts and causing a host of angry creditors to denounce them. Smith and his converts fled farther west to frontier Missouri where they began the process of resettlement.

The Missouri settlers proved even less tolerant than the people of New York or Ohio, and trouble broke out almost immediately. Embittered by the experience in the East, Smith vowed to his flock: "Our rights shall no more be trampled with impunity." He told the Mormons at their July 4, 1838, celebration that "the man, or set of men, who attempt it, does it at the expense of their lives. And that mob which comes on to us to disturb us, it shall be between us and them a war of extermination, for we will follow them till the last drop of their blood is spilled, or else they will have to exterminate us." This declaration did nothing to endear Smith's group to the Missourians, and within a few months bands of anti-Mormon guerrillas were roaming the countryside, robbing and beating the Saints and burning their homes. Smith appealed to Governor Lilburn Boggs for protection but the Governor proclaimed that the Mormons "must be exterminated or driven from the state, if necessary, for the public peace." Attacked by frontier ruffians and state officials alike, the Mormons in early 1839 retreated east into Illinois.

There the discouraged members of the Latter-day Saints began to rebuild. Their new community of Nauvoo grew rapidly and with fifteen thousand inhabitants by 1845 had become the largest city in the state. Despite the obvious envy and distrust of its neighbors, the community might have enjoyed peaceful relations had news that the Mormons were practicing polygamy not gotten out. Joseph Smith continued to receive "revelations," and plural marriage was one of these. Few Nauvoo leaders actually practiced polygamy but it became the issue that tore the community apart. Mormons who objected published a newspaper attack on Smith in Nauvoo and church officials ordered the press destroyed. This brought a near riot, and Smith and his brother were arrested and jailed at nearby Carthage. There a mob stormed the jail and killed the brothers. Then, amid increasing raids by gentile mobs, the bulk of the Mormons united under Brigham Young, who negotiated a tenuous peace by agreeing to be out of the state in 1846.

Young and other church officials led the faithful across the Mississippi River into Iowa, and by the end of 1846 thousands of Mormons had settled there. The next year, however, Young himself took his followers farther west and the group reached the Salt Lake Valley in July 1847. Once in Utah, church leaders worked desperately to create a new home in the desert for their embattled followers. Large-scale irrigation, communal economic practices, and incredible industry secured the region for the Mormon pioneers. But even there they were not entirely free from suspicion and harassment.

The Mormons had gone west to escape the United States and had settled in the Salt Lake Valley, then part of Mexico. But within two years, after the end of the Mexican War, the entire area was ceded to the United States, which had also just acquired Oregon from Great Britain. The Mormons were not immediately threatened because they were so far from other American communities, but Salt Lake City lay squarely on one of the main overland routes to California, which had also been obtained as part of the settlement with Mexico. California would become the scene of great expectations, and a magnet for hundreds of thousands, after President James K. Polk informed the nation in 1848 of the great gold discovery there. The mines, he said, were "believed to be among the most productive in the world."

MANIFEST DESTINY

It was not only gold that attracted Americans to the West. Ideology and agricultural and commercial needs played even more crucial roles. Desire to acquire Western territory in the 1830s and 1840s moved President Andrew Jackson to attempt to purchase Texas and the San Francisco area from Mexico. Missionary reports coming back from Oregon, describing the incredible richness and fertility of the soil in the Willamette Valley, whetted the appetites of American farmers. The agricultural possibilities stimulated an "Oregon fever" and wagon trains from Missouri headed west to the Pacific.

Commercial and manufacturing interests also promoted expansion. The harbors of present-day Seattle, San Francisco, and San Diego lay in territory owned by Great Britain and Mexico, and Americans coveted these warm-water ports and coaling stations that could serve as springboards for commercial ties with the Orient. That these lands were controlled by foreign powers did not disturb Americans, who genuinely believed, as a later expansionist would write, that "God, with infinite wisdom and skill [was] training the Anglo-Saxon race" for its ultimate destiny. Americans were certain that the Almighty wanted the United States to spread its institutions across the continent to the Pacific, and then "move down upon" Mexico and Latin America and "out upon the islands of the sea, over upon Africa and beyond."

In the 1840s, however, this spirit of "Manifest Destiny" extended mainly to the Pacific and the Caribbean, and James K.

"American Progress." This 1873 illustration reflects the nineteenth-century vision Americans had of the westward movement and their belief in the glory of American progress. (*Library of Congress*)

Polk was elected to the presidency in 1844 on an expansionist platform. During his four years in office he divided the Oregon Territory with Great Britain, ensuring that the United States received all of the valuable agricultural land below the 49th parallel as well as the superb Puget Sound harbor; he also took the country to war with Mexico, ultimately acquiring the present-day Southwest along with the harbors of San Francisco and San Diego as part of the spoils of war. In his 1848 State of the Union address to Congress President Polk described the great benefits that would accrue to the nation from its recent acquisition of territory:

> No section of our country is more interested or will be more benefited than the commercial, navigating, and manufacturing interests of the Eastern States. Our planting and

farming interests in every part of the Union will be greatly benefited by it. As our commerce and navigation are enlarged and extended, our exports of agricultural products and of manufactures will be increased, and in the new markets thus opened they can not fail to command remunerating and profitable prices.

Yet the acquisition of the new territory from Mexico would also lead, indirectly, to the greatest political upheaval in the nation's history. A little-known congressman, David Wilmot, arose in the House of Representatives in August 1846 and proposed, as an amendment to an appropriations bill under consideration, that "neither slavery nor involuntary servitude shall ever exist in any part" of the newly acquired Southwestern territories. Although not many recognized its significance at that time, the so-called Wilmot Proviso opened a hornet's nest in American politics. Almost every major piece of domestic legislation considered by the Congress during the next fifteen years would in some way touch upon the expansion of slavery, and the issue ultimately led to the Civil War. In the 1840s, however, few people realized that the acquisition of so much new territory would mark the beginning of the end of slavery in the United States.

4

Immigrants and Nativists
(1840s–1880s)

THE ACQUISITION OF over 1,200,000 square miles of territory in the West coincided with the accelerated pace of agricultural and industrial growth in the United States. Practically every segment of the economy mushroomed in the years preceding the Civil War. Production of corn, wheat, and cotton increased rapidly while the riverboat and port cities quickened the pace of their activities. The total value of imports and exports in the nation rose from $125,250,000 in 1843 to $687,200,000 in 1860. Domestic trade alone multiplied tenfold during these years and on the eve of the Civil War exceeded $10 billion. Massachusetts with its textile and shoe factories, Maine with its lumber mills, Pittsburgh with increased iron and coal production, and the Midwest in general reflected the dynamism of the decade. (Most of the increase in railroad trackage, from 8,500 miles in 1850 to 30,000 miles in 1860, connected the agricultural markets and industrial centers of the region with the Atlantic port cities.) The American population grew from 23,000,000 in 1850 to 31,000,000 ten years later, while during this same period the number of foreign-born practically doubled from 2,200,000 to over 4,000,000. The most dramatic growth occurred in the

Midwest; Minnesota, for example, increased its population 2,760 percent in the 1850s. Every section shared in the prosperity. Southern exports of cotton leaped from 2,469,000 bales in 1850 to 4,387,000 bales in 1860, and even the region's manufacturing output showed impressive gains: production of steam engines and machinery rose 387 percent, while the production of agricultural tools increased 101 percent and that of boots and shoes 80 percent. California's gold output surpassed the half-billion dollar mark between 1848 and 1857. The 1850s also saw national production of coal and railroad iron increase by 182 percent and 100 percent respectively, and the amount of wheat exported from Illinois leap from 9 million to 24 million bushels. Possibilities for still further expansion in the American economy remained for energetic entrepreneurs who would turn visions into accomplishments.

Americans in the mid-nineteenth century believed that unequaled opportunities awaited the enterprising. A wilderness stood ready for conquest, cities yearned for growth, and industries and mines had barely been developed. Farms had to produce more food stuffs, but first a better system of transportation was needed to move goods and people more quickly from place to place and workers had to be found to man the machines and till the soil. Industrialists and state governments therefore made extensive efforts to recruit settlers both at home and in Europe. This expansionist philosophy would grip Americans through World War I. After subduing the continent visionaries looked abroad in search of sources for raw materials and outlets for agricultural and industrial products. New inventions like the sewing machine, refrigeration, and incandescent lights would stimulate whole new industries while industrial geniuses like John D. Rockefeller, finance capitalists like J. P. Morgan, and the development of business bureaucracies and scientific management would lead to significant growth in employment opportunities for Americans and foreigners alike.

Fortunately for the United States this industrialization coincided with a similar process in Europe whereby millions were

Table 4.1

MAIN SOURCES OF EUROPEAN IMMIGRATION
TO THE UNITED STATES, 1841–1860

	1841–1850	1851–1860
Belgium	5,074	4,738
Denmark	539	3,749
France	77,262	76,358
Germany	434,626	951,667
Great Britain		
England	32,092	247,125
Scotland	3,712	38,331
Not Specified	229,979	132,199
Ireland	780,719	914,119
Netherlands	8,251	10,789
Norway ⎱ Sweden ⎰	13,903	20,931
Switzerland	4,644	25,011

uprooted. Famine and poverty, agricultural enclosure movements, and industrial development that drew people from farms
but failed to provide enough employment in cities combined to
force thousands from their homes. Once people started moving
there were no limits to their search for an ultimate destination.
The news of "fortunes" to be made in America, along with the
reality of deprivation in Europe, induced more than four million
Europeans to cross the Atlantic between 1840 and 1860 (see
Table 4.1). Approximately 75 percent of the migrants in this
period came from Ireland and the German states. The overwhelming majority of the newcomers sought greater economic
opportunities in the United States; only a small percentage left
their homes because of religious or political persecution.

Emigrants from Europe frequently endured the most harrow-
ing conditions during their ocean voyages. This was especially
true before steamships started replacing sailing vessels in the
1850s, for on the older boats the journey generally lasted more
than a month. With the newer ships the time was cut in half,
and then in half again. By the advent of the twentieth century

it took European emigrants less than a week to cross the Atlantic Ocean. The earlier journeys, however, aroused serious criticism from both passengers and humanitarians. Fourteen Norwegians who traveled on an English ship in 1853 later detailed their treatment on board. It was a month, they recalled, "of bruised heads, broken ribs, a broken collar-bone, and teeth knocked out as a result of brutal treatment by seamen whose orders, given in English, they could not understand; of food thrown to the emigrants as if they were dogs, and of the emigrants fighting for it like wild animals; of bunks full of lice; of dangers of assault upon wives, sisters, and daughters." The passengers who survived such incivilities were quite relieved to reach America.

SETTLEMENT PATTERNS

Practically all of the Europeans landed at one of the five major American ports. As the figures in Table 4.2 indicate, New York City always received the lion's share. Immigrants too poor or too despondent to go farther remained in these cities, the others followed the established transportation patterns inland. From New York City foreigners either sailed up the Hudson River to the Erie Canal and then moved westward or made the journey by rail.

Every region and major city in the United States during the middle of the nineteenth century saw its immigrant population

Table 4.2

IMMIGRANTS ENTERING AMERICAN PORTS

	Total	New York	Boston	Phila-delphia	Baltimore	New Orleans
1846	158,000	98,000	13,000	7,000	9,000	22,000
1851	408,000	294,000	25,000	18,000	8,000	52,000
1855	230,000	161,000	17,000	7,000	6,000	20,000

New York City percentage of total immigrants:
1846—62%
1851—72%
1855—70%

mushroom. By 1860 the foreign-born and their children constituted a majority in New York, San Francisco, New Orleans, and
Chicago. Industrial and commercial needs dictated the patterns
of settlement. Cities with good harbors increased their trade and
needed stevedores and laborers, and fledgling manufacturing
communities sought unskilled hands. River ports and railroad
depots facilitated development, and territorial and economic
growth in turn stimulated the need for additional laborers in the
nation's factories, and mills.

Immigrants responded to these needs and went where the
jobs were. New England attracted many, especially the Irish,
who landed at Boston before the Civil War and were in the
process of obtaining a solid footing there by the 1880s. French
Canadians crossed the northern border to work in the numerous
textile mills and shoe factories of Massachusetts and Rhode
Island. The Middle Atlantic states housed more newcomers
than any other section. New York City, the nation's premier
port, welcomed more immigrants than did all other ports combined, and the city also provided numerous jobs for each succeeding boatload of newcomers. As a result it housed the largest
Irish and German populations of any American city in the
nineteenth century. Philadelphia also provided opportunities for
these groups, especially before the Civil War. The first Midwestern cities to receive large numbers of immigrants were, like
Cincinnati and St. Louis, connected via the Ohio and Mississippi
rivers to New Orleans. After the completion of the Erie Canal
in 1825 and of the transcontinental railroads in the post–Civil
War era, the northern Midwestern cities became major immigrant terminals. St. Louis, Cincinnati, and Milwaukee were
known for their German populations, although other groups
settled there as well, and Germans and Scandinavians predominated in the upper Midwest. Chicago boasted of its large German and Scandinavian populations, but by the time of World
War I it also housed large colonies of every European minority.

In comparison, the Southern states did not attract many immigrants. New Orleans, the exception, was the region's only

cosmopolitan city. The South had little industrial development to attract job seekers, and since good farmland had already been acquired by plantation owners, there was relatively little acreage available for independent entrepreneurs. In addition, a large number of Germans and Scandinavians regarded the South's climate as unhealthy and felt more comfortable in the northern Midwest where the soil and the weather were more akin to that in their homelands. As a result of these factors the foreign-born comprised only about 2 percent of the region's population at the close of the nineteenth century. French, Germans, and Irish lived in New Orleans, however, and a variety of other peoples were scattered elsewhere. The South, for example, tried to attract Chinese laborers because whites thought the Chinese would work more efficiently than blacks for the same or lower wages. Some Chinese settled in Mississippi, as did other immigrants, but generally the Southern states remained the home of America's black population and old-stock whites.

Although most of the immigrants went to urban areas, many others found farming, mining, and fishing more to their taste. They often settled in the northern Midwest or the Far West. In the late nineteenth century Wisconsin had the largest percentage of foreign-born of any state east of the Mississippi River. Those of German stock predominated within its population but Scandinavians, especially Norwegians, were not far behind. Iowa, Minnesota, Kansas, Nebraska, and the Dakotas also proved attractive to these same groups and for the same reason: the availability of good farmland. Germans and Scandinavians also helped populate the state of Washington, going there primarily for farming and fishing. The mining areas of Utah contained over twenty-five different nationality groups and Salt Lake City also had a diverse population.

THE GERMANS AND THE IRISH

None of the immigrant groups outnumbered the Germans, equaled their scope of influence, or settled in a larger and more varied number of locations. They went to both urban and rural areas and to every section of the country, working as farmers and laborers, skilled craftsmen, and professionals. By 1900 they constituted the largest single foreign element in Wisconsin, California, Kansas, Missouri, New Jersey, New York, and twenty other states, and they were the most prominent ethnic group in eight of the nation's ten largest cities. Only in Philadelphia and Boston were the Irish more numerous.

The nineteenth-century migrants represented all classes of Germans. They included intellectuals, radicals, and labor union organizers, but the overwhelming majority were peasants and artisans intent on improving their economic positions. The Germans had a reputation for hard work, thrift, and determination, and they made every effort to maintain their Old World culture. The hardworking Germans also relaxed with verve and their communities overflowed with beer gardens, breweries, concert and lecture halls, and a variety of theaters, singing societies, and athletic organizations. The German *Gymnasien* stressed the development of both a sound mind and a sound body. In religion Germans were divided among conservative Catholic, Lutheran, and Reformed churches, with a sprinkling of anticlericalists and freethinkers. The German Christmas, a church holiday celebrated with lavish foods, joyous songs, and a beautifully decorated tree, was not only transplanted intact from the Old World but proved so appealing to others in the United States that the dourness of the New England Yankees and the rowdiness of some of the more boisterous Southwestern communities all but disappeared as ways of celebrating the Savior's birth within the next few generations. Although many Germans went into politics, they were not an especially political people. They did not deluge almshouses or charity hospitals either, and they engaged in few activities outside of their ethnic associations that would bring them into social contact with other peoples.

In contrast to the varied groups, classes, and values of the Germans, the three million Irish who also made their initial impact in American society in the 1840s and 1850s were almost exclusively poor, downtrodden, and Roman Catholic. Their entry into the United States aroused great anxiety and hostility because they were the first non-Protestant group to arrive in such large numbers within a comparatively short time. Their Catholicism, at the core of all of their values, came into direct conflict with the Protestantism of old-stock Americans and most of the other European immigrants. They believed in the subordination of the state to the church ("Religion overrides all other sovereigns, and has the supreme authority over all the affairs of the world," one of their spokesmen proclaimed) and that Catholicism was the only true faith. Moreover, they subscribed to that aspect of Catholic doctrine that declared "no man has or can have a *religious* or *moral* right to be of any religion but the true religion." These views certainly constituted heresy in a nation strongly of the opinion that the *Protestant* God looked over the United States and that, in theory at least, all men had the right to worship, or not, as they pleased so long as they did not disturb their neighbors.

The Irish, unlike the restless Americans ever searching for new frontiers to conquer, were also content to accept their station in life. They felt, historian Oscar Handlin tells us, that "they were victims of incalculable influences beyond their control" and therefore resigned themselves to whatever fate had set out for them. These opinions also conflicted with the optimistic strain in American society that preached that man could make of himself what he would.

Finally, the Irish were the poorest and most degraded of the mid-nineteenth-century immigrants from Europe and apparently worked like brutes at whatever menial tasks were available. Many had fled Ireland rather than starve during the Great Hunger of the 1840s and they arrived penniless. Packed into the Eastern port and industrial cities with little money and few skills, they soon comprised a large part of the working-class population. In city after city Irish names appeared more frequently than those of any other native- or foreign-born ethnic group on lists of paupers and criminals, and these factors alone would have made them unwelcome even had there been no national or religious prejudice against them. Indigent American workers despised the urban Irishmen and complained that by working for low wages they took jobs away from "honest" men. In city after city they dominated the ranks of common laborers but avoided commerce and the skilled crafts. In addition, the Irish thought that their children should contribute to the household rather than waste their time in school. As a result the Irish had the lowest incomes, lived in the worst conditions, and received a disproportionate amount of public charity. Some Irish did succeed in American terms, but in numbers and proportions they lagged behind the Germans, English, and Scandinavians. In a country motivated by material advancement the Irish turned to the church for salvation and security and this only increased Protestant opposition.

During the 1850s the Germans and Irish constituted the two major immigrant groups in the United States; their combined numbers approximated 2 million people. The British ranked a distant third with about 300,000 emigrants reaching the United States during the decade. The massive Irish influx totaled over a million people for the years 1847–53, whereas the German figure did not exceed 100,000 until 1852. By 1854 Irish emigration had begun to wane while the German totals that year exceeded 200,000 for the first time. Thereafter German immigrants outnumbered all others in every year except three through 1892.

THE COMING OF THE CIVIL WAR

The Civil War temporarily disrupted the flow of immigration. The war was also the most serious domestic crisis since the American Revolution. The issue of slavery came to a head during this decade and the continual agitations and disruptions in the political arena channeled national concerns into an attempt to put a permanent end to the problem of the "peculiar institution." The acquisition of vast new territories between the Rocky Mountains and the Pacific Ocean raised the issue of extending slavery. Southerners demanded the right to transport their human property westward but many Northerners, more responsive to moral and political pressures at home, refused to concur with the Southern point of view.

The political debates of the 1850s aroused the nation, destroyed political parties, and gave rise to the emergence of new leaders. Out of chaos came the Republican party, founded in 1854 and dedicated to preventing the expansion of slavery beyond its existing limits. The party failed in its first national effort in 1856 but broadened its base four years later by supporting some economic benefits for almost all Northerners and many likely immigrants. It added to its program a homestead plank that offered free land to anyone who would till the soil and improve it for five years, a protective tariff, and the promise of a transcontinental railroad. Next it turned to a moderate candidate, Abraham Lincoln, who had supported the Fugitive Slave Law passed in 1850. That legislation called for the return of all runaway slaves, no matter where they were found, to their lawful owners. In addition, Lincoln had promised not to touch slavery in the states where it existed. He believed in white supremacy and favored the colonization of blacks abroad. Because of his conservative views on the race issue, some radicals distrusted this "slave hound" from Illinois.

Yet Lincoln opposed the expansion of slavery and had said a nation could not endure half slave and half free. He thought that industrial progress would be slowed and the nation remain divided until the agitation over the expansion of slavery ceased. His election in 1860 frightened militant Southerners and some states seceded from the Union. Lincoln's decision in April 1861 to reinforce Fort Sumter, an American army base at Charleston, South Carolina, precipitated the Civil War. Despite the president's insistence that the struggle was to save the Union and not abolish slavery, this distinction became blurred as the war progressed.

The war disrupted the economy. It hurt some industries but aided others. Railroad building fell, but large-scale demands for food, uniforms, blankets, shoes, weapons, and so on, spurred economic growth and necessitated more labor. Congressional legislation raising the tariff, thereby protecting newly established factories, and granting land for railroad expansion, education, and homesteading also promoted extensive growth. The departure of Southerners from Congress gave free reign to the spokesmen for industrial expansion. Thus, in spite of the dislocations of the war, it in fact settled the issue of whether the nation would be slowed in its quest for economic growth by Southern interests. Industrial forces gained control of the national legislature and ever since have had predominant influence in the shaping of national legislation.

BLACKS AND THE DOMESTIC CRISIS

Thus the war that had started to save the Union ended with the triumph of industrial forces as well as the abolition of slavery. Practical and military concerns certainly had more to do with both of these results than did moral considerations. President Lincoln had originally said that he did not intend to interfere with slavery; rather, the war was a struggle to preserve the Union. When the war came black volunteers rushed to serve the Union cause but the federal and state governments rejected them. The Providence, Rhode Island, police even declared that they would break up groups of drilling blacks as "disorderly gatherings." When General John C. Frémont declared martial law in Missouri and freed the slaves, Lincoln overruled him. The president worried about public opinion in the North and the reaction of the border slave states, which, despite much pro-Confederate support, had not joined with the states of the Lower South. If freedom were to come, Lincoln wanted compensated emancipation and not unilateral action by military commanders. Radical abolitionist criticism was unable to move the president.

Circumstances, however, and Lincoln's changing attitude gradually pushed the federal government in the direction of employing black troops and ending slavery. First, the war did not go well for the North. Heavy casualties and military failures made the use of black troops seem more appealing. Second, the slaves themselves created a problem for Northern generals. Large numbers fled the plantations and poured into the Union lines. Perplexed generals did not know what to do with these "contrabands," as they were called. Some suggested returning them to their masters, others fed and cared for them, and a few wanted to use them against the Confederacy as laborers or soldiers. In the Sea Islands of South Carolina, occupied by the Union, General David Hunter in May 1862 freed the slaves and impressed them into the army. But Lincoln countermanded the order. Although the president declared his opposition to the use of black troops as late as the summer of 1862, he soon allowed Northern commanders to recruit them in segregated units.

Lincoln had hoped to compensate slaveholders as an inducement for emancipation and had suggested colonization for the newly freed blacks. Congress abolished slavery in the District of Columbia, granted $300 per slave compensation, and indicated its support for the president's proposals for the border states. By the summer of 1862, however, Lincoln had resolved to end slavery. In September he issued the preliminary Emancipation Proclamation and on January 1, 1863, the final one. The proclamation freed only those slaves under rebel control, but slavery disintegrated as the Union armies pushed South.

Many Northern whites did not want to see slavery terminated because they believed abolition made the South fight harder and hence prolonged the war. Others simply did not care whether blacks were enslaved. Competition between whites and blacks for jobs did not help either. On several occasions during the war angry white workers assaulted blacks and burned their homes. In Buffalo, where blacks were employed as longshoremen, white workers killed three blacks and severely beat twelve

others. Cincinnati, Chicago, Detroit, Cleveland, Boston, and
Harrisburg all experienced riots, but the worst outbreak occurred in New York City in July 1863. Aroused by grievances
over the draft and the frustrations of the war, whites, especially
the Irish, who contended against blacks for jobs, rioted. Thousands roamed the city, burning and looting. Several blacks were
lynched and a mob destroyed the black orphanage. Fortunately,
the attendants managed to get the children out. Not until the
draft was temporarily suspended in New York and federal troops
brought in did the riots cease. All told, perhaps seventy-five people died as a result of the onslaught.

After the riots ended the public could once again focus on the
war and its progress. By 1864 the end was in sight; it was only
a matter of time before the North would emerge successful. It
seemed almost certain that Northern victory would result in
the abolition of slavery and, it was hoped, allow the entire
nation to unify in its goal of industrial expansion.

The war ended in April 1865, but before unity could be at-
tained some efforts had to be made to help the former slaves
move productively into the new society. Three years of wrangling between Andrew Johnson, who had succeeded to the
presidency on Lincoln's assassination in April 1865, and the
Congress over the appropriate federal legislation and administration prolonged the healing period. Congress did succeed,
however, in establishing a Freedman's Bureau to provide temporary assistance to the former slaves, and the nation later
adopted the Thirteenth, Fourteenth, and Fifteenth amendments
to the Constitution, which, respectively, outlawed slavery, ostensibly protected civil rights, and prevented black men from being
denied the vote. These amendments were intended to help ease
the paths of the erstwhile bondsmen into the free world, but
insufficient education, an overwhelmingly agrarian background,
lack of land redistribution, and racism thwarted the progress of
the blacks. This racism sometimes erupted into violence during Reconstruction. The Ku Klux Klan, for example, attacked
blacks, especially when they attempted to vote and exercise

their civil rights. Federal authorities helped protect blacks' civil rights, and they were able to vote and hold office during the Reconstruction period. But the white South, aided by the Klan, overthrew the Reconstruction governments. As a result blacks remained politically powerless and, as workers on Southern farms, had few opportunities from the expansion of the nation's industries. The failure of the attempt to bring a degree of racial democracy to the South eventually ended in a torrent of racism after 1890 and made the Fourteenth and Fifteenth amendments dead letters until after World War II. To be sure, most white Southerners were economically deprived as well, but many members of the old planter class and their descendants seemed to land on their feet. Those planters who survived, and the new industrialists who exploited white and black workers alike, ruled the South.

Although Afro-Americans failed to win equality, the Reconstruction period and after did see the growth of black institutional life in the American South. First the black family, which had no legal status under slavery, received the sanction of law. Thousands of freedmen took advantage of the new situation to legalize their unions. "My husband and I have lived together fifteen years and we wants to be married over again," explained one wife. Many who were parted from their mates and children during slavery now searched for their loved ones. Some took to the roads seeking their families; others advertised in the newspapers. A white correspondent for a Northern journal reported encountering one freedman who had walked nearly six hundred miles in two months in search of his wife. Not all spouses could be reunited, but the Reconstruction era did see the stabilization of the black family in ways impossible under slavery.

While the legal restrictions against the black family were removed so were those against Southern black churches. After the Civil War thousands of black freedmen left the slave galleries in the churches of their former masters and flocked to the all-black Baptist, Methodist, and Holiness churches that grew substantially in the aftermath of slavery. Their own churches were important to blacks, for here they could be free from the watchful eyes of whites. No wonder that a number of black politicians and other leaders were clergymen. After the elimination of blacks from Southern politics in the 1890s they functioned politically by determining policy and choosing leaders in their churches.

For Southern blacks the churches also provided an outlet for their culture. Through Afro-American religious music and the services themselves, blacks expressed their own experiences and longings for the future. The singing of Afro-American spirituals and the shouting characteristic of services in the slave era continued, but they declined among the educated elite, who preferred to forget connections to slavery. In a later era the spirituals were replaced by gospels. While the spirituals emphasized the Hebrew children and deliverance from slavery, the gospels recognized the sorrows of this world, but, as the following piece suggests, also promised hope for the future:

> The Lord will provide,
> The Lord will provide,
> Sometimes another, the Lord will provide.
>
> It may not be in my time,
> It may not be in yours,
> But sometimes another, the Lord will provide.

Not all Afro-American culture was expressed in religion. Southern blacks used song as well as humor and other oral traditions. The songs were sung by black workers to provide a rhythm for work, but they also talked of love and life. In the late nineteenth century Afro-Americans produced jazz and later blues; these musical forms spread to the North and became popular in the twentieth century.

POSTWAR IMMIGRATION

Once the controversy over slavery ended, economic growth, as measured by industrial expansion in the 1880s and after, re-

Table 4.3

MAIN SOURCES OF IMMIGRATION TO THE UNITED STATES, 1861–1890

Europe	1861–1870	1871–1880	1881–1890
Austria-Hungary	7,800	72,969	353,719
Denmark	17,094	31,771	88,132
France	35,986	72,206	50,464
Germany	787,468	718,182	1,452,970
Great Britain			
England	222,277	437,706	644,680
Scotland	38,769	87,564	149,869
Ireland	435,778	436,871	655,482
Italy	11,725	55,759	307,309
Norway	71,631	95,323	176,586
Sweden	37,667	115,922	391,776
Switzerland	23,286	28,293	81,988
USSR	2,512	39,284	213,282
Asia			
China	64,301	123,201	61,711
America			
Canada and Newfoundland	153,878	383,640	393,304

sumed. This expansion, as well as the Homestead Act of 1862, which granted free land to people who would settle and develop it, gave rise to increased immigration from Europe (see Table 4.3). As in the mid-nineteenth century, the Europeans were responding not only to opportunities in the United States but to industrial and political changes in their own homelands. Industrialization attracted people to the cities but failed to provide sufficient jobs there, and laws requiring military service and the lifting of emigration restrictions also contributed to the flow westward to the United States. After the Civil War most immigrants continued arriving from the German states, Ireland, and England, but a substantial increase was noted from Scandinavia, where a series of crop failures provided a spur. Whereas before 1860 annual immigration from Scandinavia exceeded 4,000 only twice, after the Civil War a great surge ensued. More than 200,000 arrived between 1866 and 1874, over a million came between 1880 and 1892, and another 500,000 or so landed in the United States in the decade preceding the outbreak of World War I in 1914. Altogether more than 2 million Swedes, Norwegians, and Danes moved to America after 1860.

Swedes and Norwegians comprised nearly 90 percent of the total Scandinavian migration, with the former outnumbering the latter by a ratio of approximately two to one. Most of these people settled in the upper Midwest. The Swedes were the most urban of the Scandinavians: in the twentieth century census tracts regularly found 60 percent or more of them concentrated in cities. Chicago housed the largest Swedish contingent in the world outside of Sweden, and sizable groups of Norwegians took advantage of job opportunities there as well as in New York, Cleveland, Minneapolis, and San Francisco.

Less noticed than the large numbers of Germans, Irish, and Scandinavians were the 1,600,000 people coming from England, Scotland, and Wales in the years between 1870 and 1900. Unlike so many foreigners, these newcomers spoke English as a native tongue and did not feel as strange in the United States as did members of other national minorities. Immigrants from the United Kingdom were often welcome in America because they had valuable skills, especially for the iron and steel industry, textiles, and mining. A few industries, like pottery, relied almost totally on British skilled workers. Even in growing cities experienced English workers soon found themselves at the top of the working class. Thus their cultural similarity and relatively easier economic adjustment made their experiences considerably less harsh than those of the Irish or even of the Germans and the Scandinavians.

FINDING EMPLOYMENT

The first task confronting the foreigners was finding employment. Whether they stopped in a city or moved into rural areas in search of farmlands, no other aspect of their lives was of greater concern. Those who did not work did not eat and could not support their families. To be sure, even many of those employed earned insufficient sums to maintain a decent life for either themselves or their families. The immigrants usually arrived with little capital and few skills and so employers took advantage of them. Although industry and commerce were booming, thereby providing millions of new jobs, there were always more people willing to work than there were jobs available. The reservoir of cheap unskilled laborers frustrated the attempts of unions to raise wages and improve working conditions. Real wages did improve in the late nineteenth century, but they still remained low. Almost every account of workers in these years details their pitiful salaries. In an era when $500 to $600 a year was considered the minimum necessary to support a family of five most laborers earned less. Women received even lower wages while working longer hours than men. In New York City a skilled tailor might make $6 to $10 working fourteen hours a day, six days a week, while a seamstress rarely took home as much as $3 in her good weeks! Maids and other domestics whose daily toil totaled upwards of sixteen hours had the opportunity of earning $4 to $10 a month plus a basement or attic room and board.

The abundant supply of foreign laborers contributed to the growth of cities and accelerated transportation development in the United States. Many foreigners, especially the Irish, were collected in the Eastern port cities and taken to distant construction sites to build railroads, bridges, tunnels, and canals. In Philadelphia, Chicago, and New York—but not Boston—the Irish were represented in various aspects of the construction business aside from common labor. The industries of some cities soon became identified with particular ethnic groups. Hence the Germans in Milwaukee and Cincinnati were thought of in connection with brewing and wine-making while in Boston the Irish operated 900 of the city's 1,500 liquor stores in 1850. In Ohio, one historian tells us, drugstores with German proprie-

The arrival of immigrants at Castle Garden, allegedly to take the place of American strikers. Castle Garden at the tip of Manhattan was the point of arrival for many immigrants before Ellis Island opened. A persistent fear of Americans was that immigrants took jobs from native-born workers. From *Leslie's Magazine*, 1882. (*Library of Congress*)

tors were thought of as "a guarantee of reliability, for only German pharmacists had been trained in the fundamentals of chemistry."

Overall the Germans had a smaller percentage of common workingmen than the Irish and a larger number of skilled craftsmen in most of the cities where they lived. German tailors, cabinet-makers, and small shopkeepers abounded in every section of the country except New England and the Far West. Some Germans were domestics and unskilled laborers but these categories are more frequently associated with the Irish. For example, one third to one half of all Irish immigrants were classified as domestics or unskilled workers in New York City in 1855, whereas only 15 percent of the Germans appeared in those occupations. In Boston in 1860, the Irish constituted 7,000 of the city's 8,500 laborers. In New Orleans the Irish who arrived in the 1840s and 1850s (more prosperous Irish had come earlier in the century) also worked in the most menial positions. They frequently toiled outdoors in subtropical sun and muddy swamps laying out streets and digging canals.

But immigrant experiences varied from city to city. Philadelphia, which was a textile center, a port city, and the hub of a wide railroad network, had a variety of economic enterprises—one wit noted that everything from battleships to bonbons was manufactured there—and greater opportunities for advancement existed. The Irish thus progressed more rapidly in Philadelphia than they did in Boston or New York. In Savannah, Georgia, in 1860, foreigners owned most of the dry goods and clothing establishments, retail groceries, saloons, cigar and tobacco shops, barber and hairdressing salons, bakeries, confectioneries, hotels, and expensive stores. Almost half of the city's population was foreign-born, and six of its nine banks had foreign-born directors. In the 1850s a Frenchman opened the first bakery in Dallas, Texas. And in cities like New York, Philadelphia, Boston, and Cincinnati, German Jews utilized the newly developed sewing machines in setting up factories for mass-produced clothing.

Artisans from Great Britain used their skills in the manufacturing of textiles. When the United States increased its duties on silk after the Civil War, owners of British factories took their machines and workmen to America to begin anew, virtually destroying the industry in England. English skills were also evident in mining. As news of better wages in American mines spread in Great Britain, many left to seek a new way of life. English miners worked in the coal fields of eastern Pennsylvania and Welsh miners found jobs elsewhere. Among the most famous of the British miners were those from Cornwall. The Cornish immigrants put their knowledge to good use in places like Wisconsin and the hardrock mines of the American West. In the nineteenth century Britain made many improvements in metallurgy, and English workers brought knowledge of these advances with them to the New World. Although the British immigrants included a high percentage of skilled craftsmen, many of them also had to work for low wages in unskilled jobs.

Not all immigrants found employment in industrial and urban America. Among the old immigrants few Irish but large numbers of Germans and Scandinavians took up farming in Pennsylvania, Wisconsin, Ohio, Illinois, Texas, and other states. Life was not easy in rural America. Clearing the land, avoiding hostile Indians, and enduring inclement weather, which included freezing blizzards and blistering droughts, discouraged alien and native-born farmers alike. Often they had little money and so had trouble starting a farm. Although free land was available under the Homestead Act, others often owned the best land and there were tools and supplies to purchase. The long hours of toil and loneliness added to the tribulations of farm families. Many children, accustomed to workdays lasting from 4 A.M. to 10 P.M. and long winters of virtual isolation from friends and relatives, had no desire to spend their adult lives in similar circumstances. The twelve-hour workdays in industry and the opportunities for social intercourse that urban areas provided seemed to offer a much more stimulating existence. Hence many of the new city dwellers were migrants from a radius of no more than 250 miles.

LIVING CONDITIONS

The type of work the breadwinners did and the amount of their earnings determined the family's living conditions. Most frequently the workers' homes were inadequate and unhealthy. On the frontiers and in rapidly growing new towns, families often made do with badly built facilities. A Dutch emigrant recalled constructing his sixteen-foot cabin in Milwaukee in 1846 "out of rough common lumber. The boards were lapped and nailed on like siding, without anything else being added inside or out, and the roof was of the same material. There was also a so-called upstairs which was reached by climbing a home-made ladder. Not much of a manse this—and it was certainly an uncomfortable dwelling during a storm or in weather below zero." Irish workers who helped build Illinois canals lived in log huts and mud cabins.

The majority of newcomers suffered in pestilential tenements in the nation's largest cities. They got off the boats, found work, and then sought homes nearby. To cope with this influx specu-lators converted old mansions and factory lofts into housing units while others hastily built cheap tenements. As a result rents were high and the living units lacked even essential features. Often they had no floors—just dirt, feathers, or patches of straw. Air and light were luxuries and sewage accumulated both inside and outside of the dwellings in New York and other cities, where dwellings for the poor had no indoor toilets and backyard privies overflowed frequently, breeding disease. In 1850 three quarters of the city had no sewers and waters over-flowed into the streets. The first bathtub in the United States appeared in Cincinnati in 1842. Some newspapers called it a plaything of the rich; Philadelphia prohibited its use between November 1 and February 28; and Boston banned the bathtub unless prescribed by a physician. "Men of medicine and men of God," one chronicler tells us, warned that the practice of bathing "would wash away a man's virility and a woman's virginity."

HEALTH, WELFARE, AND COMMUNITY LIFE

Under these circumstances diseases and epidemics abounded in the major cities. Cholera, smallpox, malaria, tuberculosis, pneu-monia, typhus, and typhoid were common afflictions of the poor, and especially of the Irish. In New Orleans 12,000 people died during the summer of 1853; among them were 4,000 Irish, and St. Patrick's cemetery reported a shortage of gravediggers. Epidemics hit the new immigrants more severely than the Americans because they were already physically debilitated from their ocean crossing and also because a greater percentage of them congregated in the stifling and unhealthful urban ghettos.

Immigrants also crowded the inadequate public facilities and from the 1830s on consistently totaled more than 50 percent of the inmates of the almshouses, insane asylums, and jails. Picked up as vagrants, drunks, or general nuisances, they were also victimized by unjust administration of the laws. Young immigrant women were looked upon as fair prey by their employers or "gay blades" about town. A far too typical example of exploitation was the case of a New Orleans girl plied with liquor by a band of rascals who then seduced her. She was sentenced to jail for public drunkenness while her abusers went free.

Insensitive community officials failed to make constructive criticism. Instead they condemned the victims and blamed them for the ills of society. "The Irish suffered the most," one New York City Board of Health official concluded in 1832, because they were "exceedingly dirty in their habits, much addicted to intemperance and crowded together in the worst portion of cities." In the 1858 annual report of the New York Association for Improving Conditions of the Poor the author noted: "Our city, operating like a sieve, lets through the enterprising and industrious, while it retains the indolent, the aged, and infirm, who can earn their subsistence nowhere, to become a burden, and often because of their vices, a nuisance to the community."

This type of prejudice gave the newcomers all the more reason for clinging to one another for support. The Americans, who would not associate with the immigrants in any case, then assailed them for their clannishness. More importantly, however, the immigrants felt more comfortable with those of similar backgrounds and experiences. The enclaves where they clustered were beginnings of the urban immigrant ghetto. It has been the place where recent immigrants and their children felt comfortable and coddled, and the place that second- and third-generation adults moved away from, having been given in their earlier years the succor that would ease their paths into the dominant society at the appropriate time.

The advent of the Irish and the Germans marked the beginning of the large ghettos of the foreign-born. In New York, Cincinnati, St. Louis, Chicago, and Milwaukee, to name but a few communities, one found *Kleindeutschlands* (Little Germanies), where all of the shopkeepers spoke German, where the daily life almost duplicated that of the old country, and where traditional customs prevailed. In the 1850s Milwaukee had its "German market," a shopping center and a clearinghouse for local gossip. When American women from "Yankee Hill" patronized the shops one could hear the Germans calling out, "Da kommt die englische Dame!" or "Die Dame von Yankeberg!" Lutheran church services conducted in German and parochial schools perpetuated the language among the children.

Almost every ethnic group had a benevolent society to assist immigrants at the dock. Frequently these provided food, shelter for a night or two, travel assistance, and job information. The Irish Emigrant Society of New York and Die Deutsche Gesellschaft were among the busiest in the middle of the nineteenth century, but also active were the Scots St. Andrew's Society, the Hebrew Benevolent Society, and the French Benevolent Society.

Other associations and organizations, ranging from benevolent to quasi-military to special interest, also arose. To some extent these were established to promote group solidarity and continuity but another factor, sometimes overlooked by observers, concerned immigrant disdain for the apparent lack of culture and refinement in the United States. Many Germans, for example, who had a rich heritage of music, art, and literature as well as a standard for civilized behavior, regarded the Americans as uncouth and bizarre. One historian of the German Americans, Carl Wittke, tells us that some of them

> ridiculed such American habits as rocking in chairs, chewing and spitting tobacco, standing up to a bar to down a drink, getting "eye-openers" each morning, wearing hats

An early Norwegian Lutheran church in Crawford County, Wisconsin, about the mid-1800s. (*State Historical Society of Wisconsin*)

crooked, and sticking feet on tables and window sills. They were not impressed by the "anarchical noise" of Fourth of July or firemen's parades, or by the muddy streets, the corrupt shirt-sleeve, tobacco-cud politics of the cities, and the "human bull fighting" known as pugilism. They preferred sausage and sauerkraut to pie and pork and beans. They were shocked to find slavery firmly established and nativism rampant in a free republic. They hated American sabbatarianism, blue laws, and "the temperance swindle," and the more radical ridiculed what they called the religious superstitions of the American people. They were determined to preserve their language and customs and to resist assimilation to an inferior culture.

Hence the restricted social contacts involved in community athletic groups, picnics, dances, lectures, and intellectual meetings served the dual purpose of providing recreational outlets while still preserving a valuable heritage. The songfests of one group of German organizations, the *Sängerbunds*, or singing societies, proved so popular that national meetings of German *Sängerbunds* were held in cities like St. Louis and Cincinnati.

Some groups, especially the Irish, established fire and militia companies. In 1846 an observer commented, "There is scarcely a city of any note in the United States in which an Irish volunteer corps is not to be found, clothed in the national colour and ornamented with the harp, shamrock, and other national emblems." For the Irish St. Patrick's Day dictated a massive turnout for fun, parties, and parades of militia companies in full and colorful regalia.

Immigrants from Great Britain also formed their own groups. Although fluency in the language and Protestant background gave them an entry into American society, they too felt different from Americans and sought each other out. The Welsh had their own style of Protestantism and loved to attend their *eisteddfod*, a festival of singing and literature. The Scots, too, had their associations. The various groups from Great Britain, like other foreigners, also published their own newspapers. One factor that unified the newcomers from the United Kingdom was hatred of the Irish, and not a few joined the ranks of the growing anti-Catholic, anti-Irish movements of the nineteenth century.

ANIMOSITY TOWARD BLACKS AND FOREIGNERS

The hostility expressed toward the Catholics seemed, to some extent, to be generally applicable to all foreigners. Although immigrants aided American industrial growth, old-stock Americans resented them. They were regarded as unsavory and inferior beings merely because of their European heritage. "What has annoyed me most in my associations with the Americans," one Norwegian wrote back home,

> is their prejudice against Europe, which they regard as hopelessly lost in slavery and wretchedness. Three fourths

of the people in the East and ninety-nine hundredths of the
people in the West are fully convinced that the other side
of the Atlantic is nothing but a heap of medieval feudal
states, which, indeed, show some slight indication of reform here and there, but have not made much political
progress and have not enough vitality to rise from the
abyss of misery and corruption into which they have fallen
as the result of centuries of ignorance and despotism; their
doom is inevitable.

Americans regarded themselves, on the other hand, as privileged and generous people who were willing to share their
destiny with the less fortunate Europeans who chose to leave
their homelands. In return for this "generosity," however, they
expected recent arrivals to relinquish their old ways and values.
And "until they have become morally acclimated to our institutions," Horace Mann, the Boston educator, declared, they
were simply unfit for participation in American society. One
of the ways that Mann and others expected the foreigners to
"become morally acclimated" to American customs was through
the common school, which would instill among all youth the
values and outlook of "real" Americans. To some, however, the
very idea that Europeans could adapt seemed absurd. "Our
Celtic fellow citizens," a New Yorker confided to his diary,
"are almost as remote from us in temperament and constitution
as the Chinese." A New Englander expressed still another
attitude toward the foreigners. He did not much mind them but
he found them somewhat amusing. In verse he mocked the
habits and accents of the Germans he saw about him:

> Mine cracious! mine cracious! shust look here und see
> A Deutscher so habby as habby can pe!
> Der beoples are dink dot no prains I haf got;
> Vas grazy mit trinking, or someding like dot.

Animosity toward foreigners probably developed out of discontent with national economic adversity. The Jacksonian era
may have been a time of great opportunity for the "common
man," but it was also a time of periodic economic dislocation.

Cartoonist Thomas Nast's view of St. Patrick's Day, 1867. Nast—along with many other Americans—viewed the Irish as ugly, brawling drunkards. From *Harper's Weekly*, 1867.

The increased emigration from Europe, which started in the 1820s, thereafter contributed not only large numbers to the ranks of the unemployed but, according to the estimates of one scholar, "came close to creating a permanent semi-pauperized working class." In cities like New York, Philadelphia, Baltimore, Cincinnati, and Washington this led to an increase in poverty-stricken people, crime, and public disorder. The periods of economic difficulty coincided with the increase in riots and labor disturbances. "Americans in the nineteenth century," one scholar tells us, "engaged in economic conflicts with their employers as fierce as any known to the industrial world." This was certainly true of the Jacksonian era.

More significant in regard to ethnic relations, however, was the increased number of racial and religious conflicts. Instead of venting their wrath on the entrepreneurs who owned the factories and the government and courts that supported capitalists and suppressed labor organizations, the working people blamed foreigners and minorities. Throughout America's history the majority has unquestioningly followed the patterns set in an Anglo-dominated colonial America and has been suspicious and resentful of those who failed to adapt rapidly to the prevalent customs. During times of contentment and prosperity immigrants who did not conform were usually left to fend for themselves, but in times of emotional or economic adversity they have been victimized. Sometimes they have been labeled as the causes of the national difficulties; at other times they have stood in for elite groups as a more socially acceptable outlet for the release of high tensions.

In Jacksonian America a contracting economy precipitated the battles. Whereas there had been only some twenty-odd riots between 1828 and 1833 the number increased to sixteen in 1834 alone, and thirty-seven in 1835. Abolitionists who wished to end human bondage, free blacks, and the Irish served as targets for the rowdies, who were often unemployed, underemployed, or on the brink of poverty. Sometimes skilled Protestant workers fought with unskilled Catholics, and both persecuted free blacks. Labor troubles preceded the burning of a black church and other violence perpetrated on abolitionists and blacks in New York City in 1834. In 1835 and 1839 economic hardship led to attacks on blacks in Washington and Cincinnati respectively. In Philadelphia five major riots against blacks broke out between 1829 and 1850, and a notorious struggle in 1844 between Protestant and Catholic workers continued for four days in the streets of the Kensington section of the city. The Kensington riot occurred not only because of economic discontent but because Protestant Americans were incensed that school authorities had succumbed to Catholic pressures to allow the Catholic Bible to be read in the public schools along with the King James version. Before three thousand troops entered the fray to restore order the rioters had burned more than thirty buildings and had injured or killed at least fourteen people. In spite of the militia's arrival, Protestants set fire to two Catholic churches and several other buildings. The Kensington riot, and many others as well, happened during a spell when a combination of heat, humidity, and stench frustrated people of the lower classes beyond endurance. In "the city of brotherly love," however, it took more than the weather to incite such aggression. Problems during the Jacksonsion era were so severe that one historian has observed, "By any measure, the period from 1835 to 1850 was the most violent in Philadelphia's history."

ANTI-CATHOLICISM

Important as economics and race were in the development of American hostility toward minorities, the outstanding ingredient in pre–Civil War nativism was the vehement fear and dislike of Catholicism and particularly the Irish Catholics. Boston erupted with numerous anti-Catholic demonstrations in 1823, 1826, and 1829, and local roughnecks burned the Ursuline Convent at Charlestown, Massachusetts, in 1834. The convent stood as a symbol of growing Irish competition for jobs and was a little-understood institution in the community. Rumors of dungeons and torture chambers there inflamed the prejudices of the local rowdies who ravaged the building. The general public disavowed the violence, the governor offered a $500 reward for evidence leading to the capture of the perpetrators, and thirteen men were arrested. Of these eight were tried but only one was convicted; he received a life sentence. It is difficult to know how much this particular incident reflected local problems, but it certainly was not an isolated example of hostility toward Catholics.

There were several other indications of anti-Catholicism during the pre–Civil War decades. The Protestant Association in New York City leveled a continuous stream of attacks at Irish Catholics, and the *New York Protestant* printed these items regularly. In 1834 Samuel F. B. Morse, now famous as the inventor of the telegraph, published a series of letters entitled *A Foreign*

Conspiracy Against the Liberties of the United States. In it he denounced an Austrian Catholic missionary society for sending men and money to America. The next year the Reverend Lyman Beecher followed Morse's epistle with *A Plea for the West,* in which he accused the pope of plotting to dominate the American West by sending hordes of Catholic settlers there. Although others may not have been as specific in their charges as were Morse and Beecher, the simple truth was that most American Protestants believed Catholicism to be incompatible with American ways. The Irish are "our natural enemies," claimed one editor, "not because they are Irishmen, but because they are the truest guards of the Papacy." Prominent Catholics in the United States did little to assuage existing fears; instead, their actions encouraged Protestant hysteria.

Archbishop John Hughes, the leading spokesman for the American Roman Catholic church in the 1840s and 1850s, tried unsuccessfully to obtain state aid for Catholic parochial schools. The Catholics objected particularly to the use of the Protestant Bible in the public schools, but they also wanted to isolate their children from non-Catholic influences. Of course in a nation of true religious freedom no child would have been required to engage in offensive religious practices in the public schools, but the church's objections merely confirmed the views of American Protestants that Catholics were subversive elements in society. After all, Protestants regarded the public schools as one of the best ways of assimilating foreign children to the dominant culture. The *Minnesota Chronicle and Register* observed in 1850 that the common school

> takes the child of the exile of Hungary, of the half-starved emigrant from the Emerald Isle, and of the hardy Norwegian, and places them on the same bench with the offspring of those whose ancestors' bones bleached upon the fields of Lexington. . . . As the child of the foreigner plays with his school fellow, he learns to whistle "Yankee Doodle" and sing "Hail Columbia," and before he leaves the school-desk for the plough, the anvil or the trowel, he is as sturdy a little republican as can be found in the land.

But the Roman Catholics did not want that kind of assimilation. Archbishop Hughes frightened American Protestants when he announced: "Everyone should know that we have for our mission to convert the world." This was exactly what the Protestants in the United States feared; it squarely opposed their beliefs that it was the *American* mission to convert others to the American way of life. The 1853 annual report of the Boston School Committee summarized the Protestant argument: "The ends of government . . . require that religious instruction should be given in our Public Schools. . . . The whole character of the instruction given must be such and such only as will tend to make the pupils thereof American citizens, and ardent supporters of American institutions."

Catholic schoolchildren who did attend the public schools were victimized by Yankee schoolmarms who incorporated society's views into their instruction. Boston's Cardinal O'Connell later recalled how those "good women" barely concealed the bitter antipathy they "felt toward those of us who had Catholic faith and Irish names. For any slight pretext we were severely punished. We were made to feel the slur against our faith and race, which hurt us to our very hearts' core." It did not help Irish Catholics either that in a reform era they opposed temperance, abolition, and public education while they supported slavery and the Fugitive Slave Law.

POLITICAL NATIVISM

Battles over the public schools were not the only signs of nativism. Anti-Catholic feeling had been manifesting itself in violence for decades before the Civil War. No doubt these episodes of public disturbances were partly triggered by books, newspapers, and pamphlets warning of the Catholic "menace" to American civilization; such accusations not only flourished from the 1830s through the 1850s but also surfaced once again at the end of the nineteenth century and would reappear more strikingly for a third time during the 1920s. On each occasion the anti-Catholic paranoia would be reflected in the political arena.

The Know-Nothing party of the 1850s was the largest of a variety of local nativist groups emerging during the 1840s and 1850s. Nativism in American politics was not unusual; hostility toward Germans, Quakers, Scotch-Irish, and other ethnic minorities had cropped up during the colonial era, and hostility toward foreigners had resulted in the passage of the Alien and Sedition Acts in 1798. But a nativist political party was a product of the 1840s. The acquisition of Western lands, the forceful removal of the Indians beyond the frontier, and the organization of Nebraska territory in 1854 exacerbated the anxieties of those people who feared Catholic encroachment. "Everyone knew," the authors of one American history observed with tongue in cheek, "that the Pope had his eye on America, for who would dwell in decaying Rome when he could live in the Mississippi Valley?" Obviously the United States had to protect itself. Some of the bigots joined openly hostile organizations, but many preferred the secretive Know-Nothings. (When members were questioned about the goals of their party they would respond, "I know nothing.") Under the banner of anti-Catholicism and antiforeignism the Know-Nothings achieved some success at the polls, especially in the elections of 1854 and 1855 when they won impressive victories in a few of the Northeastern states and sent 64 men to Congress. By the election of 1856, however, many of the party's members had already switched to the new Republican party, but those who remained loyal gave their votes to the American party, as the Know-Nothings then called themselves. The party collapsed after 1856 because Southerners had gained control of the organization, passed proslavery resolutions, and failed to give anti-Catholicism the prominence many Northern Protestants thought it deserved. As a result the political aspects of Northern bigotry achieved little, and the Know-Nothing movement disintegrated in the late 1850s, when the slavery controversy overshadowed American concerns about immigration and Catholicism. Besides, the Crimean War, improved economic conditions in Europe, and the conflict over slavery resulted in lower immigration totals after 1854. During the Civil War, when immigration fell still further, and when the foreigners proved themselves loyal citizens of both the Confederacy and the Union, anxiety about immigration considerably lessened.

It was not the slavery issue and the Civil War alone that killed pre–Civil War nativism. Although many Americans were alarmed by the newcomers, not all objected to their arrival. Industrialists, railroad builders, and other businessmen generally supported immigration. The need for unskilled laborers who would accept minimal wages assured immigrants of some welcome from the business community. At the same time, more people meant higher sales of goods and services and a stimulus to the national economy. Others besides business people welcomed Europeans into their communities. The nineteenth-century ideas of growth and progress meant that state, territorial, and even city governments worked to attract people. More than a score of states, including Michigan and Wisconsin, opened offices in New York to lure immigrants west as they disembarked from their ships. Finally, Americans believed that their nation was the home of the politically and religiously oppressed and that America had a unique world mission to aid those seeking asylum.

The fears of immigration and hatred of different ethnic groups, although waning, did not disappear in the 1860s, and resurged in the late nineteenth century. At that time different patterns of immigration brought large numbers of southern and eastern Europeans to America. The rising anxiety accompanying this shift eventually led to considerable conflict and major changes in the open-door policy for immigrants.

5

Burgeoning Industrialism
and a Massive
Movement of Peoples
(1880s–1930s)

INDUSTRIAL EXPANSION

THE INDUSTRIAL EXPANSION of the mid-nineteenth century stimulated further economic growth in subsequent decades. Although the Panic of 1873, the recession in the middle of the 1880s, and the terrible depression in 1893–94 punctuated the advances, the aggregate accomplishments are impressive. New industries like oil refining and iron and steel, new processes of economic organization like trusts, and new overseas markets all led to greater manpower needs. Whereas in 1860 total investment in United States industry approximated $1 billion, by 1890 it had increased to $6.5 billion, and by 1910 the figure exceeded $13 billion. National wealth practically doubled in the first decade of the twentieth century while the worth of foreign investments multiplied fivefold between 1897 and 1914. The nonagricultural work force jumped 300 percent between 1860 and 1890, when the numbers employed in factories, mines, construction, and transportation topped eight million. Twenty years later, in 1910, these same industries recorded almost fifteen million employees. The native birthrate and the movement from farms to cities simply could not provide the labor demanded by this fantastic economic explosion.

Besides labor, the United States needed several other ingredients before embarking on further industrial expansion. Capital, natural resources, and technological developments were necessary as well. The first, capital, was available in abundance. Wealthy Europeans, especially English, invested in railroads and mining. The United States government assisted the railroads with loans and generous grants of land. The Homestead Act of 1862 enabled farmers to get free land while other federal laws and policies permitted timber and mining interests to purchase valuable tracts at bargain prices. Federal concern showed itself further in the passage of protective tariffs and banking laws to help business. The government also refrained from intervening in contractual relations between employers and employees or demanding safety and sanitary precautions. At the state and local levels, governments provided tax abatement for industry while minimizing their efforts to regulate working conditions. The lack of governmental support for the laborers maximized profits and allowed for the increased accumulation of capital. Recessions during the 1870s and 1890s and the Great Depression of the 1930s hurt business, but generally profits were sufficient to feed the growing industrial plants and generate new capital. A case in point was the experience of the Pullman Company. For the year ending July 31, 1893, wages paid out came to $7,223,719 while dividends to stockholders totaled $2,520,000. Because of a terrible depression that ensued the following year sales and total income fell, and wages were reduced to $4,471,701. Nevertheless, the business slump did not affect the dividends, which increased to $2,880,000.

The industrial society also benefited from an abundance of natural resources. The Ohio, Mississippi, and Missouri rivers spanned most of the continent and connected with the Gulf of Mexico and the Atlantic Ocean, thereby facilitating commerce.

Excellent harbors in New York City, Philadelphia, Boston, Baltimore, New Orleans, Charleston, Tampa, San Diego, San Francisco, and Seattle further contributed to the prosperity of manufacturing and commerce. The fertile lands of the Southern states yielded the cotton for the textile industry while the production of farms increased sufficiently to feed the industrial and urban populations and even generated enough food for export. The rich coal and iron-ore lands were crucial to the growth of the steel industry, and the Western states contained enormous deposits of gold, lead, silver, copper, and other valuable minerals. As new materials were required in the twentieth century, the nation found them. Oil, so important for economic development in the last century, was first produced in Pennsylvania, but drillers later discovered larger deposits in Texas, Oklahoma, and off the shores of California and the Gulf Coast states.

In technology the United States also rose to the occasion, at first borrowing heavily from abroad and then producing its own practical scientists. A nation that counted people like Thomas Edison, Alexander Graham Bell, and Henry Ford among its inventors had no shortage of creative ideas. The incandescent light, the telephone, the automobile, and numerous other inventions propelled the industrial society. Even farming methods were transformed by technology. There were the machines— thrashers, reapers, cotton and corn pickers, and the like—then various fertilizers, irrigation, and ways of controlling crop and animal diseases.

As important as capital, resources, and technology to the industrial transformation was an energetic labor force. Many white farmers moved to the cities in search of work, but there were not enough of them. A few businessmen suggested hiring blacks, but most employers preferred to use whites, at least until World War I. Fortunately the United States had another source of labor: between 1880 and the onset of a worldwide depression in 1930, over twenty-five million immigrants came to the United States (see Table 5.1). In so doing they made a vital contribution to the building of the modern society.

Table 5.1

IMMIGRATION TO THE UNITED STATES
BY DECADE, 1880–1930

1881–1890	5,246,613
1891–1900	3,687,564
1901–1910	8,795,386
1911–1920	5,735,811
1921–1930	4,107,209

UPROOTED PEOPLES

The process of industrial expansion occurred throughout the world. In the 1890s the Russian economy was perhaps the fastest growing one in Europe, but other nations on the continent and in Latin America, Asia, and Africa were also experiencing the impact of industrial upheaval. Innumerable technological changes affected millions of people. Industrialism uprooted many from their traditional way of life, but it also presented heretofore unanticipated opportunities for movement. At best, the changes offered possibilities for a more prosperous and secure life; at worst, they meant exchanging agricultural desperation for industrial drudgery.

Europeans and Asians went to the United States, Africa, and Latin America; freed slaves and their children moved north; and American Indians, after near annihilation, were penned into reservations in the North Central and Southwestern states. Many of these population movements overlapped. Europeans and Asians arrived in the United States throughout the nineteenth century but their numbers soared dramatically between the 1880s and World War I and then again in the 1920s. Blacks tried to fend for themselves in the South during the late nineteenth century but several hundred thousand moved north during the Progressive era (1900–1917)—and continued to migrate in the 1920s—primarily to fill a labor shortage created by the curtailment of European immigration during World War I. Starting in the twentieth century, hundreds of thousands of

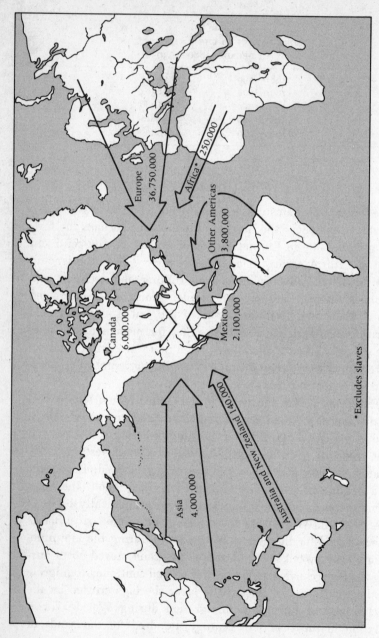

Europe
36,750,000

Africa *
250,000

Other Americas
3,800,000

Canada
6,000,000

Mexico
2,100,000

Asia
4,000,000

Australia and New Zealand 140,000

*Excludes slaves

Immigration to the United States, 1820–1990

Immigrants on the deck of an Atlantic liner in 1906. (*Library of Congress*)

Mexicans crossed the American border in search of a better way of life.

A diversity of peoples came to, or moved through, the United States seeking economic opportunity. The state immigration bureaus eagerly recruited Europeans. Railroads sent agents to Europe with promises of free or cheap land and passage, and steamship lines, hungry for the profits of the carrying trade, actively sought immigrants to sail on their lines. During the Civil War Congress enacted a contract labor law that enabled agents to scour the European countryside for workers, but this law was repealed in 1885. Yet illegal labor agents operated for many years in Europe.

Many northern and western Europeans succumbed to the inducements, but by the end of the nineteenth century the sources of labor changed as the bulk of the population move-

Immigrants lining up to be processed at Ellis Island, about 1900. (*United States Immigration and Naturalization Service*)

ment shifted to southern and eastern Europe, while a revolution in Mexico led to an influx of people fleeing a troubled society. Included among the most numerous of the twentieth-century arrivals in the United States were over three million Italians, three million or more of the various Slavic peoples, two million eastern European Jews, more than one million Mexicans, and hundreds of thousands of Asians, Hungarians, Greeks, Armenians, Syrians, Turks, Christian Arabs, Bulgarians, Latin Americans, Portuguese, and French Canadians.

An exact count of the immigrants is impossible. Slavic groups from the German and Austro-Hungarian empires were frequently mislabeled by American immigration inspectors as Germans, Austrians, or Hungarians although they might have been Serbs, Slovenes, Croatians, Czechs, or Montenegrins. (Europeans also had problems with identification. One Slovak writer complained in 1915: "The Magyars say we are Magyars, the Czechs that we are Czechs. But we are Slovaks!") Italians who lived in the Austrian Tyrol were recorded as Austrians while

A newly arrived immigrant, about 1900. (*National Archives*)

Poles were not listed separately between 1899 and 1918. Mexicans who arrived in the Southwest by land were not counted
until 1907, and even after that hundreds of thousands merely
crossed the border at places other than official immigration
stations. Jews came in classified only according to nation of
birth, so one can only estimate their numbers from Russia, Aus-
tria, and Rumania. Therefore, figures used in immigration
statistics and census tracts only approximate the numbers of
different peoples who arrived in the United States.

WHERE THE IMMIGRANTS WENT

The patterns of settlement remained similar to those of the mid-nineteenth century. The Middle Atlantic region housed more newcomers than any other section. New York City continued to be the nation's premier port for immigration and the city's population swelled. In 1930, some 75 percent of the New Yorkers consisted of foreigners and their children. Italians and eastern European Jews predominated but enclaves of almost every other ethnic group, ranging from Arabs to Yugoslavs, lived there. The city's overflow population gravitated toward Connecticut and New Jersey factories and Pennsylvania manufacturing and mining communities. The Slavs in particular found that the Pennsylvania mines provided the best paying unskilled jobs and many of them went to the Pittsburgh area. Buffalo, a port on the Great Lakes connected to New York City via railroad as well as the Hudson River and the Erie Canal, received many Poles and Italians. It also served as one of the gateways to the Midwest, where Chicago attracted just about everyone. A Lake Michigan port, the nation's railroad hub, a center for the grain and lumber trades, livestock processing, and meat packing, and the home of breweries and iron and steel mills and the Midwestern garment and financial center, Chicago almost always needed labor. Successive waves of foreigners and blacks filled its needs. By 1900 those of German stock constituted 35 percent of its population; those of Irish stock, 17 percent; and Scandinavians, 14 percent. As the century progressed an extraordinary diverse number of peoples found their way to the "Windy City." In the 1920s Chicago included the largest colonies of Scandinavians, Persians, Poles, Czechs, Serbo-Croatians, and Lithuanians in the nation; it ranked second in numbers of Germans, Greeks, Slovaks, Jews, and blacks.

Other Midwestern cities also attracted migrants from Europe and the American South. Detroit, Cleveland, and Milwaukee proved particularly attractive to Slavs from the Austro-Hungarian empire. Cleveland's prosperity rested on its Lake Erie loca-

Eastern European immigrants in the marketplace of Stevens Point, Wisconsin, about the turn of the century. Although most eastern Europeans migrated to the industrial centers of the Northeast and Midwest, they could be found in smaller towns like Stevens Point as well. (*State Historical Society of Wisconsin*)

tion and on its iron and steel foundries, blast furnaces, and rolling mills. In 1906 it was estimated that one of every five Cleveland inhabitants was German or Jewish, and one of every six of Slavic background. Detroit, the nation's most important point of entry for both English- and French-speaking Canadians, also claimed a polyglot population. In the mid-nineteenth century the city's early settlers mingled with French Canadians, Germans, and Irish, but by the 1890s eastern European Jews and Poles started coming. Within the next few decades Detroit witnessed the growth of black, Rumanian, Greek, Armenian,

Lebanese, Bulgarian, and Macedonian colonies. Milwaukee, Omaha, Duluth, and Minneapolis–St. Paul grew originally as centers for Germans and Scandinavians, but after the 1880s immigrants from southern and eastern Europe settled there. The "Head of the Lakes" region in northern Minnesota, Wisconsin, and Michigan housed the largest concentration of Finns anywhere in the world outside of Finland.

The South was less hospitable to the new immigrants than it had been to the old, but foreign-born workers and their enclaves appeared throughout that region. New Orleans remained an ethnically diverse city, and the state of Florida had contingents of Cubans, Spaniards, Greeks, and Hungarians. Prior to 1905 Florida had even sought people of Italian, Chinese, and Japanese descent because of a desperate labor shortage. There were also Italian agricultural colonies, as in the sugar cane fields of Louisiana, and scattered pockets of foreigners in cities like Atlanta, Richmond, and Memphis.

THE NEW IMMIGRANTS

The Italians were the most numerous of the new immigrants. Mostly poverty-stricken people from southern Italy, more than 75 percent settled in New York, Pennsylvania, and New England, but significant numbers went to every section of the country, with colonies in Detroit, Chicago, New Orleans, Denver, and San Francisco. Many of the Italian men came for temporary work and then returned home during the slack season. From 1908 to 1916 more than one million Italians went back to Italy, but the immigration restriction legislation of the 1920s halted the commuting.

Italian peasants left southern Italy to seek a better life in the United States. Poverty gripped their land, and between 1884 and 1887 cholera epidemics killed more than 55,000 people while frightening thousands of others. Beginning in the late 1880s increased citrus production in California and Florida cut American imports of Italian lemons and oranges, ruining the

Italian street market in New York City, about the time of World War I. (*New York Community Service Society*)

export market of farmers in southern Italy, and France put a high tariff on imported wines that also hurt the Italian economy. Conditions became so bad that some peasants dwelled in hovels of wattle and daub or straw. Those Italians who had gone to America told friends in the old country of plentiful jobs and high wages. Such news from the United States, received at a time when conditions were so bad, swept through southern Italy. "Once this movement got under way," notes one historian, "it seemed like an avalanche to gather momentum and carry all before it until whole districts had been depopulated of their males." Sometimes entire villages left together and once in the United States settled in the same neighborhoods. Calabrese, Venezians, Abruzzese, and Sicilians isolated themselves in separate areas. Americans may have lumped them together as Italians, but their group identification did not extend beyond their village associations. In America they discovered that they were all regarded as one people!

Once in the United States, the Italians found work in construction and heavy industry, on the railroads, and in the mining camps. Soon they gained a near monopoly of the fruit and vegetable business in New York City and New Orleans and engaged in truck farming on both East and West coasts. In California they were generally more prosperous than in other sections and many of their vineyards and fruit orchards became quite successful. Despite the fact that some prospered, most were common laborers.

Two million Jews comprised the second largest body of immigrants arriving in the late nineteenth and early twentieth centuries; like the Italians, they could be found throughout the country. Also like the Italians, their largest contingent (over 75 percent) remained in New York City, New Jersey, Pennsylvania, and New England. The Jews made up at least half of all Russians entering the United States between 1890 and 1914, and perhaps 90 percent in some of those years. Ninety-five percent of the emigration from Poland in 1920 was Jewish. Victimized by the industrial transformation, the rise of Pan-Slavism with its nationalistic emphasis, and the rampant pogroms in Russia, Poland, and Rumania, the Jews cherished a desire to fit in the United States.

For centuries Jews had been a minority group in other nations and this experience helped them in the United States. Although most of the men were skilled or semiskilled laborers, their meager earnings in the United States still kept them near the brink of poverty. Jews worked in New York City's garment district as well as in cigar and toy factories and printing plants in a number of cities, but many prospered as retail tradesmen, accountants, lawyers, and doctors. In the United States they pioneered in the manufacturing of ready-to-wear clothing; they started the film industry in New York City and later in Hollywood; and they achieved prominence as major department store merchants in New York City, Philadelphia, Chicago, Dallas, Birmingham, and elsewhere. Because so many Jews have become prosperous in recent decades, it is often overlooked that a majority of their forebears arrived impoverished. Only a few made spectacular successes, and it took two to three generations before most Jewish families found a niche in the middle class. As a result of the massive Jewish movement from Russia, Austrian Galicia, and Rumania, American Jewish life changed from a predominantly German to an overwhelmingly eastern European style.

The third major group arriving in the twentieth century, the Slavs, settled mainly in an area stretching from Connecticut to Minnesota (see Table 5.2). The term *Slav* includes Poles, Bohemians (Czechs), Ruthenians (Ukrainians), Slovaks, Russians (but not Russian Jews), Bulgarians, Serbs, Croatians, Montenegrins, and Slovenians. The western division of Slavs includes Bohemians, Slovaks, and Poles; the eastern and southern Slavs comprise the Russians, Ruthenians, Bulgarians, Serbs, Croatians, and Slovenians. The last three, along with the Montenegrins, are also the groups that live in Yugoslavia.

The United States received possibly over four million Slavs, but that figure would be at best an uncertain estimate. One difficulty in calculating the number of Slavs in the United States is the fact that so many returned to Europe. Some estimates indicate that 50 percent or more of the Slovaks, Slovenes, and Croatians went home, and the figures for the other Slavs are problematic. The Czechs, who came with their families and included a goodly proportion of professional and skilled workers, artisans, and small businessmen, were more likely to remain in America than the Serbs or Poles, who came singly, intent on saving their money before returning home to buy property and settle down. The outbreak of World War I in 1914 altered the future of hundreds of thousands who had originally planned on returning to Europe.

One cannot discuss the Slavic immigrants without indicating the significant cultural, linguistic, historical, political, and reli-

Table 5.2

SLAVIC GROUPS

	Religion	Language	Alphabet	Major regions of settlement in the United States (1880–1930)
Poles	Roman Catholic	Polish	Latin	Chicago, New York, Detroit, Milwaukee, Pittsburgh, Buffalo, Cleveland
Yugoslavs				
Slovenes	Roman Catholic	Slovenian	Latin	Cleveland, Milwaukee, Chicago, Joliet (Ill.), Pennsylvania
Croatians	Roman Catholic	Serbo-Croatian	Latin	Chicago, Pittsburgh (New York City after 1945)
Serbs	Serbian Orthodox	Serbo-Croatian	Cyrillic	Chicago and Detroit
Montenegrins	Serbian Orthodox	Serbo-Croatian	Cyrillic	
Macedonians	*	**	Cyrillic	Detroit
Russians	Russian Orthodox	Russian	Cyrillic	New York and Pennsylvania
Bulgarians	Bulgarian Orthodox	Bulgarian	Cyrillic	Detroit
Czechoslavakians				
Slovaks	Roman Catholic	Slovak	Latin	Pennsylvania (mostly Pittsburgh area); also Illinois, New York, Ohio, New Jersey
Czechs	Roman Catholic	Czech	Latin	Chicago, Cleveland, New York City
Ukrainians	Ukrainian Orthodox	Ukranian	Cyrillic	Pennsylvania, New England, Chicago

* Macedonians were from Yugoslavia, Greece, and Bulgaria. They belonged to the Serbian Orthodox, Greek Orthodox, or Bulgarian Orthodox church, depending on the country in which they lived.
** In Yugoslavia they spoke Serbo-Croatian; in Greece, Greek; in Bulgaria, Bulgarian. In the recent past efforts have been made to use the Macedonian language.

gious differences among them. Although belonging to the Indo-European peoples, each group had a different cultural and historical experience. The Poles, Croatians, Slovenes, and Slovaks were Roman Catholics; the Serbs and Montenegrins, Greek Orthodox; the Russians, Russian Orthodox; and the Czechs were divided between Roman Catholics and atheistic freethinkers. The groups came from different, although often contiguous regions of Europe and frequently regarded one another with suspicion. The Poles and Czechs started going to the United States in the nineteenth century and had already established some colonies before the Civil War. The Croatians from Dalmatia also had some settlements in America as early as 1820. They pioneered in the oyster industry in New Orleans and southern Louisiana and in the tuna industry in San Pedro, which is about twenty-five miles south of Los Angeles, California. Most of the Dalmatians in California live in this area and work in fishing or related industries.

One of the characteristics of many of the Slavic peoples, and the eastern and southern Europeans in general, except for the Jews, is that a large percentage regarded the United States as a place to earn some money before returning to their native countries and settling down. The Jews, who really had no homeland to return to, did not think in these terms and only about 5 percent of them went back to Europe. The non-Jews, though, roughly 70 to 80 percent of whom came over as single men, thought otherwise and something like 60 to 80 percent, depending on the individual ethnic group, returned to their homes after a stay in the United States.

Other groups that arrived in large numbers included Hungarians, Greeks, Lithuanians, Hollanders, Portuguese, Armenians, Middle Easterners, and French Canadians. Almost all came for greater economic opportunities but some, like the Armenians, sought to escape annihilation.

The Hungarians may be cited as among those people who planned to stay only temporarily in the United States. Although 1.8 million of them arrived between the 1880s and

World War I, the 1910 census recorded only 500,000 or so in the country. The records for the years 1908–14 indicate, however, that 64 percent of those who emigrated to the United States from Hungary subsequently returned. Hungarian enclaves could be found in New York City, as well as in mine and steel furnace regions of Ohio, Pennsylvania, New Jersey, and West Virginia. The cities of Cleveland, Chicago, and Detroit, which housed numerous colonies of Slavs, also developed sizable Hungarian populations. These immigrants were for the most part members of the peasant class and quite devoted to their church. Most of those in Cleveland were Roman Catholic, but other Hungarians could be found of the Reformed, Lutheran, Baptist, and Greek Orthodox faiths.

The Greeks also came to the United States with the intention of "making a killing" and returning home. As with so many others, however, they changed their minds once they arrived, or else circumstances altered their plans, and less than half made it back to Greece. The Greek exodus, about 10 percent of that nation's population between 1900 and 1925, occurred primarily because of the curtailment of the overseas currant market in the 1890s and the failure of the crop in 1907. Families scraped together whatever they could to send their young men to America to make some money that could be sent home. The men came alone with "their families' pool of silver coins sewed to their rough goatskin underclothing." Tied to their lapels were identification tags indicating their destination in America and the name of the relative or labor agent who would receive them and help them find work. The Greek immigrants, like so many others, looked outlandish with their tags, carrying bundles or straw suitcases, but once in America they worked with the fervor of zealots.

Most of the 500,000 or so Greeks went to New England, Chicago, New York City, Detroit, and San Francisco, but they could also be found in Milwaukee, Atlanta, and Salt Lake City, in the mines and mills of Colorado and Wyoming and the copper pits of Butte, Montana, and on the railroad track gangs in the Far

West. Some even cleared sagebrush in Idaho, and others prospered as sheepmen in the Rocky Mountain area. The Greeks despised working for others and sought, as soon as they could, to establish their own businesses. By the 1920s they owned over 2,000 restaurants, 150 grocery stores, several hundred shoeshining and hat-cleaning parlors, and numerous flower shops. They dominated the manufacturing and sale of candy in Chicago and were well represented in the sweets business throughout America. Whenever they could they also purchased buildings and properties. In Atlanta in the 1920s about 50 percent of the Greeks owned their own businesses, although many had been in the United States less than five years. Ninety-five percent of the Greek immigration to the United States originally consisted of men, those who wished to remain in America often went home to choose a bride. But the immigration restriction acts of the 1920s made this more difficult and the custom of "picture brides" developed. The depression of the 1930s affected the Greeks in the United States like everyone else, and many returned to their homeland during that decade.

The Lithuanians, Portuguese, and Dutch are among the other European groups who participated in the massive movement from Europe to the United States. The Lithuanians, often mislabeled as Russians, Poles, and Germans, sent hundreds of thousands of people to America between 1870 and 1930, but somehow the census bureau and Lithuanian spokesmen reached outrageously different figures. In 1918 Lithuanians estimated that at least 750,000 of their countrymen were in the United States, but the 1920 census takers found only 135,000 of them! In the 1930s Chicago housed a colony of about 100,000 Lithuanians, probably the largest concentration in this country. Most of them were of the Roman Catholic faith. Originally blue-collar workers, their respect for education and ambition to advance in society stimulated their children to seek other endeavors.

The Dutch, famed for their settlement of colonial New Amsterdam, now New York City, came in much greater numbers during the industrial era than they had in the colonial period. On the eve of the twentieth century there were over 100,000 Hollanders in the United States. Thirty thousand lived in Michigan, Illinois housed about 22,000, and Iowa, 10,000. In the hundred years between 1820 and 1920 more than 300,000 Dutch immigrants reached the United States, but as stern Calvinists who settled for the most part in farming communities away from urban centers, they attracted considerably less attention than those who engaged in industrial pursuits.

Fewer than 100,000 Portuguese, 98 percent of whom were Roman Catholic, came to the United States, but those who did gravitated mainly to New Bedford, Massachusetts, where the whaling fleets are docked, and to Rhode Island and California. In fact, about one third actually settled in the Golden State. Their focal point originally was the San Francisco Bay area, but they spread out from there to the Sacramento and San Joaquin valleys, and a number planted roots in Oakland. Many of those who were not seafarers became successful farmers. By 1950 most of those of Portuguese stock were in the rural areas of the state, and in southern California they ranked second only to the Dutch in the dairy industry. One Portuguese immigrant, J. B. Avida, a native of the Azores, arrived in the United States sorely missing one of his favorite vegetables. In 1888 he bought acreage near Merced, California, and started cultivating it. His crop grew well and he sold it to restaurants wherever he could. The San Francisco restaurants served it first but then it made an impact throughout America. Soon Avida was known as the "Father of the Sweet Potato Industry."

Like the Portuguese, the Armenians also numbered fewer than 100,000 immigrants, and also like them, settled in Massachusetts and California. But there the similarities end. Armenians, who also found homes in New York, Pennsylvania, Illinois, Wisconsin, and Michigan, were mostly peasants and unskilled laborers and they escaped not only from poverty but from the brutalities of the Turks, who massacred them like whites slaughtered bisons on the Western plains in the United

States. Armenians found work in New England textile mills and shoe factories, in the Pennsylvania foundries, and on the farms or in the packing houses, canneries, or cement works of California. More than 8,000 lived in Fresno, California, in 1915.

Often overlooked among those who chose to come to the United States are the approximately 450,000 Middle Easterners, mostly from Syria and Lebanon, but also from Yemen, Iraq, Arab Palestine, and other sections of the region. Over 125,000 were Lebanese Maronites (affiliated with the Roman Catholic church); there were also 100,000 Greek Orthodox, 50,000 Melkites (a combination of Roman Catholic and Greek Orthodox), 25,000 Moslems, 10,000 Protestants, and 140,000 unaffiliated or members of smaller Christian sects. Turkish persecution of Syrians had led to their exodus from the Middle East. Some arrived as early as the middle of the nineteenth century, but the majority came after the 1890s. They formed colonies in New England, New York, Pennsylvania, Michigan, and Ohio, making every effort to blend with the American churches of their respective sects. As Christians in the Ottoman Empire they owed no allegiance to a secular state, region, or culture, and they were neither Arabs nor Turks, neither Asians nor Assyrians. They were usually shopkeeping and lower-middle-class Semitic Christians influenced by economic difficulties and persecution to seek a better life in the United States. Once here they obtained whatever work they could but made every effort to improve their situations. They disliked working for others and started their own businesses as soon as they could. Some became peddlers and others merchants; some owned grocery stores; and a number owned and operated large trucking, clothing, amusement, and food enterprises. Many adopted American- or French-sounding names and attended local American churches.

French Canadians, or Franco-Americans as they prefer to be called, are associated with a particular region in the United States even though they established settlements in Illinois, Wisconsin, Louisiana, and New York. Nonetheless, one thinks of them in connection with New England, where over a quarter of a million were firmly entrenched by 1900, most in textile and industrial towns. The French Canadians left economically distressed Quebec because agriculture presented such a dismal future and because of the comparatively high wages available in the United States, although once in America they worked for sums that others disdained. The French Canadians were of the Roman Catholic faith and only the Irish, among ethnic groups, outnumbered them in New England.

BLACK MIGRATION NORTH

Foreigners may have contributed the largest numbers to the movement of people within the United States, but after 1880, and especially after 1910, American blacks from the South engaged in a major migration of their own as they left their homes for jobs in the North (see Table 5.3). The failure of the Reconstruction Congress to provide the freedmen with land precluded them from developing a solid economic base, and this ultimately caused the black exodus.

A common arrangement for black farmers that emerged during the Reconstruction era was sharecropping. Under this system blacks, and many whites as well, contracted to work on someone else's land and pay the owner a share of the proceeds after the harvest. The planter would advance money for tools, seed, food, and other supplies that the cropper might need; he in turn would pay for these advances at high interest rates after

Table 5.3
BLACK POPULATION OF SELECTED NORTHERN CITIES

City	1880	1890*	1900	1910	1920
Boston	5,873	8,590	11,591	13,564	16,350
Chicago	6,480	14,852	30,150	44,103	109,458
Detroit	2,821	3,454	4,111	5,741	40,838
New York	19,663	25,674	60,666	91,709	152,467
Philadelphia	31,699	40,374	62,613	84,459	134,229

* Includes Chinese, Japanese, and Indian.

the crop, usually cotton, was harvested and marketed. The sharecropper could also raise his own food, and if the crop was bountiful and the price of cotton high, he could pay his debts and perhaps have enough left over to purchase some land. Yet few made profits when the accounts were settled. Indeed, most remained in debt after the annual reckoning. Another disadvantage the sharecropper suffered was that the planter kept the books and the illiterate cropper was sometimes cheated outright or left confused by the financial settlement.

Many blacks, hoping to clear enough profit to buy land, preferred this arrangement to its chief alternative, gang labor for wages, which was too reminiscent of slavery. Other blacks did not engage in sharecropping but hired themselves out instead; still others rented and tilled the soil. These systems, however, left the capital-short black farmer at a disadvantage; all that he could sell was his labor, and that went cheap.

Staying on the land did not inevitably mean that blacks remained on the plantations of their former masters. A considerable migration of freedmen took place from the seaboard states to those farther west or to the cities and towns. Even before the end of the Civil War blacks were on the move. They poured into cities like New Orleans, where they were wretchedly poor, hungry, and ill-housed. Urban blacks did make economic progress, although many of them also had a difficult time making a living. Some of the skilled, who had learned their trades as slaves or as free blacks before the war, found work and little discrimination in wages, but many of the unskilled and newly arrived from the plantations either had to accept exceptionally low-paying menial and servile positions or else did not work at all. Some unskilled laborers learned a trade and earned higher wages than before, but other skilled workers lost their hold on some crafts or were paid less than whites for the same work. In 1902 W. E. B. Du Bois claimed that white painters in Atlanta received $2.30 per day while blacks got $1.80 and that white electricians earned $5.00 per day but blacks only $3.50. In Memphis Du Bois found that black stationary engineers made

Black sharecroppers in Alabama, 1937. (*Library of Congress*)

between $2.00 and $2.50 per day while whites made $3.00 to
$4.50. White unions, with few exceptions, wanted no part of
black workers. At the beginning of the new century only 40,000
of the nation's 1,200,000 union members were black, and in
many cases white unions barred black members or insisted on
racial segregation. Although unions like the United Federation
of Miners in Alabama resisted segregation, in other instances
white workers went on strike to protest the hiring of blacks.

Some blacks went to the North. After the end of the Reconstruction era, in 1879, thousands found new homes in Kansas,
while still others drifted to New York City and Philadelphia.
Most black Americans remained in the South, however, relent-
lessly trying to sustain themselves on the soil. But after 1914,
when European immigration declined as a result of the disrup-

tions caused by World War I, blacks streamed into the Northern cities to take the unskilled jobs formerly held by the immigrants. From 1910 to 1920 more than 500,000, and in the next decade nearly 750,000, blacks moved North. In those years they generally followed the railroad routes to New York City, Philadelphia, Chicago, and, to a lesser degree, Detroit, Cleveland, and Pittsburgh. Blacks moving to the cities preferred the North, but the nation's capital, Washington, D.C., also received a sizable influx as did Southern cities like Atlanta, New Orleans, and Birmingham.

Like the European, Asian, and Latin American minorities, black Americans were drawn to the cities for economic reasons, but other factors also account for their movement. Southern racism, especially acute from 1890 to 1920, made the North seem like the Promised Land. Chronic Southern poverty, always worse for the blacks, was the push factor, while the lure of jobs in the cities was the pull. Conditions were especially bad in the generally poverty-stricken South of the early twentieth century, for the boll weevil, sweeping north from Mexico across Texas, ravaged cotton crops and ruined many farmers. In some counties virtually the entire planting was destroyed in a single season. In 1915 floods ruined thousands of farm acres in Alabama and Mississippi. With a labor shortage in the North during World War I, industries that had relied on European immigrants now recruited blacks. Black newspapers, like the *Chicago Defender*, also urged their readers to come North, where the wages were good and discrimination less severe. Letters from those in the North often repeated the message.

With millions of people moving about the country and communities continually expanding and having to make room for and adjustments to the newcomers, it is no wonder that massive tensions existed. Periodically these tensions resulted in strains too difficult for the changing communities to cope with peacefully. For both migrants and natives the process of adaptation was fraught with unanticipated perils. The story of this adjustment will now be dealt with.

6

The Process of Adjustment
(1880s–1930s)

THE PROCESS OF ADJUSTMENT for the immigrants and urban blacks varied widely. The degree of prejudice encountered, the education available, and family values all contributed to the individual experiences. Most blacks and immigrants, regardless of cultural background, never moved beyond working-class status. The big differences occurred among the immigrants' children and grandchildren, with many factors contributing to mobility. For blacks progress was especially slow. The immigrants and migrating blacks usually moved with the desire of improving their economic conditions. A better life meant jobs that paid well, or at least more than the immigrants could have earned in their home countries or blacks could have made in the rural South. During the rapid pace of industrialization in the United States in the late nineteenth and early twentieth centuries, positions for the unskilled existed in every section of the country. As one Greek wrote home, "Work is everywhere. Your two hands are all you need." When immigration fell off at the time of World War I, blacks found greater opportunities.

THE LABORERS' LOT

Although some people knew exactly where they wanted to go, others relied on labor agents to help them. Among the Italians, Greeks, and Syrians, *padroni* assumed that responsibility. Some *padroni* traveled to Europe to recruit workers; others made the initial contact in the United States. They negotiated deals with employers, sent the workers off to their destinations, and collected and distributed the men's salaries after deducting their service fees. Some *padroni* also provided housing, wrote letters, and interpreted the American scene for their innocent charges. If the immigrants were lucky the *padrone* was fair; if not, they had to deal with a scoundrel. No matter what the character of any individual *padrone*, he served the purpose of bringing laborers to jobs in a day when public employment bureaus were few. In the East, where most of the immigrants first touched American soil, a network of American labor agents supplemented the *padroni*. Often these agents also engaged in practices that many today might consider reprehensible. For example, their letterheads included phrases like "Strike Orders Handled on Cost Plus Basis," indicating that they provided strikebreakers for industrial firms.

It would be impossible to discuss in detail the destinations and occupations of the more than twenty-five million immigrants who reached American shores between 1880 and 1930, but certain generalizations can be made. Most people knew where they wanted to go or could go and what kinds of work they would accept. Unskilled foreigners and blacks obtained most of the menial jobs on the railroads and in every mining and manufacturing center of the nation; they also dominated the ranks of toilers in American agriculture. The Irish and Poles consider peddling and needle crafts either beneath their dignity or occupations for women, but both of these groups regarded as "manly" heavy work calling for physical strength and prowess. As a result many Irishmen went into construction during the middle of the nineteenth century, and many relatives and friends joined them later. There was a good deal of truth to the jocular remark of that ficitional humorist, "Mr. Dooley," who claimed that on entering the United States, "a shovel was thrust into me hand and I was pushed into a street excyvatin' as though I'd been born here." By the end of the nineteenth century, and into the twentieth, the steel mills and mines throughout the country were desperate for brawny males, and so they recruited Poles and other Slavs, who accepted the long hours and low pay without much protest.

In many industries the social composition of the work force changed with the passage of time. On the railroads, for example, after 1880 Italians, Greeks, and Japanese replaced the earlier Chinese and Irish laborers, and they in turn gave way to Mexicans in the twentieth century. New York City's garment district at one time employed Germans and Irish, later Jews and Italians, and more recently blacks, Puerto Ricans, and Chinese. After 1910 on the West Coast Mexicans and Filipinos practically ousted the Chinese and Japanese from many areas of agricultural production. A number of Mexicans and blacks also moved into Midwestern industry in the 1920s as the Slavs moved up to supervisory positions. It did not always work out well for the minorities. As one steel foreman put it, "We have Negroes and Mexicans in a sort of competition with each other. It is a dirty trick."

Although immigrants and blacks often had no difficulty finding unskilled jobs, few worked a full fifty-two–week year or earned decent wages. Every industry had its periods of unemployment. In New England's textile towns most immigrants could count on no more than a forty-week year. In 1889 a survey of a quarter of a million railroad laborers disclosed that 70 percent worked fewer than 200 days during that year and 40 percent of those people had an annual income of less than $100. Wages in other industries were also insufficient to meet family needs and job security was just as uncertain. By 1910, when $900 a year was considered necessary for a family of five to maintain a modest standard of living, only one out of seven of the foreign-born earned that much. According to one survey, taken before World War I, the average annual *family* income of immigrant peoples was:

Armenians	$730	Greeks	$632	Ruthenians (Ukrainians)	$569
Jews	$685	Poles	$595	South Italians	$569
North Italians	$657	Syrians	$594	Russians (non-Jewish)	$494
Lithuanians	$636	Slovaks	$582	Serbs	$462

Wages, although four to ten times higher than they were in Europe, were nevertheless wretched since prices were high. Adult males sometimes earned $2 or more a day but rarely averaged $455 for the year. Blacks fared worse than immigrants, earning the lowest wages for the most menial and degrading work, and the newcomers sometimes took the better jobs away from black workers. Other blacks migrating to the Northern cities were exploited because of their eagerness to seek jobs. Discrimination by trade unions also diminished the changes of blacks getting skilled work. Given the low wages of the era, it is no wonder that people from all over the world flocked to Detroit following Henry Ford's 1912 announcement that he would pay assembly-line workers $5 a day.

Although Ford may have done something for the auto workers, the situation in other industries remained deplorable. In the ring-spinning and carding rooms of the New England textile mills, for example, dust, dried sputum, heat, moisture, poor air and light, and carbon monoxide produced conditions that cut years from the weavers' lives. A third of the spinners in Lawrence, Massachusetts, died before having worked ten years, half of them before they were twenty-five years old. For some death came instantly, as accidents were common during the making of industrial America. Working in the mines and on the railroads was particularly hazardous. In 1910, for example, approximately 3,000 railroad workers were killed and over 95,000 injured.

Working and safety conditions were especially bad for women

and children. "At the bottom of the industrial system," we are told, "was a body of sweated, underpaid women, of overworked children, and of hard-driven day-laborers whose lot often seemed worse than that of dumb beasts." There are tales of Polish children earning $2.68 for a sixty-hour week in the Shenandoah coal mines and of a fifteen-year-old girl in Chicago taking home $27 for 245 days of labor. Slavic women and boys earned 75¢ to $1 a day in Pittsburgh's spike, nut and bolt, and steel wire factories. Women also sweated for ten hours daily, at wages of 10¢ an hour, in the city's steam laundries. They stood continuously in pools of water with their shirts soaking from the steam. One worker complained of the hot manglers and washing machines: "The work's too hard, and you simply can't stand the heat." In Chicago and New York City Italian females just about monopolized the home finishing of cloaks in the garment trades. One factory paid girls as high as 12¢ for a finished garment, each of which usually took one and a half hours, but 5¢ to 7¢ per coat was a more common figure. When one scans salaries, sums like $1.35 for a full week's work and $9.37 for thirteen weeks' labor crop up frequently. Most unbelievable is that many Italian women continued working fifteen- and sixteen-hour days in which all they received for their efforts was 50¢ or 60¢. One explanation, perhaps, is that they had no choice. With some exaggeration a contemporary observer wrote that their husbands and fathers were desperately anxious to bring money into the home and women were regarded as instruments to advance this end. The Italian male thought "his women belong to him as much as his feather bed and the copper saucepans he brought with him from the homeland. As a thinking, human being, acting independently, the southern Italian immigrant woman does not exist. She obeys absolutely the will of her nearest male relative and he is driven by the concrete vision of a dollar."

Most black and many immigrant families could not have survived without the wages of wives and children: the 1910 census recorded over two million child laborers. The cultural background as well as the poverty of each group dictated who would, and who would not, be allowed to seek gainful employment. Italian children were pulled out of school as early as possible; boys went out to seek jobs; girls remained at home to help their mothers. Italian women usually worked at home or in a family business, but in cities like New York, Buffalo, and Chicago their husbands and fathers permitted them to get jobs in carefully selected factories. The Irish, Poles, and French Canadians thought that everyone should contribute to the family coffers, and they too saw no point in an extended education. Dutch and Greek women did not work outside of the home unless it was in a family business. Greek males believed it was humiliating not to be able to support their wives, mothers, daughters, or sisters. French-Canadian women worked in factories but not as domestics. Irish, German, Bohemian, Scandinavian, and Slavic women did both factory and domestic work. Mexican women could work in fields but not in factories or someone else's home. Polish women worked wherever they could find jobs; marriage and family were not necessarily valid reasons for ending their wage-earning. There is the story of a Polish woman in a West Virginia mining community who, although pregnant, did not let her delicate condition interfere with her duties as mistress of a boarding house. One evening the woman retired to her bed, gave birth at three o'clock in the morning, and then was up at six o'clock preparing breakfast for her thirteen ravenous boarders and fixing lunches for their dinner buckets. Black urban women had little choice, for their husbands earned so little that the wives had to work. In New York City around the turn of the century, nearly 60 percent of the black women worked compared to 27 percent for the foreign-born and 24 percent for native-born white women. Mostly they found jobs as domestics or in other low-paid occupations. For black women to work was nothing new; during slavery they had traditionally worked on the plantations of the South.

Low wages for long hours in abysmal surroundings were thus the common experience of immigrants and blacks, both male and female. The miserable factory and mining conditions

Child laborers working in the mines. The utilization of child laborers reached its peak in the early twentieth century. (*Library of Congress*)

stimulated the development of labor unions, but because of the overabundance of labor, discrimination, employer opposition, and public and governmental indifference or hostility, unions were not very successful in the late nineteenth century. In the 1870s the Knights of Labor sought to organize nearly all American workers into one big union, but the Knights lost some key strikes, were identified with radicalism, and were poorly managed and divided; hence they collapsed. The most successful labor union to emerge during the late nineteenth century was the American Federation of Labor (AFL), led by Samuel Gompers. The AFL concentrated on organizing the skilled craftsmen and negotiating benefits from employers; most workers, especially the immigrants and blacks, were left out. From 1870 to World War I working and safety conditions gradually improved, and during the Progressive reform years after 1900 unions won more acceptance. During World War I the government urged business to recognize unions and union contracts in order to stimulate war production by avoiding strikes. As a result, trade union membership grew to over five million by the end of the Great War, only to suffer serious reversals during the anti-union climate of the 1920s.

Members of almost all the immigrant nationalities and some of the blacks participated in union activities at one time or another, but their experiences were not uniform. In the nine-teenth century Germans dominated the labor movement among the skilled craftsmen; in the 1880s, after the formation of the AFL, the Irish ranked high among the second and third echelon of leaders. The newer groups from southern and eastern Europe had a reputation for shunning union activities, although the Pennsylvania anthracite coal strike of 1897 was dominated by Poles, Lithuanians, Slovaks, and Ukrainians. In that strike even the women participated, and the *Wilkes-Barre Times* editorial-ized that their presence was "a novelty of a not very pleasing nature." In the twentieth century, eastern European Jews fig-ured prominently among the founders and leaders of the Inter-national Ladies' Garment Workers' Union and the Amalgam-ated Clothing Workers' Union. Most immigrants, however, did not at first join unions and were willing to allow employers to co-opt their services regardless of circumstances.

Employers in every part of the country used immigrants as strikebreakers. A North Adams, Massachusetts, shoe factory hired seventy-five Chinese to replace striking employees in 1870; packing plants in Omaha brought Japanese and Greek scabs there in 1904; and Mexicans went to Chicago for the same purpose a generation later. In the Carbon County, Utah, mines, Italians and Slavs replaced English strikers in the late nine-teenth century; Greeks replaced the Italians and Slavs who went on strike in 1903; and Mexicans were used when the

Greeks walked off the job in the 1920s. Foreign-born minorities who appeared as scabs in one place often led strikers elsewhere. Mexicans were prominent among the railroad, copper mine, and agricultural strikers in the twentieth-century West, while Italians, who were often discriminated against and refused admission to some unions that they wanted to join, like the stonecutters, provided the backbone of the Lawrence, Massachusetts, textile strike in 1912.

For blacks the situation was somewhat different. Unions usually excluded them or else segregated them into separate locals. Hence a number of blacks showed no hesitation crossing picket lines. Negroes were employed to break strikes along the waterfront as early as 1855 in New York City, and the tradition continued for decades. In 1903 New York City subway contractors replaced protesting employees with imported black workers, and at about the same time meat packers in Chicago did the same.

Hostility to black laborers kept them out of numerous industries, except as strikebreakers, but in some areas the barriers were less formidable. They worked in the bituminous coal fields of West Virginia and Alabama, and in 1907 the Immigration Commission reported that blacks, concentrated in Alabama and Maryland and to a lesser extent in Virginia, Tennessee, and Kentucky, made up approximately 40 percent of the Southern steelworkers. By 1910 some 350,000 Southern Negroes were factory workers. In the cities blacks also managed to find jobs as longshoremen and in some of the skilled crafts and building trades. Others worked for the railroads. In nearly all of these jobs, however, black workers faced considerable discrimination. They usually were common laborers in the industries where they were employed and were paid less than whites. Immigrant workers competed with them for some of the better jobs, forcing many blacks to seek employment as menials or as domestic servants in the homes of white folks.

A number of industries preferred not to use blacks at all. Those Southern proponents of a New South, which was to be based on industries and cities, attempted to recruit immigrant labor. State governments, railroads, industrialists, and even planters tried to entice foreigners to the South. South Carolina set up the first Southern state immigration agency in 1866, and other states followed. The Southern Immigration Association of America was organized in Louisville in 1883 and held its first annual meeting in 1884. Although it became defunct in a few years, other groups tried to promote immigration to the South.

Planters wanted Chinese laborers because they allegedly worked better for lower wages than Europeans would accept. But few came and other Southerners expressed reservations about bringing another racial group to the region. Several state immigration bureaus actually contracted to bring in Poles, Greeks, Italians, and Portuguese, but not in large numbers. Federal law prohibited contract labor, but more important was the reputation of the South among foreign workers. Some did come, lured by labor agents in the North, but upon arrival they often found wages lower than had been stipulated. Furthermore, for those immigrants interested in farming, better lands were available in other sections of the United States. Immigrants, often shrewd about economic opportunities available, accurately believed that the South offered less than other regions.

Thousands of immigrants and blacks in the South were also victimized by one of the most oppressive systems of labor imaginable—peonage, a form of involuntary servitude. Peonage existed in practically every state of the Union but was centered in the Southern cotton belt from the Carolinas to Texas, in the turpentine areas concentrated along the contiguous borders of Florida, Georgia, and Alabama, and in the railroad construction camps, the sawmills, and the mines of the South. The peons included unsuspecting immigrants who had been promised good pay and working conditions and Southerners who had been fined or imprisoned for some petty offense. The system offered large employers of labor low unit costs of production and enormous profits. No one with any moral scruples would have exploited workers in such a cruel fashion, for peonage was in many respects worse than slavery had been. Whereas in ante-bellum days slaves had some monetary value, and their illnesses and deaths resulted in pecuniary losses, peons required no investment and only minimal expenditures for food and shelter. Hence they were kept only as long as they could toil and then dispensed with in a variety of notorious ways, including murder.

The brutality of life for the peons knew no bounds. Many blacks, often illiterate, were made to sign contracts that gave planters "the right to use such force as he or his agents may deem necessary to require me to remain on his farm and perform good and satisfactory services" and "the right to lock me up for safe keeping." With or without such documents those who used peons employed armed guards, who did not hesitate to threaten, maim, or shoot their charges. When laborers ran away they were searched for with bloodhounds and, when caught, severely whipped, often chained, and then brought back. An escaped immigrant peon, kept in jail with a vagrant while awaiting trial, asked her, "Do they flog men everywhere in this country?" "No," she replied, "just down here in the South where they used to flog niggers." Locked and barred stockades, which were sometimes converted chicken coops or horse stalls, provided shelter during the workers' off hours. In some railroad camps locked boxcars without cots or even straw housed the laborers at night. "In the woods," one peon later recalled, "they can do anything they please, and no one can see them but God."

The institution of peonage, begun sometime after slavery ended, continued into the twentieth century. It attracted nation-wide attention in 1906 when the federal government began an investigation in Florida and found conditions resembling "slave-labor" camps. In the 1920s, after heavy floods in Mississippi, over 5,000 blacks were retained in refugee camps behind barbed wire until someone would come and promise to give them a home, a job, and prevent them from becoming "a public charge." No one knows how long peonage continued or how many blacks and immigrants were impressed, but between 1958 and 1963 the federal Justice Department received over 170 complaints concerning involuntary servitude from thirty states including California (home for many Mexican migrants), Florida, Georgia, Alabama, Mississippi, Texas, and Arkansas.

As a result of the abominable treatment so many workers received in the South, especially in the late nineteenth and early twentieth centuries, as well as misrepresentation by labor agents and entrepreneurs, foreigners shunned most of the former Confederate states and the region could not even hold on to the relatively few immigrants who were enticed there. The 1900 census showed over 620,000 foreign-born inhabitants in the South; ten years later the figure had declined to half a million. That was only 2 percent of the region's population compared to 20 percent for the rest of the country. New South industrialists therefore sought laborers among the old-stock Southerners. English, Scottish, and Scotch-Irish names, seemingly of the "purest" Anglo-Saxon heritage, were found on the payrolls of Southern mills and in the iron, tobacco, and other industries. Southern industrialists could recruit these workers for the mills and factories because rural conditions were so miserable and afforded limited opportunities for poor whites.

These native-born whites in the South fared only slightly better than blacks and immigrants. Workers in the New South's industries were among the worst paid and most exploited laborers in America. Especially appalling were the cotton mills, which employed women and children. Youngsters of eight and nine years toiled twelve hours a day for pitiful wages. The Southern states claimed more than half of all of the child laborers in the nation, and in 1900 the census found more than one million employees under the age of sixteen in the South. While Northern states were beginning to outlaw child labor, Southerners were reluctant to do so. One Mississippi senator branded such legislation "part of a hellish scheme laid in foreign countries," and another politician insisted the elimination of child labor "would destroy the home. It would destroy a civilization based on the Bible." The use of child labor declined after 1920, but conditions in the company-run mill towns remained shocking. One critic of such towns said the boss "owns the community and he regulates the life that goes on there after the day's work is over in his mill. He has the power to discharge the worker at the mill, to refuse him credit at his store, to dump a worker's furniture out of a house, to have him expelled from church, to bar his child from school, and to withhold the service of a doctor or hospital." A mill manager spoke more succinctly: "We govern like the Czar of Russia."

Conditions of a similar but less extreme nature existed in parts of the North as well. Public sentiment was sharply hostile to lower-class workers before the 1930s and especially to laborers who were also ethnic minorities. Bosses hired thugs to beat strikers and law officers often helped the roughnecks or watched in amusement. During the Chicago garment workers' strike of 1910 Irish policemen "cracked the heads of 'Kikes,' 'Dagoes,' and 'Polacks.' " One observer noted "mounted policemen plunging over the sidewalks and trampeling [sic] peaceful workers." Five years later the mayor of Chicago defended similar episodes of police brutality. When a citizens' delegation came to protest such incivilities Mayor "Big Bill" Thompson told them, "With these Poles and other foreigners, one cannot do anything else."

The abuses perpetrated against immigrants and blacks did not go unnoticed. Many thoughtful citizens tried, in a variety of ways, to improve their lot in the United States. Muckraking journalists in the Progressive era, during the early years of the twentieth century, wrote about some of the worst evils, and, along with other middle- and upper-middle-class reformers, sought to better the conditions of working-class Americans through legislation by the local, state, and federal governments. Beginning in the 1870s, and reaching a peak in the years before World War I, states enacted laws curbing child labor, improving factory safety and working conditions, giving greater protection to women, providing some pensions for needy widows with small children, and generally improving the quality of life for those most severely affected by the abuses of the industrial system.

THE TENEMENT DISTRICTS

Among those in the forefront of the fight to improve the laborers' lot were the social workers. Jane Addams, the most famous of those dedicated and well-educated Americans who opened up settlement houses in the immigrant communities, established Hull House in Chicago in 1889. No tasks were too menial or too insurmountable for the settlement-house workers. Whatever they felt the community needed, they fought for. Jane Addams had herself appointed garbage inspector so that she could legally require landlords to clean up their houses. The most important function of the settlement houses and leaders, though, was to provide a refuge from the harshness of the outside world. A variety of recreational and educational facilities such as libraries, arts and crafts classes, social clubs, music and theater groups, gymnasiums, playgrounds, and day nurseries were available to those who lived in the community. Emotional succor, often the most necessary form of assistance, also ranked high among settlement-house offerings. The settlement workers did not restrict their activities to the local community, though their goals almost always reflected community needs. They petitioned government officials at all levels to help alleviate the worst abuses of factory and city life. One of their main objectives was to improve the physical environment in which they and the immigrants both worked and lived. They succeeded, to some extent, when a state like New York passed new housing laws requiring windows in every bedroom and plumbing facilities in each tenement apartment, but such new legislation took effect gradually, while the dwellings that already existed remained in use.

Tenement housing may be described but the full impact of its wretchedness simply cannot be conveyed in words. New York City, the mecca for most of the immigrants, had, according to a knowledgeable reformer of the Progressive era, "the worst housing conditions in the world." Tenements were overcrowded with an average of 15.6 persons per dwelling unit in

1910, compared to 9.1 in Boston and 8.9 in Chicago. Sometimes it is difficult to imagine how bad New York must have been when one hears about conditions in other cities. In Philadelphia an investigator discovered 30 Italian families with 123 persons living in 34 rooms; in Chicago the Polish district averaged 339.8 people per acre; and a physician in Los Angeles found 23 Mexicans sleeping in one room. In Pittsburgh one reporter described the dwellings of Slavic laborers as "so noisome and repulsive that one must visit the lower quarters of Canton to meet their like." The Polish district in Chicago was reputedly "nothing more than an infested wall-to-wall carpet of rotted wood and crumbling concrete." Tenements in city after city were without indoor plumbing, and the outdoor toilets overflowed into basement flats during heavy rains. In 1903 the floors of many Chinese homes in San Francisco were found to be rotting away because the broken sewer pipes and cesspools that lay underneath them had saturated the lots with human excrement. In most cities the stench from piles of outdoor garbage and horse droppings and the presence of chickens, goats, and cows housed along with horses in buildings adjoining residential dwellings is simply too pungent to describe.

The worst housing in the cities was reserved for the black migrants coming from the South. Owners preferred to rent to the white immigrants rather than to blacks, and black families sometimes encountered violence when they tried to move outside their growing ghettos. Black renters usually found quarters in dilapidated older buildings left by whites, and the growth in the Northern urban black population during the Great Migration of 1910–20 strained available facilities. To pay their rent regularly, blacks, even more than most immigrants, had to take in boarders. Various studies reveal that in Northern ghettos in the early twentieth century about one third of black families took in boarders or lodgers. In the Pittsburgh ghetto half of the single black men lived three or four to a room and less than 40 percent had a bed to themselves. Half slept two in a bed and sometimes three and even four shared a bed. No wonder then

Child laborers stripping tobacco in a tenement house. Not only was the employment of children in violation of the law, but the odor of tobacco that permeated the tenements made life unbearable. (*Library of Congress*)

that the health of black Americans was worse than that of others. Blacks were more likely than whites to suffer pneumonia as well as tuberculosis and other crippling diseases. In 1910 the black death rate was 21.7 per 1,000 while the white rate was 14.5 per 1,000, and between 1915 and 1920 the infant mortality rate of blacks was 50 percent higher than that of whites.

VOLUNTARY ASSOCIATIONS

One is often amazed that the immigrants and black migrants managed to survive their experiences in urban America, but they did. Social reforms and a gradually rising standard of living helped, but perhaps the main reason for their ability to overcome the day-to-day hazards in their lives was the enormous aid and support that they received from their own people, their churches, and the numerous organizations that had been set up to sustain them during their transition period. Blacks and members of almost every immigrant group participated in some of the activities of an organized and cohesive ethnic community, and this not only helped their own adaptation but also provided their children with the strength to go out into the dominant society. As one sociologist observed, "The highly organized community life was . . . the means by which the minority group met the problems of adjustment with which it was confronted."

Most of the immigrant groups desired to retain their traditional culture for themselves and their children while at the same time adjusting to life in the United States. They made every effort to have the Old World characteristics transmitted intact to succeeding generations. Language was held on to tenaciously, community newspapers proliferated, and parochial schools were established. Traditional holidays were marked with appropriate festivities and organizations were formed to keep members of the group together. At the same time, however, thousands of voluntary associations, societies, lodges, benevolent groups, cultural clubs, *Gymnasiums*, literary guilds, choirs, and theatrical circles stood ready to help the newcomer bridge the gap between the Old World and the New. In part these organizations were indispensable to those in a bewildering society who needed security; but immigrants also designed these groups to thwart complete assimilation into the dominant society. A perceptive scholar noted recently that the popular notion that immigrants came to the United States ready to assimilate "is a myth. The specter of 'Americanization,'" he continued, "troubled more immigrants than historians have been willing to admit."

Immigrant associations anticipated subsequent governmental welfare agencies in helping some to find jobs and homes and others to obtain transportation to distant cities. Some groups provided relief, others sustenance. A number gave unemployment insurance; most offered some kind of death benefits. The Irish

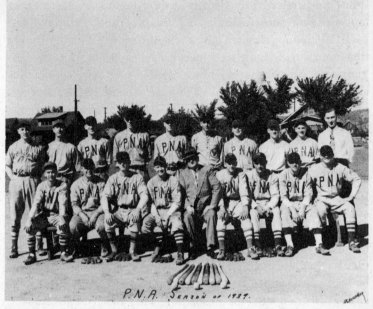

Baseball team of the Polish National Alliance, 1939. (*Immigration History Archives*)

Benevolent Society of Lawrence, Massachusetts, proclaimed, "We visit our sick, and bury our dead." In 1914 the largest of such societies, the Deutsch-Amerikanischer Nationalbund, counted over two million members. Women's organizations, mainly devoted to charitable activities and the promotion of the traditional culture, also proliferated. Among the most active were the Polish Women's Alliance, the Jednota Ceskyck Dam (Society of Czech Women), and the National Council of Jewish Women.

Although it would be impossible to discuss all of the myriad minority societies, one might look at the Polish National Alliance (PNA), founded in 1880, and the Polish Roman Catholic Union (PRCU), founded a few months later, as prototypes. Both organizations began on the eve of the great migrations from Poland. They helped the immigrants on their arrival, published newsletters, provided insurance, organized libraries, established museums, maintained youth programs, sponsored trips back to Poland, promoted education, and were influential in getting monuments built in American cities celebrating the past glories of Americans of Polish descent such as Tadeusz Kosciuszko and General Kazimierz Pulaski, who fought in the American Revolution. The PNA's annual calendars, replete with useful information and Polish proverbs, were avidly sought by American Poles. But the two organizations differed in their emphases. The PNA's main goals were to develop support for an independent Poland while at the same time instilling loyalty to the United States in Polish Americans. The PRCU, on the other hand, dominated by Catholic priests, emphasized the separateness of Poles from other Americans and discouraged participation in non-Polish Catholic activities. Like all such groups that refused to recognize that the Old World culture could not be transplanted intact and American-reared children could not be kept in complete ethnic isolation, the PRCU fought a losing battle. In 1935 when the PNA claimed a membership of over 280,000 people, the PRCU had only about 150,000.

BLACK ASSOCIATIONS

The two most well-known black organizations founded in the early twentieth century, the National Urban League and the National Association for the Advancement of Colored People (NAACP), stressed the need for full equality and better living conditions for blacks. The NAACP called for immediate civil rights and combated racism in the courts and legislatures. During World War I the Association, while reluctantly accepting a Jim Crow army, tried to get more black officers and improved training and social facilities for black troops. In the 1920s the NAACP unsuccessfully lobbied for the enactment of a federal antilynching law. The Urban League was less political and concentrated on helping rural migrants adjust to city life by getting decent housing and jobs.

While both the NAACP and the Urban League tried to integrate blacks into the mainstream of American life, other groups and individual blacks promoted black culture. In the late nineteenth century a few blacks, such as Methodist Bishop Henry Turner, rejected the notion that blacks could become part of American culture and urged instead emigration to Africa. In 1892 Turner wrote from Liberia, "One thing the black man has here, that is manhood, freedom, and the fullest liberty; and he feels as a lord and walks the same way." Few blacks went to Africa, but some began to study their African and Afro-American heritages. Black authors began to collect materials about the experiences of blacks in America. The most influential group was the Association for the Study of Negro Life and History, founded in 1915, which published the *Journal of Negro History*. Other organizations, like the Society for the Collection of Negro Folk Lore, gathered materials about black culture.

The most spectacular leader urging black pride and concern about Africa was Jamaica-born Marcus Garvey, founder of the Universal Negro Improvement Association, who arrived in New York just before World War I. With fervent oratory Garvey urged freedom for Africans, a back-to-Africa movement, and pride in being black and chided those who advocated social equality and assimilation. He told blacks to build up their own businesses and organizations, and he built a mass black movement with a special appeal to the black masses who had recently moved to the cities. In the 1920s this flamboyant leader ran afoul of the law and his black shipping business ran into financial difficulties. Following his conviction and deportation his movement fell apart, but he was the first black in America to build a genuine nationalist movement.

CULTURAL AND RECREATIONAL ACTIVITIES

Numerous cultural endeavors also afforded outlets for social intercourse in an ethnic setting. Many minorities formed marching bands that led parades to Sunday picnics. For some groups, like the Greeks, national identification was so strong that they took their flags along with them. Other recreational opportunities were made possible by the coffee houses, saloons, beer gardens, musical organizations, athletic teams, and drama societies that proliferated within most of the immigrant communities. The Swedes, Poles, and Czechs had an ethnic theater, as did the Germans, whose earliest performances were staged in local taverns without props. The Italians, who had a profound love of opera, also participated in other dramatic and musical productions. Antonietta Pisanelli Alessandro organized one of the better-known Italian-American theatrical companies in San Francisco in 1904. The Yiddish (Jewish) theater, the most famous of the ethnic drama groups, originated in the 1880s in New York City and lasted for more than half a century. The theater was the "great cultural passion" of the Jews and acting provided a release for a good deal of their creativity. Eventually a large number of actors, writers, and directors from the Yiddish theater achieved fame in New York City's commercial theater as well as in the motion picture industry in Hollywood. In the 1920s and 1930s several American theater critics upheld aspects of the Yiddish theater as models of accomplishment and seriousness.

Blacks also produced important cultural works. During the 1920s the success of a group of novelists, poets, and dramatists asserted the presence of "the New Negro." Writers of what was known as the "Harlem Renaissance" explored folk themes and black identity and rejected white standards. Yet it was in the area of music that black culture made its most original and major contribution. Some black groups studied and sang spirituals while other black musicians composed the black musical revues so popular after 1910. Coming up from the South were jazz and blues musicians. "Jelly Roll" Morton recalled that around the turn of the century in New Orleans, "Music was pouring into the streets from every house. . . . Little boys and grown-ups would walk along the avenues, swaying and whistling jazz

Sauk City Wisconsin Dramatic Company, a German-American group, in 1904. The immigrant theater helped many groups to maintain their own cultures. (*State Historical Society of Wisconsin*)

tunes." Many of the great black musicians like Louis Armstrong had little formal training, but they grew up in the black musical tradition and their genius and creative styles found eager audiences in the growing urban ghettos. By 1910 a black theater had opened in Harlem and it began to feature blues singers. Records made the blues popular in the 1920s and 1930s. A creation of black society, the blues, with their themes of pathos, were relevant to the black condition. While the writers associated with the Harlem Renaissance appealed to an elite group, the blues were popular among both the rural and urban black masses. From 1920 to 1940 over five thousand blues records were issued featuring over one thousand black musicians. These records were mainly purchased by blacks.

A traditional New Orleans funeral procession. Mourners, accompanied by a jazzband, march from the funeral parlor to the cemetery. (*Louisiana Tourist Development Commission*)

THE CHURCHES AND PAROCHIAL EDUCATION

Of all the ethnic institutions none was more important than the church. Whether black or white, Protestant, Catholic, or Jewish, religious bodies exerted an influence far greater than any of the other community affiliations. The Lutherans were strong among the Scandinavians and the Germans, but many of the former later became Baptists and Methodists. The lives of the eastern European Jews were at first almost totally circumscribed by religious dictums. Roman Catholicism contained by far the largest number of immigrant adherents and had more parishioners than all the other immigrant churches combined. The faithful included an overwhelming majority of the Irish, Poles, French Canadians, Lithuanians, Croatians, and Slovenes, as well as a goodly number of Germans and Czechs. Mexicans and Italians were also Catholic, but the former followed practices that were unfamiliar to those of European descent while the latter did not have much respect for the church or its hierarchy. Blacks were mostly Protestants, usually Methodists or Baptists.

Black Protestants usually attended segregated churches. Whites had not welcomed them to their services even when they were few and continued to exclude them as a large number of Southern blacks began pouring into the cities. When a neighborhood became predominantly black, whites abandoned their churches to the blacks. Older established black churches witnessed a big growth in membership and they and some of the newer congregations developed social programs for the migrants. The Reverend Reverdy Ransom's church in Chicago, for example, ran a day nursery and an employment office. Perhaps equally important among the religious institutions were the numerous storefront churches that appeared in the expanding urban ghettos. These evangelical groups had great appeal to the poor, less-educated rural blacks, who found in their services a similarity to the emotional worship of the rural black churches. There the service would be fervent with the traditional shouts and music; it was a bit of home in the city.

Just as the black churches adapted to the needs of their parishioners, so too did those organizations serving the immigrants. The Catholic hierarchy in the United States, dominated by those of Irish ancestry, established thousands of parallel social, educational, and athletic groupings designed to keep Catholics separated from non-Catholics and free of assimilationist influence. Most Catholics were willing to go along with this policy and some, notably Germans, French Canadians, and Poles, isolated themselves still further on national bases. The Italians also wished to remain by themselves, but the church played little role in their lives.

No groups were more devoted to, or involved with, the Roman Catholic church than the Irish and the Poles. It was the center of their world and the priest was the authority in the community. The Irish, of course, had come first, and in the church they found the only American institution both familiar and willing to accept them. As Archbishop Hughes remarked about the Irishman in the middle of the nineteenth century:

> It is only when he has the consolation of his religion, that he feels comparatively happy in his new position. If on the Sunday he can be present at the holy sacrifice of Mass, if he can only see the minister of his religion at the altar and hear the word of God in the language to which his ear was accustomed from childhood, he forgets that he is among strangers in a strange country.

The church was no less important for the Poles. As one wrote, "Without the Church we would have lost our identity." Polish children were educated in the parish school, which was conducted in the Polish language and taught by Polish priests and nuns. Polish culture had to be preserved but nationalism and Catholicism were so intertwined that Poles could not separate one from the other. For Germans and French Canadians the parish school, conducted in the familiar tongue, was also important. One Catholic missionary priest in Milwaukee observed in 1852, "German Catholic schools are the crying need in this country because German children, if Anglicized, by some strange fate generally become alienated from Catholic life."

In fact many ethnic groups conceived of education as the means with which to preserve the Old World language and culture. In spite of their poverty, Jews, Greeks, Swedes, Japanese, and Chinese, to mention a few, either set up day schools for instruction in traditional ways or else had afternoon or summer schools for that purpose. The tenacity with which the immigrant groups held on to their schools can be observed from the eruptions in 1889 and 1890 when lawmakers in Illinois and Wisconsin required basic instruction to be conducted in the English language. In Wisconsin both Catholics and Lutherans united in opposition because they saw the laws as attempts to destroy parochial education. As one German put it, his children

The congregation of a Polish Catholic church in St. Paul, Minnesota, 1918. (*Immigration History Archives*)

had to be educated in the "language of Luther." In both states strong opposition to the enactments soon brought their repeal.

PUBLIC EDUCATION

No amount of devotion to the Old World and its needs, however, could counteract the "baneful" effects of an American education on the children and grandchildren of the immigrants. Not that this education was consciously destructive to Old World ties—although in many cases it certainly weakened them—but for children born and reared in the United States attachment to the Old World culture came to consist only of their love for their parents and for the traditions in which they were raised. To a certain extent, of course, parochial schools still promoted the history and culture of the old country, and in the major urban centers, where most children attended the public schools, educators also had to acknowledge the presence of the immigrants. In the nineteenth century eight Midwestern states allowed German to be used as the language of instruction where there was a sufficient demand. This policy was continued in some of the states until 1917. Kansas counties in the 1890s had schools conducted in German, Swedish, Danish, Norwegian, and Czech; some San Francisco elementary schools provided Italian, German, French, or Spanish; and practically every state in the country at one time or another offered elective courses in a variety of foreign languages. But in an American urban setting the children came in contact with many divisive influences. Moreover, children growing up in the United States thought of themselves as, and wanted to be, Americans. This was not done to spite their parents but out of a real conviction that regardless of their backgrounds, their destinies lay in America and the faster they achieved the status of "American" the better off they would be.

Parents and ethnic leaders alike recognized the Americanizing influences of the public school, but members of different groups did not have a uniform response to the threat. Some, however reluctantly, accepted the fact that their offspring would become Americans; they valued education too much to deprive their children of it. The determining factor in a child's future success in the United States often hinged on whether the child's culture prized education in itself or because of what it could do for the individual. Armenians, Bulgarians, Czechs, Dutch, Germans, Greeks, Jews, Lithuanians, Macedonians, Asians, Rumanians, and Yugoslavs thought that their sons should be well educated and were willing to make sacrifices to help them along. Other groups, mostly Roman Catholics like the French Canadians, Irish, Italians, Mexicans, Poles, and Slovaks, saw little advantage in education aside from learning the rudiments of reading and writing, or as a necessary aspect of inculcating the faith, and pulled their children out of school and sent them to work as soon as the law allowed or the children could get jobs.

Many immigrant parents subscribed to the views expressed by a Catholic prelate, Father René Holaind, that "all the child is entitled to is to receive the education necessary to live in comfort in the condition of his parents." A number of Catholics also saw the public schools as "a huge conspiracy against religion, individual liberty and enterprise, and parental rights." Poles regarded public schools as "unchristian, pagan and demoralizing institutions" that would rob their children of a priceless heritage. Daniel Patrick Moynihan tells us that the Irish had no respect for intellect and possessed a "contempt for learning." Some southern Italians had unique ideas about education. The offspring of one wrote, "Mother believed you would go mad if you read too many books, and Father was of the opinion that too much school makes children lazy and opens the mind for unhealthy dreams." Another Italian American, who attended college, recalls friends and relatives pointing out to his father that it was a "scandal" for the healthy son of a packing-house worker, who should be out working, to get so much education.

Many blacks who moved North wanted their children to get an education, but they found conditions inhospitable for schooling. Whereas educators were eager to get the children of immigrants into the schools to "Americanize" them, they were frequently indifferent to black youngsters. Hence school boards spent much less money to educate them. In the South, where fewer than 40 percent of all youngsters regularly attended schools before World War I, fewer than one in seventy black children reached the eighth grade. Black schools remained apart because of segregated housing, and school boards even used gerrymandering to make the racial lines more rigid. In Indianapolis in the early 1920s, white parents, despite black protests, induced the school board to build a separate high school for blacks. The few blacks who escaped the ghettos and were admitted into the public universities of the North found segregation and discrimination in their dormitories and other facilities.

THE MINORITY PRESS

The foreign-language and black newspapers supplemented the education offered in the schools and exercised a considerable influence on their readers. Next to the church and the school, they served as the single most important social and educational institution in the immigrant and black communities. People who had never read anything in Europe or on Southern farms accustomed themselves to reading the daily or weekly newspaper. In fact, the first newspaper published in the Lithuanian language appeared in the United States, not in Europe. The newspapers helped develop a sense of group pride and group awareness among people who may never before have thought of anyone as "kin" who did not live in the same village. In addition, some helped the foreigner adjust to the United States. They instructed their readers about registering to vote, taking out citizenship papers, and conforming to the proper American modes of behavior. The foreign-language press exerted a powerful influence in the immigrant communities. In Cleveland, we are told, "No movement whether social or political could succeed among the immigrant groups without the approval of their press. To be ignored or 'teased' by these papers meant complete failure for any business or political venture." The immigrants also became sophisticated in their own use of the newspapers. In Pittsburgh Croatian leaders organized several meetings with local journalists to explain to them who the Croatians were and what they wanted. Blacks in the cities also discovered the virtues of their own press because white newspapers printed derogatory news or else ignored them. In addition to discussions about items of group interest, newspapers like the *Chicago Defender* provided lists of "do's and don't's" in city life for recently arrived Southern blacks.

MAINTAINING OLD WORLD TIES

The newspapers also kept readers informed about events in their native lands and tried in numerous ways to preserve involvement with, and love of, the old country. Special organizations sent money back for various good causes and individuals also made contributions. Between $5 million and $10 million annually went to Mexico in the 1920s; Greeks sent $121 million to Greece in 1921; and the amount that went back, over the years, to Ireland and Germany probably exceeded $1 billion. Even the groups with relatively few immigrants in America contributed to the fatherland. In 1910, for example, Finns in the United States donated $3,500 to the "Fight for Finland's Freedom Fund." Raising such money was never very hard. As one commentator noted, "Who was there with soul so dead he would not say a prayer, shed a tear and give a dollar for the cause of old Ireland?"

The greatest outpouring of feeling occurred during wartime. Money was raised for relief and immigrants frequently returned home to fight for the cause. During the Balkan wars in 1912 Serbs and Greeks went back to Europe to battle the Turks, and Serbs, Croatians, and Slovenes participated in World War I. The Bohemian National Alliance in the United States even influenced Congress to amend the immigration laws so that Americans of Czech descent who joined the French legions during the war would be allowed to return to this country without difficulty.

World War I also stimulated intensified efforts by American immigrants to obtain independence for their homelands. Irish nationalism had been strong in the United States for decades, but during and after the war the Irish put great pressure on President Woodrow Wilson to support an independent Ireland. American Poles, with better results, applied similar tactics to create a united Poland free of German, Austrian, or Russian political control. Some groups used their influence to create new states. Croatians, Slovenes, and Serbs held numerous rallies promoting the establishment of Yugoslavia; some Jews hoped to obtain a homeland in Palestine; and Czechs and Slovaks launched a drive for the formation of the state of Czechoslovakia.

During the 1930s and World War II, Greek, Polish, and Jewish groups, to name but three, helped compatriots and lobbied in Washington for the benefit of friends and relatives in Eu-

Czechs and Slovaks demonstrate their loyalty to the American cause in World War I. From the U.S. War Department General Staff. (*National Archives*)

rope. The Poles protested the new boundaries for Poland determined at the Yalta Conference in 1945, and American Jews tried to obtain favorable interpretations of immigration legislation as well as new laws to help refugees after World War II. They also used their influence to win American support for the establishment of the state of Israel in 1948.

POLITICS

Ethnic minorities could exert influence on the United States government because they had learned how to function in the American political arena. No group proved more sophisticated or adroit in manipulating the system to its own needs than the Irish, who had a keen understanding of political power and how to use it. For two centuries they had been oppressed by the English in Ireland, and during that period they had learned how Anglo-Saxon law could be manipulated to satisfy the ends of those who governed and work against those who did not. As the only major immigrant group to arrive in the United States with this knowledge, they had an advantage over people from continental Europe, Asia, and Latin America. Their initial experiences in the United States further convinced them that they would have little control over their own destiny unless they obtained political power. Since within their own group positions of political importance carried high status, group approval coincided with practicality.

One aspect of their heritage that helped the Irish when they entered politics was their allegiance to the Roman Catholic church. From this attachment they knew how a disciplined and cohesive organization functioned and how much could be accomplished when each member of the group accepted the guidance of established authorities. The urban political machine, set up according to hierarchical principles, may be likened to the church organization, with the political ward being equated with the local parish and the powers of the urban boss being similar to those of the archbishop. The members of the party, like the parishioners in the church, gave undeviating loyalty to the institution. In return those who exercised authority could forgive almost any human foible except disloyalty and could also dispense favors to those deserving them.

When the Irish first came to the United States in large numbers, they found the Democratic party more congenial than the Whig party. The latter housed a large percentage of Protestant bigots, whereas the former seemed to have a much more tolerant and broader-based constituency. Once in the party, the Irish helped to fashion it into the more attractive political party for most of the immigrants who came after them. Not every Irish immigrant became a Democrat; many in Philadelphia and Rochester, New York, for example, joined the ranks of the Republicans after the Civil War. Nor did every immigrant follow the

Irish in their allegiance—the Swedes, for example, were prominent Republicans—but over the next century or so the overwhelming majority of immigrants, and blacks after 1933, found the Democratic, rather than the Republican party more suitable to their needs.

Irish politicians understood the immigrant ethos and this facilitated their dealings with the newcomers. Unlike the Republicans, many of whom wanted "to civilize, to Christianize and Americanize these people," Irish Democrats wanted only to exercise political influence in the choice of elected candidates. As a result, by the end of the nineteenth century the Irish came to dominate the Democratic party and the local political scene throughout most of urban America, including Boston, Chicago, New Orleans, New York City, and San Francisco.

The Irish political boss may be likened to a modern social welfare agency. He helped his constituents from the moment of their arrival in America and he remembered those who remained loyal to him. One Boston ward boss had agents stationed at the pier waiting to assist the immigrants coming down the gangplank; thereafter he did not have to worry about obtaining their support when he needed it. Ward bosses also provided jobs on the public payroll, posted bond for those held on criminal charges, obtained exemptions from city ordinances and speeded the process for those who wanted peddling licenses, sent food baskets at holiday times, appeared at social gatherings, and were available as friends during any emergency. The boss, although usually Irish, knew that his position depended on the votes of his ward or precinct and he tried not to show favoritism to any ethnic group. As one New York City boss put it, "It makes no difference to me whether I take my hat off in a church or put it on again in a synagogue." Chicago bosses often boasted of putting various southern and eastern Europeans on the public payroll, and while "Big Bill" Thompson was mayor of the city in the 1920s he hired so many blacks as "temporary employees" that cynics referred to the City Hall as "Uncle Tom's Cabin."

One of the most colorful of the Irish bosses, Boston's Jim Curley, was especially good at providing jobs. Under Curley streets were fixed, hospitals built, and playgrounds and beaches laid out. Although he had his faults, and his administrations were careless with funds, one historian reminds us that "much of what he did needed to be done." The cost would be excessive, the payrolls padded, and corruption ignored—yet "without him most of these projects would never have been undertaken."

Irish bosses, like many others who obtain power and positions of prominence, also aroused opposition. They angered those who envied their power, and their use of influence for personal gain frequently bordered the thin line between immorality and illegality. They were not adverse to accepting bribes or "favors" from those who received their largesse. They also had to protect their flanks, sometimes in ruthless and despicable ways, from others who wanted to obtain the power that they possessed.

In Chicago in the 1920s, one man of Czech ancestry, Anton Cermak, successfully battled the Irish machine within the Democratic party and between 1927 and 1933 enjoyed the powers and prestige that Irish mayors had both before and after his administration. Like the Irish, the Czechs in Chicago put a premium on political power and through Cermak they saw the chance to obtain the recognition they coveted. Enraged at being lumped together in the public mind with southern and eastern European immigrants, the Czechs longed for separate—and favorable—appraisal. They were sufficiently literate, cohesive, and stable to work together to achieve their goals.

Cermak, at first a ward boss, fulfilled his own ambitions and at the same time capitalized on Czech aspirations. In the 1920s other Democrats were beginning to resent Irish domination of the political scene and Cermak benefited from this discontent. One of the main gripes against Irish political domination was that the choicest political plums, and sometimes two thirds of the elected positions, went to those of Irish descent. Once Cermak, who had proclaimed himself a leader of all of the foreign-born, achieved his goal of becoming mayor, Irish domination ceased and good jobs were more evenly distributed to members of other

ethnic groups. Under Cermak, Slavs, Italians, and Scandinavians received greater recognition than they had had in the
past and, in his boldest stroke, the mayor headed the state Democratic ticket with a Jew, who won election to the governorship
in 1932. In 1933 an assassin's bullet, aimed at President-elect
Franklin D. Roosevelt, struck Cermak, who was riding in the
same automobile, and the Irish once again resumed control of
Chicago's City Hall. They held on to it until the death of Mayor
Richard Daley in 1976.

Like any leader, the political boss could retain his constituents' loyalties only so long as he moved in the direction that his
followers wished to go. During the Progressive era, the immigrants supported most of the political and economic changes
proposed. They backed, for the most part, reforms such as a federal income tax amendment to the United States Constitution,
laws to regulate business, workman's compensation, mothers'
pensions, safety legislation, the establishment of bureaus of labor statistics, and regulation of wages and hours, especially for
women; some, but certainly not all, even came around to accepting women's suffrage, although many regarded women in
politics as a degrading thing and a threat to the family structure.

But the one "reform" that evoked almost unanimous opposition from every immigrant group except the Swedes was Prohibition. To so many minorities, especially Irish, Germans, Czechs,
Poles, and Yugoslavs, the saloon or beer parlor was a place to
meet friends, exchange tales and jokes, read newspapers, and
imbibe a few drinks. Most immigrants attached no moral stigma
to these places and in fact considered them to be indispensable
social institutions. But WASP Americans believed that the con-
sumption of alcoholic beverages led to poverty and moral degra-
dation and, galvanized by the Anti-Saloon League and the Wom-
en's Christian Temperance Union, they fought ferociously to
outlaw it. The successful campaign climaxed with the passage
of the Eighteenth Amendment to the Constitution in 1918 during the patriotic fervor aroused by American entry into World
War I. The president of one German-American group had pro-

claimed earlier that "Prohibitionism is a fight against the Germans," and many Americans later interpreted it that way also. German Americans had assumed, and time proved their assumptions correct, that the approval of prohibition would be only the first step in the path of future xenophobic legislation. And so the Germans, as well as most other immigrant groups, battled to preserve their liquid pleasures. But the moral commitment that erupted during World War I overrode their objections.

SOCIAL MOBILITY

The culture that the immigrants tried so hard to maintain, and the values that they strove to preserve, dissipated with each succeeding generation. Their children, and to a lesser extent their grandchildren and great-grandchildren, clung to some traditions, but the "pull" of American society proved too difficult to resist. Most immigrants came to America for economic reasons and instilled the drive for success in their children. To succeed in American society, however, meant that the English language had to be mastered and used and that American customs had to be followed.

For some groups, cultural needs and values coincided with American goals and therefore their children progressed quickly. The Greeks, for example, placed a high emphasis on work, status, and achievement. Parents wanted their children to move to a higher station in life than the one to which they were born and they stimulated them to advance. The professions, especially law and medicine, were held up as attractive positions. Germans regarded work as a necessary concomitant to life, and they instilled that idea in their children. Each was expected to do his utmost to master his tasks. As a result German children knew that only first-rate performances were acceptable. There is a story of the accomplishments of the children and grandchildren of one immigrant German family that suggests the enterprising nature of the Germans:

Of the five sons and one daughter of Max and Anna Goettsch, two received M.D. degrees, three received Ph.D. degrees, and one received a degree in engineering. The daughter was not allowed to go to high school. Of Max's seven grandchildren, five received M.D. degrees, one received a Ph.D. degree, and one received an A.B.

The most striking feature of the second generation is the educational attainments of the women. Five of the seven grandchildren were female. Of these five, three earned M.D. degrees, one earned a Ph.D., and one earned an A.B.

Of the groups that prized education none achieved as much, or moved as quickly out of the working class, as the Jews. The traditional culture weighed very heavily in Jewish accomplishment. For the eastern European Jews a life devoted to study was the social ideal and the most respected members in the community were the men who pursued that goal. No one else, no matter how wealthy or skilled, could compare in status with the Talmudic scholar. He was treated with the greatest deference in the ghetto regardless of whether he was rich or poor, and parents sought learned men as husbands for their daughters. In the United States Jewish immigrants did not exalt their rabbis and scholars as they had in Europe, but the tradition of respect for learning continued. Jewish children, especially sons, were encouraged to achieve intellectually. That they did so can to some extent be confirmed. A higher percentage of the children of eastern European Jewish descent graduated from high school and college, when given the opportunity to do so, than did children from any other ethnic background. A 1911 survey of New York City, where large numbers of both Jews and Italians lived, revealed that 16 percent of Jewish children were finishing high school. This was the highest proportion among immigrant groups. Practically no Italians finished high school. Five years later Jewish enrollment constituted 13 percent of Columbia University's student body, 44 percent of Hunter College's, 73 percent of City College's, and 21 percent at the Roman Catholic Fordham University. In his studies of social mobility in Boston, Stephan Thernstrom found that 75 percent of the children of eastern European Jewish immigrants entered the middle class after starting out in the working class. This total was higher than for any other group.

It is impossible to pinpoint which cultural characteristics stimulate mobility and which do not, but among those that seem to make a difference are education, family values, and religious affiliation. Offspring of Protestant and Jewish immigrants progressed faster in American society than other Europeans. The groups whose economic achievement was slowest were those whose attachment to the Catholic church was strong or where parents equated American education with the destruction of family values. Thernstrom's study found that the Irish and Italians in Boston had the least mobility, and he suggests that parochial education in some way failed to stimulate the necessary ambition. In Chicago, the Poles moved up the socioeconomic ladder most slowly. Perhaps Robert Cross's study of the Catholic church at the end of the nineteenth and early part of the twentieth centuries reveals the reason for this; Cross notes that "to the Catholic conservatives, the only proper response to social difficulties was devout passivity." We also know that not only did the Poles and Irish invest much of their resources in their churches; they also insisted that their priests were the ones from whom guidance on the most crucial matters should be sought. And most of the Catholic priests subscribed to the view that only within the Catholic community, and only by accepting Catholic doctrines and outlook, could salvation be achieved. The descendants of Catholic immigrants gradually came to accept the value of social mobility, but the immigrant church did not emphasize this goal as did many Protestants and Jews.

Another retarding factor in mobility has to do with family attitudes toward individual achievement. Mexicans, French Canadians, Poles, and Italians cherished views that would scarcely induce their offspring to surpass them in attainments. Children were taught that individual accomplishment had to be subordinated to family needs; that education in itself had little value;

and that gainful employment, at the earliest age, was a positive good. Mobility, children learned, took one away from one's family and threatened traditions. Also, none of these peoples stressed the advantages of learning English, either for themselves or for their children. In each of these groups, moreover, there were individual mores that limited progress. Among the Mexicans, for example, the culture dictated that an individual refrain from trying to do something he could not master. One sociologist tells us that among Mexican Americans, it would be better "not to try to reach a goal barred by serious obstacles than to pursue a goal at the risk of failure. Not to try does not reflect negatively on their manliness and honor but to try and fail does." Finally, individuals in these groups who educated themselves and moved up in American society were regarded as outcasts. As one Polish-American historian writes, "Members of Polonia feel bitter toward their educated class, resent its attitude, and consider it ungrateful."

These differences among the cultures of the various immigrant groups blurred with the passage of time. Succeeding generations, exposed to the nationalizing influences of the public school, and, increasingly after the 1920s, to the media, grew up with similar ideas about life in the United States. Their goals, their heroes, and their attitudes toward success showed a greater resemblance to a homogenized Americanism than to the foreign cultures that had been so supportive for their parents.

It makes a great difference, of course, whether children grow up in a culture that encourages them to achieve in American terms or one that does not. Members of both categories have been successful in the United States, but the numbers coming from the former group are much greater than those coming from the latter. Almost all children of immigrants, except Mexicans before World War II, showed progress in social mobility from one generation to another but the pace of that progress was to some extent retarded or advanced by the values in which the children were reared. Of course even children with a desire to achieve cannot easily overcome institutionalized bigotry. Nor can they be oblivious to, or remain untouched by, a worldwide depression such as occurred during the 1930s. And finally, despite group influences and emphases, not every individual conforms to the stereotypical behavior of the minority to which he or she belongs. Nevertheless, most of the ethnic offspring did move to a station above that of their parents.

Whereas the children of immigrants progressed above their parents, blacks usually did not. The black standard of living did rise, but no matter how hard their families pushed them or how much education they had, blacks were unable to advance much prior to World War II. Racial discrimination practiced by white Americans proved an insurmountable obstacle. The small black elite in business and the professions catered largely to the poor crowded into the growing urban ghettos. Just as the Irish had competed with blacks in certain jobs in the mid-nineteenth century, many immigrants from southern and eastern Europe competed with them in the twentieth.

ASSIMILATION

With mobility came assimilation. The higher one's income and the more prestigious one's position, the more likely it was for the ethnic ties to be loosened. The factors promoting assimilation in fact were so powerful that the descendants of the immigrants could scarcely resist them. The Americans, despite their rhetoric of tolerance, demanded conformity before accepting the newcomers, and the immigrant children and grandchildren hastened to meet the standards of the dominant community. Organizations set up to aid those in need, like the Illinois Immigrants' Protective League and the North American Civic League for Immigrants, were concerned primarily with integrating their charges into American society. Employers like Henry Ford in Detroit, and cities throughout the country instituted English classes and "Americanization" programs for foreigners. At the school in the Ford Motor Company the first thing immigrants were taught to say was "I am an American." One prominent

Immigrant adult-education class, about 1920. Governments and voluntary agencies ran thousands of classes and programs for immigrants in an effort to Americanize them and prepare them for citizenship. (*Library of Congress*)

educator in New York City enunciated the prevailing sentiments when she said that the immigrants "must be made to realize that in forsaking the land of their birth, they were also forsaking the customs and traditions of that land; and they must be made to realize an obligation, in adopting a new country, to adopt the language and customs of that country."

The dominant elements in the Catholic church hierarchy in America, mostly Irish, also promoted "Americanization." They too frowned on the babel of tongues in the ethnic parishes and tried to assimilate all of the Catholic newcomers into one large American Catholic church. But Germans, Poles, Lithuanians, and French Canadians, loyal Catholics though they might be, resented Irish control and the attempts to promote uniformity.

Most of the immigrants were neither willing nor able to relinquish their heritage. They wanted priests who spoke their languages and services that reflected the flavor of the Old World. Many Poles, for example, equated Americanization with the hated German and Russian attempts to impose their values on them in the areas that these powers ruled in Europe at the end of the nineteenth century. To Poles a free country meant the freedom to retain their Polish customs and remain Polish Catholics. As a result of these conflicting views, bickering pervaded the relationship between the various national groups and the hierarchy in the American Catholic church for several decades into the twentieth century.

Members of the second and third generations, however, did not share their parents' and grandparents' commitments to Old World values and felt more comfortable with the Americanized Roman Catholic church. While young they had no choice but to conform to their parents' standards; but as they grew up they rebelled. As one Polish American tells it, the traditional culture never had a chance to succeed with him or with his peers: "This generation, of which I am a part, never had to face the problem of pulling away from Polonia. We had never properly belonged to it. To us it was a slowly decaying world of aged folks living largely in a dream. One day it would pass and then there would remain only Americans whose forebears had once been Poles."

The signs of Americanization are readily apparent. Many foreigners changed their names. The Dutch "Kok" became "Cook," the Jewish "Greenberg" became "Green," and the Greek "Kiriacopoulis" became "Campbell." Intermarriage, the most destructive element to survival of ethnic culture, took more time to achieve. At first children feared ostracism from their communities, so they were wary of marital partners who did not have family approval. Also, some parents found ingenious devices to keep their children within the fold. There is a story of a Jewish immigrant woman in Fargo, North Dakota, which housed a tiny Jewish community. To find eligible males for her several daughters she opened a boarding house for Jewish bachelors. A granddaughter recalled, "She got husbands for all her daughters." As time passed, however, first national and then religious barriers broke down. In our own day about one third of Catholics and Jews marry those of another faith; and for most third and fourth generations of Americans national heritage has practically disappeared as a concern in selecting a mate.

The process of adjustment and Americanization varied from group to group. For the immigrants' children and grandchildren the pace was to some extent accelerated by American bigotry. Their parents had been forced to bear the burden of foreignism, but the children did not necessarily care to carry the culture of their ancestors forward—especially when to do so bore such a stigma in the United States. Perhaps cultural pluralism could have developed in the United States had there been a real spirit of tolerance. But as the next chapters will show, "difference" was not considered in neutral terms. "Different" meant "inferior," and few people growing up in American society consciously chose to be attacked or ostracized in the land of their birth.

7

Ethnic Groups
and the Development
of the West
(1840s–1930s)

THE WESTERN HALF of the United States stretches from the Missouri River to the Pacific Ocean. Because of vast distances, an often harsh environment, and a widely scattered population, the story of Western development seems at times divorced from events in the rest of the nation. This, however, was not so. True, the bitterly fought question of what to do with slavery had little overall impact on the West, but slavery was the only major issue of which that could be said. Such matters as immigration restriction, treatment of minorities, and questions related to economic development tied the region closely to the rest of the nation.

THE MINING FRONTIER

In January 1848, even before the negotiators trying to end the Mexican War completed writing the Treaty of Guadalupe Hidalgo, workmen found gold in a northern California river. Once people realized that the news of the discovery was no hoax, excitement swept through the small California settlements. "The blacksmith dropped his hammer, the carpenter his plane, the mason his trowel, the farmer his sickle, the baker his loaf, and the tapster his bottle. All were off for the mines, some on horses, some on carts, and some on crutches, and one went in a litter." Late in 1848, after people in the rest of the nation read newspaper reports of the gold finds and had their dreams of wealth supported by President James Polk's announcement of the discovery, gold fever swept the country. From every state and territory in the Union, as well as from a dozen other nations, would-be miners abandoned their pursuits and headed toward California. The population explosion was so huge that Congress admitted California to statehood in 1850 without requiring it to go through the stages of territorial government.

Although the population surge had been stimulated by fantasies of untapped riches, and although the California mines did produce massive amounts of gold, few individual miners became wealthy. Nevertheless, mining was the first important magnet to attract people in the Far West. Many migrants had no intention of working the mines but recognized that the burgeoning population needed shops and services to provide food, clothing, housing, transportation, and entertainment. In short, economic opportunity beckoned.

Exploitation of Western mineral wealth fell into several distinct eras. The first occurred from 1848 until 1858 in California, where miners learned their trade through bitter experience. Using placer-mining techniques, the men dug sand and gravel from the creek beds and banks, washed them out with water, and collected whatever gold remained. Placer mining required the least skill, technology, or capital, but was also the least efficient and productive way to extract minerals. During the 1860s prospectors spread placer mining, based on their California experience, throughout the mountain West.

Thousands of adventurers hurriedly set up hundreds of mining camps, stretching from Oregon in the north almost to the Mexican border in the south. Living in tents, caves, or shacks, the gold-seekers dug into the stream banks and hillsides with a frenzy. When picks and shovels failed to move earth fast enough to suit them, some turned to hydraulic mining, a process by which they cut down entire hillsides with powerful streams of water. However the miners pursued the gold, they came and went in a continuous stream of humanity that left scattered towns and cities throughout the West.

As placer mining diminished in California, quartz and hydraulic mining became increasingly important. Corporations, with their superior resources, moved in to exploit the more valuable and difficult to get vein gold. Often buried in quartz and other hard rock deposits, this gold had to be separated from the rest of the ore with rock crushers and other expensive equipment, which left little opportunity for the individual miner still hoping to "strike it rich" by finding gold by himself. As a result, disappointed California miners drifted throughout the mountain West looking for new mineral regions.

From 1869 to 1879 mining investment and technological advances centered largely on the famous Comstock Lode near Virginia City, Nevada, while mineral exploration in the rest of the West remained dormant. During the last decades of the nineteenth century new discoveries and investments in Colorado, Nevada, Montana, South Dakota, and Arizona kept the nation fascinated and the miners moving throughout the West.

Mining discoveries brought people, capital, transportation, and business enterprise to outlying regions, where these assets had barely been present. As early as the 1850s large numbers of Europeans had immigrated directly to the mining regions, giving camps there an ethnic flavor not often found outside the Eastern port cities and the larger Midwestern industrial centers of the time. As in the rest of the nation, many of the most highly skilled came from Ireland and from Cornwall in Britain, where mining had been an important occupation for generations. During the 1860–80 era a severe depression hit the Cornwall mines, and between one quarter and one third of the workers there left the country, many coming to the American West.

The mine operators welcomed skilled workers enthusiastically. At the Comstock Lode, for example, the census of 1880 showed that although Americans comprised more than half of the population of that community, most of the actual mining was done by the foreign-born. Of the 1,966 miners listed in the census, 691 were Irish, 543 English and Cornish, 394 American, 132 Canadian, and the remaining 206 included smaller numbers of men from several other countries.

Frequently mineral discoveries proved a mixed blessing as ore deposits became exhausted or failed to live up to the expectations of miners, business people, and investors. Hundreds of crumbling Western ghost towns stand as mute evidence to this difficulty. Nevertheless, when mining became less important in local or regional economies, the inhabitants often turned to other occupations, enabling some settlements to broaden their economic bases and survive. Thus the influx of large groups originally enticed by mining opportunities served to populate many parts of the West.

But the original lure of the West also created many unrealistically high expectations. Thus a sense of betrayal, accompanied by frustration and bitterness, lingered throughout the region. Difficulties arose from disappointed dreams of finding gold in the streets, or at least in the stream beds. In California men who had earned $15 to $20 a day in 1848 had to be satisfied with wages nearer $2 to $3 a day only four years later. Rather than thriving as individual prospectors, most became day laborers working for the newly organized mining companies. This rapid decline in personal status, sharp reduction in earning power, and the overoptimistic expectations that had lured thousands west in the first place combined to make many miners violence-prone bigots. Beginning in California, a pattern of frequent public antagonism toward blacks, Indians, Mexicans, and Asians soon spread throughout the mining camps of the West.

California led the way in the amount and intensity of this hostility. When the United States acquired that region as part of the Treaty of Guadalupe Hidalgo in 1848, it guaranteed the property rights of all Mexican residents and the retention of their Catholic faith, Spanish language, and cultural traditions. Only about 7,500 Mexicans lived in California at the time, and it appeared as if they could be absorbed easily. However, the continuation of the hatred initially aroused by the war between Mexico and the United States and the discovery of gold in California made such an accommodation practically impossible. News of rich gold deposits attracted at least 6,000 more Mexicans to the mining regions, and American miners resented having to share the wealth with their former enemies.

Bitterness grew particularly harsh in the Sonora mines of central California. There the presence of hundreds of Mexican miners aroused so much anxiety among those of European and American birth that in 1850 the latter group pushed a Foreign Miners' Tax through the new state legislature. As a result of this discriminatory law, all foreign miners had to pay a $20 monthly licensing fee for the privilege of mining gold. Aimed at both the newly arrived Mexican miners and their countrymen who were California natives, the tax succeeded in driving most of them from the gold fields. Once they left, the tax was lowered to $20 a year.

Economic frustration alone, however, does not explain the prevalent hostility. While such woes aggravated latent attitudes, American traditions must also be considered. Racism and prejudice were not indigenous only to the Californians—people brought their feelings with them from other places. California's first governor, Peter Burnett, had been a prime mover for anti-black legislation in Oregon in the early 1840s. In California he continued along the same lines, unsuccessfully urging the framers of the state constitution, and then the members of the state legislature, to exclude free blacks from residency. The lawmakers, while narrowly spurning his suggestion, nevertheless shared some of his prejudices. Hence California's first state constitution did not allow Indians, blacks, and Asians to testify against white people in the state's courts.

Unlike the racial minorities, the Europeans who arrived in California during the middle of the century—and predominant among the earliest newcomers were about 7,000 French—were accepted and expected to participate in helping the region grow.

In San Francisco, where the French clung together, failed to learn English quickly, and engaged in a "wild glorification of . . . every thing connected with their beautiful France," they had more difficulty in assimilating than did immigrants from Great Britain, who spoke English, and from the German states, who tried quickly to adapt to the prevailing customs. Chileans and Chinese also made up significant numbers of the newcomers to California's expanding population, but they were not given the enthusiastic welcome provided to Caucasians from western Europe and the eastern sections of the United States.

THE CHINESE

The Chinese in particular, about a quarter million of whom reached California between 1849 and the early 1880s, experienced discrimination and abuse. Most of them had come over as indentured or bond servants, having had their passage paid for in return for a promise to work for a stipulated period of time. In the West they worked on the railroads, in agriculture and the mines, and at domestic chores. Once the Asians arrived they came under the control of one of the "Six Companies," or Chinese governing bodies in the United States. "These companies," we are told, "controlled and governed all the Chinese in this country with an iron hand, becoming a substitute for their native village and patriarchal associations. They had their own laws, which if broken, [carried penalties that] were carried out swiftly, without regard to the laws of the United States." The Chinese immigrant, in debt to one of these companies, illiterate in English, and totally unfamiliar with the customs of the new country, succumbed to the guidance of those who watched over him and gave Californians no cause for disliking him. During his first few years in the state he was not generally scorned or victimized. A contemporary observer of the Chinese in 1850 commented that "their deportment is grave and dignified. They seem never to meddle or intervene in the affairs of others." Chinese immigrants did tasks that white men considered menial

Nineteenth-century drawing depicting Chinese laundry workers. Laundries were one of the few places where Chinese immigrants could find employment. From *Leslie's Magazine*, 1881. (*Library of Congress*)

and beneath their dignity, and hence suitable only for women and minorities, such as washing and ironing clothes and preparing meals. By 1860 the Chinese had also monopolized the making of shoes, shirts, underwear, cigars, and tinware in the state of California. In addition they owned many laundries, restaurants, and hotels.

As economic difficulties for the white men in California increased, the Chinese began to experience prejudice. Their numbers, industry, and economic success intensified white hostility. Alone among the immigrants the Chinese regularly paid the annual $20 tax that California required for foreign miners. The virtues of thrift, hard work, and responsibility, which the Chinese possessed in abundance, and which Americans praised so lavishly when displayed by WASPs, did not in any way mitigate expression of the most outrageous kinds of bigotry. Americans dubbed the Chinese "groveling worms," and accused them of eating rats and dogs and of being a "retrogressive and inferior race." Anti-Chinese spokesmen also denounced the gambling, prostitution, and opium smoking that occurred in the Chinese neighborhoods. Crowded Chinese housing conditions convinced whites that the filth and disease there would spread into the rest of society. One Caucasian complained: "The Chinese are like a sponge; they absorb and give nothing in return but bad odors and worse morals. They are a standing menace to the women of this country. Their very presence is contaminating. They have sown the seed of vice in every city, town and hamlet in this country. They encourage, aid, and abet the youths of the land to become opium fiends."

The belief that the Chinese posed a danger sprang from the conviction that Asians were innately inferior. "They are a distinct race," commented one hostile white. "They never assimilate with our people, our manners, tastes, religion, or ideas. With us they have nothing in common." Despite the existing antagonism, the Chinese continued migrating to the United States through the 1880s, when the federal government erected barriers against them.

THE RAILROADS

One reason for the growth of the Chinese population in the West was the expansion of the railroads. Practically all Western railroad building took place after the Civil War, for prior to that conflict not enough people lived in the West to justify such construction, and sufficient capital was not readily available. To remedy the latter situation Congress passed the Pacific Railroad Act in 1862. This act authorized federal loans and land grants to the Union Pacific to extend tracks west from Omaha,

Nebraska, and to the Central Pacific to lay tracks eastward from California. In May 1869 the work crews of the two railroad companies met near Ogden, Utah, thereby completing America's first transcontinental railroad. By the mid-1890s other lines—the Northern Pacific, Great Northern, Atchinson, Topeka and Santa Fe, and Southern Pacific—had been finished. With trunk and connecting lines being built at the same time, track mileage in the nation soared. In 1872 the United States had 57,300 miles of railroad track. A decade later this had increased to 114,400 miles, and by 1900 the rails stretched past 200,000 miles. The new track was by no means limited to the West, but the burgeoning railroad network had tied that region firmly to the rest of the nation by the end of the nineteenth century.

As massive construction projects that needed skilled and unskilled laborers, railroads, like the mining camps earlier, attracted people to the West. During the 1860s the Union Pacific hired thousands of Irish workmen while its Western competitor, the Central Pacific, imported about 10,000 Chinese laborers. These newcomers not only built the two lines mentioned, but many remained in the West to work on other railroad projects. To feed and house their vast work crews the construction firms provided temporary prefabricated cities—usually called "Hell on Wheels" because they were little more than shanties that could be moved from one place to another. Most of the early railroad camps were just that, but some remained as the nuclei of later settlements. Existing towns such as Omaha, Kansas City, Denver, and Salt Lake City, to mention a few, benefited from the railroad boom. Serving as supply bases, sources for labor, and banking centers, such cities prospered because of railroad building and subsequent business operations.

INDIAN WARS AND RESERVATIONS

As rails laced the countryside and mines, smelters, and towns dotted the wilderness, Caucasians came increasingly to see the Indian Americans of the West as major obstacles to regional development. Californians were particularly aggressive toward the Indians in the state. Most of the approximately 175,000 tribesmen on the West Coast were there before the gold rush, but they lived in areas heavily overrun by prospectors: the northern coastal mountains and along the Sierra foothills. Although population statistics are vague and often inaccurate, it seems likely that as late as 1850–51 nearly 100,000 Indians lived in the mining regions of California. As gold seekers, teamsters, lumbermen, and farmers poured into the state, the Indian population plummeted. Thousands died from epidemics of measles, typhoid, smallpox, and malaria, as well as from tuberculosis and from venereal disease brought in by the new settlers.

Homicide and starvation also destroyed thousands. Americans who crossed the plains and Rockies brought a hatred and fear of Indians with them. The California tribes for the most part were not hostile, but the whites failed to differentiate between those who were peaceful and those who were not. An Indian was considered "a cruel, cowardly vagabond, given to thieving, gambling, drunkenness, and all that is vicious, without one redeeming trait." As a result his life was worth little and those who killed Indians were not considered criminals. If the tribesmen dared protect themselves or avenge wrongs at the hands of the whites, vigilante groups attacked. Whenever possible the miners burned Indian villages in order to destroy their food and shelter and force the tribesmen out of the area. Such campaigns and individual acts of violence so reduced their numbers that by 1880 no more than twenty thousand Indians survived in California. In only thirty years the white flood had destroyed nearly 90 percent of the resident Indians.

Although the influx of pioneers caused rapid destruction for the California tribes, there were exceptions. Among the Plains tribes, in particular, the Indians had achieved a blending of native and European resources that strengthened their material cultures. These groups, which ranged from the Sioux, Cheyenne, and Crow in the north to the Arapaho, Pawnee, Kiowa, and Comanche farther south, had acquired horses from the Spanish

" CIVILIZED."

Late nineteenth-century view of Indians. Many whites believed that it was impossible to "civilize" the Indians and that they were shiftless or hopeless drunkards. (*Library of Congress*)

Southwest a few generations earlier, thus gaining a new mobility for hunting and warfare. Such implements as iron arrow and lance points and steel knives and hatchets, all gotten from the whites, further increased the hunting successes of the Plains tribes. Finally, by the latter half of the nineteenth century the introduction of large numbers of firearms gave the warriors an added boost in their contest with the pioneers.

By the time white Americans reached the Plains, these tribes had developed a general pattern of culture based on mobility achieved with the horse; hunting the buffalo, which provided meat for food, skin for clothing and shelter, and other materials for sewing and ornamentation; and raiding and warfare carried out against their neighbors and competitors. Their mobile culture, sophisticated use of the environment, large numbers, and skill as hunters and fighters meant that the Plains tribes could not be taken lightly. Nevertheless, between 1849 and the end of the century immigrant trails and railroads crisscrossed favorite hunting and camping grounds. A seemingly unending stream of pioneer miners, lumbermen, ranchers, and settlers flooded the land. These developments made it increasingly difficult for whites and Indians to live in peace, particularly as the large buffalo herd of the Plains dwindled rapidly.

In the twenty years following the Civil War millions of the animals were killed to feed construction crews building the transcontinental railroads and to provide leather hides for the rest of the nation. From 1872 to 1874 the hide hunters alone killed more than 3,500,000 buffaloes; during those same years the Indians killed a mere 150,000 for their food. When a group of Texans became alarmed at the slaughter and asked General Philip Sheridan to stop the carnage he declined. "Let them kill, skin, and sell until the buffalo is exterminated," he replied, "as it is the only way to bring lasting peace and allow civilization to advance." Sheridan even suggested that the Texas legislature strike medals honoring the hide hunters for destroying the Indian food supply. In 1874 Secretary of the Interior Columbus Delano noted that "the buffalo are disappearing rapidly, but not faster than I desire." The federal government's policy toward the Indians of "destroying their hunting habitats, coercing them on reservations, and compelling them to begin to adopt the habits of civilization" would have a better chance for success, officials believed, if the warriors could no longer hunt.

The government's initial steps to destroy the single most important food source for the Plains tribes coincided with a long-term effort to move the buffalo hunters onto reservations and transform them into sedentary farmers. In 1851 Congress appropriated $100,000 to negotiate with the Plains and Mountain tribes in order to secure safe travel routes to the Pacific. That same year government negotiators and Indians met at Fort Laramie and concluded treaties limiting some tribal movements in the West.

The Fort Laramie agreements called for the Indians to vacate certain areas while promising payments of goods and supplies to the tribes and peace for both groups. Tribal leaders realized that each land cession only temporarily slackened white demands for more land. The Cherokee newspaper predicted that once white settlement extended to the Indian country the government would send a negotiator "with a pocket full of money and his mouth full of lies." The government agent would use flattery, bribery, and alcohol to extract "something that will be called a treaty." Leaders of the Northern tribes also objected to repeated calls for treaties, each of which promised the Indian that this move would be his last. The oft-quoted question of Sioux Chief Spotted Tail, "Why does not the Great Father put his red children on wheels, so he can move them as he will?" showed their bitterness. Clearly many tribesmen, aware of what was happening, felt powerless to alter their destiny.

Not all Indians felt either overwhelmed or threatened by the advancing whites. Many tribal and band—a band is a subdivision of a tribe—leaders negotiated skillfully with government personnel as they sought to enrich their tribes while accepting gradually less land for their people. Some chiefs preferred withdrawal to signing more treaties or to accepting more of the whites' promises. Others, including the followers of Sitting Bull, fled to Canada for a time, and a group of the Kickapoo migrated to Mexico, where some of their descendants remain today. A few prominent leaders, such as the Comanche Quannah Parker and Sioux Red Cloud, urged their followers to come to terms with the advancing Americans, as distasteful as that seemed at the time.

Despite this range of Indian responses, interracial violence racked the West for an entire generation as some tribes and bands chose warfare as the best response to continuing white intrusions. Among many of the stronger tribes, in particular young men gained status within their villages through military exploits, so it was not long before armed clashes began. During the late 1850s sporadic raiding occurred along the immigrant trails and upon groups of miners, but it was only when the Civil War drew most regular army units east that the warriors succeeded in regaining control over large areas of the West. Usually the tribesmen lacked the numerical strength to sweep whites from the scene, so their chief tactic remained the ambush or the sudden raid, after which the attackers fled.

Most of the time the army men failed to catch their elusive foes, but when they did, better organization and heavier firepower usually triumphed. Yet Indian warriors won victories even if they lost the wars. During the summer of 1862 Little Crow led angry Sioux on a rampage across frontier Minnesota, in which at least 500 settlers and soldiers died before the fighting ended. Just four years later the Sioux destroyed Captain William J. Fetterman's command of 80 men while trying to drive the army from its forts along the Bozeman Trail, which extended through the heart of the tribal hunting grounds. This victory achieved its goal as the soldiers withdrew to the southeast and the Indians burned the empty forts. In 1876 Cheyenne and Sioux warriors annihilated five companies of the 7th Cavalry under Lieutenant Colonel George A. Custer and sent a shock wave through the nation then busily celebrating its centennial. The next year, Chief Joseph led several hundred Nez Percé Indians in a masterful flight from eastern Oregon into Montana. During the several-month trek, which covered more than 1,600 miles, the Indians completely outfought and outmaneuvered many of the best units the army could bring against them. But the end was the same as in all the other campaigns. The Indians ran out of food, horses, ammunition, and the will to fight, while the army brought fresh men and supplies against them. The Ute War of 1879, the Apache wars

Sioux Indian Camp on the River Brule near Pine Ridge, South Dakota. The photograph was taken about 1891, shortly after the "Battle" of Wounded Knee in which army troops killed two hundred Sioux, including women and children. (*Library of Congress*)

of the 1880s, and the massacre of Big Foot's band of Sioux at Wounded Knee in 1890 finished the fighting.

Before and during the decades of intermittent fighting from 1850 to 1890 white Americans hoped for the collapse of tribal societies, which would open more territory and resources in the West. But this rarely happened. The Indians recognized that their only hope for long-term survival lay in retaining their tribal lands and manipulating the system for their own benefit. Eastern tribes then living in Indian Territory (present-day Oklahoma) realized this. After the Civil War they negotiated repeatedly to grant or lease railroad rights of way as well as mineral and grazing rights to eager corporation leaders. Throughout this process it was usually mixed-blood Indians who led the so-called progressive factions into the negotiations. On the other hand, many Indians rejected dealing with the whites in this manner. Despite such divisions within the tribes, Indian leaders in Oklahoma recognized the potential benefits they could get from the corporations, and they dealt with them in the late nineteenth century.

Having tried treaty negotiations, physical withdrawal, and armed resistance in response to the continuing flood of whites moving into the West, some Indians turned their attention to religion to ensure survival. By the 1870s medicine men began offering new advice, and many Indians accepted their teachings with enthusiasm, as their ancestors had at the time of Handsome Lake and the Shawnee Prophet early in the nineteenth century.

The most important religious movement began among the Paiute tribe of Nevada. There, during the 1880s, a Paiute named Wovoka dreamed of meeting the Great Spirit and then began preaching to his neighbors. He claimed that a number of natural disasters would destroy the whites, and that the ancestors of the Indians would return and repopulate the West. To achieve this the Indians had to accept the prophet's message, embodied in ceremonies that included a modified circle dance, accompanied by a group of special songs Wovoka claimed he had learned through his visions; this was sometimes followed by fainting, when some Indians experienced visions of their ancestors. As a result the ceremonies became known as the Ghost Dance. Wovoka cautioned his followers to remain at peace, to avoid alcohol, to be just to others, but also to shun dealings with the whites whenever possible. Nevertheless, the Ghost Dance led to disaster when it swept through the poverty-stricken Sioux at Pine Ridge. There, when the local Indian agent panicked and forbade any further dancing, Chief Big Foot and several hundred followers fled the reservation to continue the ceremonies. Units of the 7th Cavalry followed, and in late 1890, when the troopers sought to disarm the Sioux and return them to the reservation, fighting broke out, resulting in the massacre at

Wounded Knee. Thus, although the Ghost Dance and other religious movements offered some consolation to the tribes, they ultimately failed to help the Indians overcome their daily problems.

While Indians tried to retain their culture, the government continued long-term efforts to destroy tribal identities. As early as the 1870s agents recruited young warriors to serve as scouts and auxillaries for the army. In 1878 Congress appropriated the first funds to operate Indian police forces on the reservations. The men serving as police had to cut their hair, wear the white man's clothes, speak English, and enforce reservation regulations. By 1883 the government had established a system of Courts of Indian Offenses, which struck at the heart of village life. Presided over by some former chiefs as well as by would-be leaders, these courts enforced reservation rules against plural marriage and participation in traditional religious observances such as the Sundance. Both the reservation police and the courts undermined customary leaders and traditions, weakened tribal unity, and provided models for those few individuals who wanted to adopt white customs.

In addition to disrupting tribal society, the reformers and government alike sought to turn all Indians into sedentary farmers. To accomplish this, the whites suggested that giving each adult Indian his or her parcel of land would force the tribal people to become individually oriented. It would also leave much "surplus" land on the reservations for frontier whites to acquire.

Even those who considered themselves friends of the Indians favored allotting land on an individual basis. For example, Captain Richard H. Pratt, the founder of the Carlisle Institute in Pennsylvania, the nation's leading Indian school, called for compulsory division of tribal lands. He believed that the individual Indians who received acreage would soon sell or otherwise squander it and would then be compelled to work for whites. Such pressures to force land ownership on the tribesmen led to the passage of a so-called Indian Homestead Act in

1875. This legislation extended to some Indians the provisions of the 1862 Homestead Act if they asked for the land. The optional provisions of this law failed to satisfy the proponents of allotment, however, and after an extended campaign they succeeded in getting Congress to pass the Dawes Severalty Act in 1887. It assigned a specific plot of land to each adult Indian, hoping to disrupt tribal use of land in common. Many tribes and individual Indians objected, but only the people of the Indian Territory delayed their land loss. They sent delegations to Washington, which persuaded Congress to exclude them from the act temporarily. In a few cases local Indian leaders subverted the policy by claiming allotments as a bloc and maintaining their communal economic practices. Nevertheless, partitioning tribal reservations proved the most successful of several methods used to destroy Indian societies.

Another area of endeavor was education. In spite of its mediocre record in the decades after the Civil War, reform leaders hoped that instruction in the ways of the dominant culture might make the Indians less unique. Schools such as the Carlisle Institute and the Haskell Institute in Kansas served as training grounds for young Indians. Upon graduation from the white man's schools, the young men and women were to return to their reservations and convince fellow tribesmen to adopt the white man's "superior" customs.

By the end of the nineteenth century the techniques to destroy tribal culture such as individual landholding, white man's education, and continuing pressures to forget old Indian customs had taken their toll. In some instances tribal identity became vague, but at the same time the Indians refused to become mere imitations of the white majority. Crowding tribal remnants together in even smaller areas increased intertribal exchanges of customs and ideas. The mixing of children from many tribes at boarding schools planted the seeds for the later pan-Indian movement, which has grown steadily in the twentieth century.

By the first decade of the twentieth century, those citizens who believed "the only good Indian is a dead one" should have been happy. Poverty, malnutrition, disease, and death stalked the shrinking reservations. By 1900 only 200,000 Indians dwelled on or near the reservations, mostly living in wretched conditions. Although the policy of assimilating the Indians had failed to get them into the mainstream of American life, it had succeeded in the other half of its task. Indians were disappearing as a distinct group. Throughout the nineteenth century many white Americans believed the "inferior" or "primitive" groups had to give way before more "civilized" ones. These people saw the steady decline of the Indian population as the proper result of this process and concluded that the tribesmen would not long remain an identifiable part of American society.

THE MORMONS

Even before the growing white population had pushed the Indians aside throughout the West, the refugee Mormons had migrated to Utah. During the 1840s and 1850s thousands of the Latter-day Saints abandoned their homes and property in the East and gathered near the shores of the Great Salt Lake. When they first tried to plow the bricklike desert soil, their plows broke in the stubborn ground. Within a few months, however, Brigham Young had organized work parties that dug irrigation ditches and diverted mountain streams into them. With water to help, the plows did their work. The Mormons used the first large-scale irrigation by Anglo-Americans in North America, and within a few decades irrigation came to be used in many parts of the West.

When they first moved to Utah, the church leaders hoped to achieve political and economic independence. They established a string of settlements from Ogden, Utah, south and west to San Bernardino, California. Mormon families considered it an honor to help set up new communities. In the eastern United States and western Europe, Mormon missionaries attracted new converts and sent them to the new western Zion. By 1856, some 22,000 Saints lived near the Great Salt Lake or along the "Mormon Corridor" to California.

While settlement took place church leaders also hoped to achieve immediate statehood, so that they could protect their community from outside interference by federal officials. Accordingly, in March 1849 Brigham Young called a constitutional convention, and this body adopted a constitution for the would-be state of Deseret. The Mormons, claiming all of Utah, most of Arizona and Nevada, and parts of California, Idaho, Wyoming, and Colorado, sent a delegation to Washington to lobby for statehood. There they met widespread opposition and in 1850 had to settle for the creation of Utah Territory, with much reduced boundaries. Fortunately for the Mormons, federal authorities appointed Brigham Young governor and four other high church leaders to administrative positions in the government. Church leaders thus continued to make nearly all political decisions for the territory.

Mormon insistence on retaining polygamy and the quarrels between church officials and non-Mormon federal officials in 1857 brought a major crisis. That year one of the federal territorial judges fled Utah and returned east, claiming that the church ran the government and that Brigham Young was a dictator who used a group of "destroying angels" to crush all opposition. With little effort to investigate, President James Buchanan dispatched an army of 2,500 men to subdue the supposedly rebellious Mormons. Frantically the Saints evacuated the women and children, prepared to burn their homes and farms rather than submit to federal occupation, and launched raids against the army supply columns. These succeeded so well that the troops failed to reach Utah that year, and the conflict ended without major fighting. Despite continuing anti-Mormon bitterness in some parts of the country, the Saints continued to attract converts and a steady stream of them populated dozens of towns and rural areas throughout the West. Thousands of Scandinavian Mormons migrated to Utah; by 1900 they made up 34 percent of the state's foreign-born and, with their children, 16 percent of Utah's population.

RANCHERS AND COWBOYS

Most people moving west had no special group motivation, as had the Mormons. Farmers, ranchers, and city folk poured into the region, but in patterns that varied drastically from earlier settlement in the East, where areas were filled with people coming from the state, county, or two adjacent to the one being settled. In the West, isolated settlements of miners, Mormons, farmers, ranchers, sheepherders, and railroad workers dotted the countryside.

Once across the Missouri River, the settlers encountered an unfamiliar and difficult climate and topography. Farmers, for example, soon discovered that much of the West was unsuited for conventional agriculture. On the Plains the hot summer winds and a shortage of moisture repeatedly damaged or destroyed crops. Immense clouds of grasshoppers periodically descended on farms, stripping orchards and fields of all edibles as well as eating the clothes off the lines and the cloth net screens off the windows. Beyond the Plains stood the Rocky Mountains and between them and the Sierras lay the arid plateaus and deserts of the basin and range country. Thus for mid-nineteenth-century farmers most of the West presented little possibility for successful agriculture.

The obstacles that discouraged farmers, however, were not major problems for ranchers and sheepherders. The almost limitless Plains had plenty of grass for either sheep or cattle, and even much of the arid region beyond the Rockies could sustain large herds of animals. Little ranching occurred in the West until after the Civil War, for until then the Indians and buffalo dominated the Plains region, and the railroads had not extended their tracks far enough west to enable cattle grazers to ship their animals to Eastern markets. By the late 1860s, and on into the next decade, these circumstances changed as a result of Indian wars, destruction of the buffalo herds, and construction of the first transcontinental railroads. By the 1870s massive cattle herds moved north from the Texas Plains to regions as far as Wyoming. Most, however, stopped at places like Dodge City and Abilene, the railhead towns in Kansas.

To move the herds north ranchers depended on cowboys. Although most Americans picture all cowboys as white, at least one quarter of them were black, and possibly another quarter were Mexicans. A typical crew on the Long Drive north to the railroad towns would consist of eight men, three or four of whom might be black or Mexican. The foreman was almost always white but the wrangler and cook could be of any background—black, white, Mexican, or, as the cowboys said, "Portugee." As long as the individuals performed their tasks well they got along with the others to some degree, but color determined the choice of leadership. One black cowboy, renowned as a rider, roper, and trail cook, lamented, "If it weren't for my damned old black face, I'd have been a boss long ago," and whites who knew him agreed. The life of the cowboys was often brutal—branding, roping, and castrating animals—and this carried over to personal relationships as well. They frequently fought and quarreled with one another and their bigotry was not reined in. "The way to handle Mexicans," one Texan asserted, "is to kick 'em in the ribs." Yet despite the prejudice and conflict the men accomplished their goals and their labors brought Eastern and foreign investment to the West, encouraged railroad building, and provided limited markets for merchants and farmers who lived near the cattle trails and towns.

By the late 1880s overgrazing, low Eastern prices, and disastrous weather ended the open range and the long cattle drives. The downfall began in the summer of 1886, one of the hottest and dustiest on record. Water holes dried up, grass turned brown, and by the end of July many streams had run low or had stopped completely. Following that summer came the worst winter ever to strike northern ranges. Temperatures fell to as low as 45 degrees below zero and some animals froze to death. Thousands of cattle died—estimates range up to 75 percent of some of the herds. After that the demoralized ranchers also had to contend with homesteaders, sheep grazers, and barbed-wire enclosures as an increased population started demarcating property lines and erecting barriers. Although the old style of ranching would not be the same again, it nevertheless remained part of the Western economy.

THE BASQUES

Sheep raising is less well known, or celebrated, than cattle ranching but is of almost equal importance to the Western economy. Practiced from Montana and Idaho in the north through Colorado and south into Arizona as well as west in Oregon and Nevada, this industry brought hatred and violence to the West for decades. Usually sheepmen hired Indian or Mexican herders, and neither group was well received by most white Americans. A foreign group, the Basques, many of whom originally went to California in search of gold, gravitated to the sheep regions after the Civil War and were later joined by compatriots from Europe. As a group, they were uniquely successful.

Sheepherding is a lonely endeavor. It requires great patience and fortitude and the ability to cope with intense boredom. The attraction that the occupation had for the Basques was probably the opportunity it afforded to be free, autonomous, and yet gainfully employed. In Europe the Basques had been fishermen, carpenters, shipbuilders, and masons, but not sheepmen. Yet in the United States they had no difficulty in adapting to the new life. Historically Basques have been independent and have maintained their separateness from other groups near whom they lived. The Basque country of the Iberian peninsula in Europe was divided and incorporated into France and Spain in the early part of the nineteenth century, but the Basques always favored their own culture and never quite fit in with either the French or the Spanish. The number of Basques in the United

States probably never exceeded 15,000, but this figure fails to reflect their importance as sheepmen in the mountain ranges and deserts of the West after the 1870s.

FARMERS

Other European groups, like the Germans, Scandinavians, and Czechs, migrated to farming regions in Kansas, Nebraska, the Dakotas, Texas, and, to a lesser extent, Colorado, Washington, Oregon, and California, where many prospered. Nevertheless, as a general rule agriculture was a risky venture in much of the West. Unaware of this, Congress in 1854 opened both Kansas and Nebraska to settlement. This brought a rush of pioneers into those territories, but the continuing difficulties with the Indians and the conflict between transplanted Northerners and Southerners, coupled with the climatic obstacles already discussed, prevented widespread settlement. In 1862 Congress passed the famous Homestead Act, which offered a 160-acre plot of land to any adult who would live on it for five years and make minimal improvements on the property. Meant to help pioneer farmers, this legislation came at a time when the existing technology and agricultural techniques were inadequate for the challenges posed by the Plains environment. As a result, thousands of homesteaders moved west only to encounter crop failures and other disasters. There is no question that eventually the Homestead Law helped to populate much of the West, but the first few decades of its operation brought misery and heartache to thousands.

It took new varieties of seeds, increased knowledge about agriculture in arid and semiarid regions, and the introduction of better equipment before farmers succeeded in much of the West. In 1862, the same year it passed the Homestead Act, Congress adopted the Morrill Land Grant Act, which provided federal land subsidies for each state and territory to use in creating or strengthening its engineering and agricultural colleges. The agricultural experiment stations, in conjunction with public

agriculture schools, introduced drought-resistant varieties of
seed as well as dry farming and crop rotation. County and state
agricultural societies and dozens of agricultural magazines and
newsletters helped spread these new ideas and techniques. By
the early twentieth century they were widely known.

Efforts by the major Western railroads to attract customers
for their land, generous federal land laws that made it cheap
and easy for individuals to get Western land, and a boom psy-
chology among farmers produced several land rushes during
the late nineteenth century. During the 1870s farmers occupied
land in Minnesota, South Dakota, western Iowa, Nebraska,
Kansas, and Texas. After the depression of the mid-1870s ended,
a new current of optimism swept thousands more west. Several
wetter-than-average years convinced would-be farmers that
they could gain large profits if only they bought enough land.
By the 1880s farmers had claimed or bought millions more
acres of federal and railroad lands in Dakota, western Nebraska,
Kansas, and eastern Colorado, an area erroneously described as
the "rainbelt of the Plains." Droughts in 1889, 1890, and 1894,
accompanied by the depression of the mid-1890s and the return
of the grasshopper swarms to the Plains in 1894, pushed many
farmers into bankruptcy. Thousands fled east or moved into
Western towns to try other occupations. Others became tenant
farmers on land they once had expected to own. Nebraska in
1900, for example, had 15,000 fewer people and 6,000 fewer
farms than in 1890.

Although real obstacles slowed agricultural development in
much of the West, farmers continued moving into the region
until the Great Depression of the 1930s, and minority groups
played an important role in Western agriculture throughout
the period. Although many blacks had agricultural experience
in the Southeast, relatively small numbers of them joined the
surge west. Homesteading, at least for former slaves, was a new
experience. In addition, court decisions and some legislation
denied blacks equal access to the public lands open to whites.
Still, some blacks did become Western farmers. In fact, during

the 1870s and 1880s substantial numbers of them migrated west into Kansas and Nebraska. Often called Exodusters, they met racial antagonism as well as some property and voting restrictions, but these difficulties failed to halt their trek. For example, it has been estimated that between 15,000 and 20,000 black farmers settled in Kansas in the year 1880. Also, several entire black communities, such as the settlers at Nicodemus, Kansas, moved from the South to the West.

THE JAPANESE

On the Pacific Coast the Chinese provided most of the stoop, or squat, labor in agriculture. A significant element in the population since the gold rush, most Chinese never earned enough money as miners or on the railroads to return to their native land. As a result many of these workers shifted to manufacturing jobs and agriculture. By 1886 the Chinese constituted about half of the farm laborers in California. Anti-Chinese feeling on the West Coast induced Congress in 1882 to pass the Exclusion Act, which suspended Chinese immigration for ten years. Since the Chinese did much of the state's menial labor, substitutes had to be found.

The growing demand for labor of all kinds in the Far West, and the need to replace the Chinese in the 1880s, led to the encouragement and temporary acceptance of Japanese immigrants. Japanese immigration to the United States, though, was unique in several regards. Unlike practically all other groups, who came solely to improve their own and their families' welfare, the Japanese exodus was in part a response to Japan's expansionist philosophy. A significant portion of Japan's ruling class perceived immigration as part of the nation's imperial and colonial policies. The Japanese rulers believed that they, along with the white races, had an aptitude for colonization, and they sought every opportunity to expand their interests abroad. Surplus Japanese laborers were encouraged to leave the country.

Not only would their departure contribute to the planting of Japanese culture overseas and provide a market for Japan's exports, but it was also assumed that these laborers would enrich the nation's coffers by returning a part of their foreign earnings to relatives in Japan. In addition, the workingmen remaining at home would have less competition, thereby raising their chances for higher wages. As a result of these views, along with the opportunities afforded to individuals who did leave, large numbers of Japanese ventured to Korea, Taiwan, and the United States. Although some of these émigrés hoped to return to Japan, many took their families along with them.

Until 1890 fewer than 1,000 Japanese had entered the United States in any single year. After that date their numbers increased gradually until 1898, when Hawaii was annexed to the United States. In the next five years over 60,000 Japanese moved from those islands to the mainland. Many of them had gone to Hawaii to work on sugar plantations and in canning plants; on the mainland most continued to do agricultural work, but others toiled on the railroads, in the mines, and as domestics. By the 1920s more than 120,000 people of Japanese ancestry lived in the United States.

Unlike the Chinese, whose center in California was San Francisco, the Japanese went mainly to the Los Angeles area. In California and elsewhere on the West Coast, they became prime factors in the farming and distribution of fruits and vegetables, eventually producing 99 percent of the celery and 95 percent of the strawberries in Los Angeles County. Many of the Japanese who settled in Oregon and Washington also engaged in truck gardening and, like their compatriots in California, wanted to become independent entrepreneurs. To achieve this goal they worked eleven to fourteen hours a day, almost starved themselves, and saved whatever they could in order to buy their own property. One immigrant recalled how difficult life was in the early 1900s: "In those days a stray jackrabbit meant a feast and a cow killed by a passing train was a Godsent banquet."

THE MEXICANS

While public attention focused on the antagonism toward Asians on the West Coast, in the early twentieth century Mexican immigrants began moving north in the United States. There were several reasons for this migration. First, in 1902 Congress passed the Newlands National Reclamation Act, which stimulated irrigated agriculture in the Southwest. The law set aside nearly all money that the government received from the sale of public land in sixteen Western and Southwestern states in a revolving fund for building and maintaining irrigation projects in those states. Within a decade farms with newly irrigated fields offered jobs to thousands of unskilled workers. Irrigation aided cotton cultivation in Texas, Arizona, and California and transformed the San Joaquin, Sacramento, and Imperial valleys into veritable Gardens of Eden. The number of irrigated acres more than doubled from 1,004,233 in 1889 to 2,664,104 in 1909 and then increased to 4,219,040 in 1919. Cotton acreage in California's San Joaquin Valley jumped from 5,500 in 1919 to 172, 400 in 1931. By 1929 California farms were producing between 300,000 and 500,000 caseloads of vegetables, fruits, and truck crops, almost 40 percent of the nation's total for these items. It was therefore fortunate for the Americans that the Mexican Revolution, which occurred in 1909, created a vast upheaval that sent as much as 10 percent of that nation's northern population to the United States. The number of farm laborers in the Golden State increased from 59,145 in 1890 to 196,812 in 1930, and Mexicans made up a majority of those workers in several areas of the state.

Official immigration figures list over 700,000 Mexican arrivals between 1901 and 1930, but the totals were at least twice that number since there were no border guards before 1924 to prevent illegal entry, and Mexicans who arrived by land before 1907 were not counted. Like most other immigrants, these people came for jobs. In the early decades of the twentieth century

Table 7.1

ETHNIC GROUPS ON NINE WESTERN RAILROADS
(Percentage of each working as track men)

	1909	1928–1929
Greeks	21.9	2.0
Italians	17.0	3.5
Japanese and Koreans	11.2	1.0
Mexicans	17.1	59.5

El Paso, Texas, served as the major distributing point for Mexican immigrants, in some months processing more than 5,000 people. Three major railroad lines passed through the city and facilitated the placement of the newcomers on farms, in mines and smelters, and on the railroads. Like the farms and mines, the railroads employed thousands of unskilled foreigners, who could be hired at lower wages than the American-born would accept. As a result the newest immigrants generally occupied the lowest rung on the economic ladder. On the Western railroads a variety of foreigners had been employed as section hands on the track gangs, but within twenty years of the Mexican Revolution, as the figures in Table 7.1 show, Mexicans dominated the field.

The Mexicans worked wherever they were needed. As World War I and the immigration restriction acts of the 1920s curtailed emigration from Europe and Asia, the Southwestern mines, the sugar beet fields of Colorado and the upper Midwest, and the steel foundries in Illinois, Ohio, and Pennsylvania had difficulty finding sufficient help. Again the Mexicans benefited. They did not have to travel far to cross the border; labor agents helped transport those who went to the Midwest and Pennsylvania; and in the Southwest they were familiar with the terrain and the increasing number of Mexican *colonias* that had developed. San Antonio and El Paso, Texas, had the largest number of Spanish-speaking people in that state, while in California El Centro, Calipatria, Calexico, and Los Angeles served as major

Mexican dwelling places. So many Mexicans moved north that in 1925 Los Angeles had a larger Spanish-speaking population than any other city in North America except Mexico City.

During the 1920s economic conditions in the United States varied widely. A postwar recession hit in 1920 and lasted two or three years in some industries. This resulted in widespread industrial layoffs of Mexican workers. For example, the Ford Motor Company in Detroit sent home 3,000 Mexican employees at its own expense during those years. In the Southwest cotton prices fell sharply, in some cases from 38¢ to 18¢ a pound, and disgruntled workers were laid off, found themselves unable to collect unpaid wages, or went on strike to protest pay cuts. Most of the strikes failed as strikers and their leaders were deported. During the last half of the decade demands for cheap agricultural labor increased the need for Mexican workers, particularly in California, and despite growing anti-Mexican feelings, these workers continued to migrate north toward the jobs.

Continuing efforts to restrict this immigration failed during the 1920s because of pressure from the railroads and the farming groups of the Southwest. The stock market crash of 1929 and the depression that followed not only ended the era of huge immigration but actually reversed the tide as thousands of Mexicans returned to their homeland. Repatriation, or sending the aliens home, seemed a simple answer to the growing unemployment caused by the depression. Some were deported by United States immigration officials; others returned voluntarily. Most, however, were forced by state, local, or federal agencies to repatriate. Many of these people went without any financial assistance, but the Mexican government helped about 5 percent of them to settle in special colonies.

OTHER IMMIGRANTS

At the same time that Mexican workers entered the United States smaller numbers of people from other lands joined the Western work force. After the United States annexed the Philip-

Filipinos cutting lettuce in Salinas, California, 1935. Filipinos, Japanese, and Mexicans were often the main sources for the backbreaking work required of farm laborers in the Southwest. By Dorothea Lange. (*Library of Congress*)

pine Islands in 1898, the islanders could move freely to the mainland. Hawaiian sugar planters and pineapple growers started recruiting Filipino laborers after the "Gentlemen's Agreement" of 1907, a pledge by Japan to halt most immigration to the United States, curtailed their supply of cheap labor from Japan. The Filipinos, who could earn four to ten times as much in the United States as at home, were happy to be recruited, although many Americans objected to their presence. In the 1920s, when Congress considered restricting Mexican immigrants as well as Europeans and most Asians, California farmers sought the Filipinos. During that decade at least 30,000 came from Hawaii and the Philippines. By 1930 estimates placed anywhere from 30,000 to 100,000 Filipinos in the United States; the census takers counted 45,208. During the depression of the 1930s many Filipinos lost their jobs to white refugees from Texas, Arkansas, and Oklahoma and as a result returned to their homeland. Those who remained in the United States established colonies in or near Seattle, Portland, San Francisco, and Stockton, California.

Several other immigrant groups also helped people the West. Italians moved to California, where they engaged in truck farming. Some became quite successful operating vineyards and fruit orchards. Of the 100,000 Portuguese who immigrated, nearly one third settled in California. Their focal point originally was the San Francisco Bay area, but they later spread to the Sacramento and San Joaquin valleys. As had the Italians, the Portuguese entered agriculture, and in southern California they ranked second only to the Dutch in the dairy industry. The Armenians who settled on the West Coast found work on California farms, in packing houses, canneries, and cement works. By 1915 more than 8,000 of them lived in Fresno. Greeks settled throughout the mountain West. The so-called Czar of the Greeks, Leonidas G. Skliris, stationed himself in Salt Lake City and there acted as the agent for the Utah Copper Company, the Western Pacific Railroad, the Carbon County mines, and other employers. He found jobs for most of the Greeks who worked in the mountain states. Over 8,500 Asian Indians, mostly Sikh indentured servants, also immigrated to the West Coast between 1900 and 1930; 5,000 of them landed at San Francisco in the first decade of the century. They worked on the railroads and in the lumbering centers of the Northwest. One group, placed in the sawmills at Bellingham, Washington, was attacked and beaten in 1907 by about 500 whites. The local newspaper explained two days after the assault that the Indians "are repulsive in appearance and disgusting in their manners. . . . Their actions and customs are so different from ours that there can never be tolerance of them."

All of those who immigrated to the American West during the last half of the nineteenth century or the first third of the twentieth did so hoping for a better life. Miners, farmers, ranchers, railroad workers, or city folk all expected economic improvement, and much opportunity in fact existed. For most, however, the myth of Western abundance and opportunity exceeded the reality. Instead of the pot of gold at the end of the rainbow they found hard work, low wages, and poor living conditions, as well as ethnic tensions that developed along much the same lines as in the rest of the nation.

8

Ethnic Tensions and Conflicts
(1880s–1945)

OLD-STOCK AMERICANS OFTEN THOUGHT that others were strange, inferior, and potentially disloyal. At one time or another many considered black slavery as natural, regarded foreigners as necessary sources of menial labor, and approved the annihilation of Indians because they allegedly blocked the progress of the white man's civilization. The belief in black inferiority grew steadily in the nineteenth century, as did contempt for American Indians. As for the foreign masses coming to American shores in the late nineteenth and early twentieth centuries, the voices of bigotry became louder. Prejudices found expression in both elaborate "scientific" theories that "proved" the innate superiority of old-stock white Americans and in crude ethnic slurs. Intolerance also manifested itself in violence as well as in social, legal, and economic discrimination.

Rapid social and economic changes in American society after the Civil War reinforced intolerance. In the 1890s American nativists began noting with alarm the shifting patterns of immigration that brought so many Jews and Catholics from southern and eastern Europe. Labor violence, such as that occurring during the railroad disturbances of 1877 and at the Haymarket in Chicago in 1886, crowded slums in the nation's fast-growing cities, and industrial strikes also created uneasiness about the stability of American society. Nativists were quick to blame foreign radicals and agitators for the unrest. During the Progressive reform era, which lasted from the 1890s until World War I, many Americans singled out the newcomers as the cause of corrupt urban political machines. If the reformers opposed the saloon and alcoholic beverages, then they saw a connection between corruption and drinking and believed that the curbing of immigration would curtail the venal aspects of American urban politics. Hence a considerable number of Progressives opposed immigration.

Many others, reformers and nonreformers alike, feared the economic impact of immigration. When depression drove wages down and threw people out of work, they blamed the immigrants for lowering the American standard of living. Many of the newcomers, themselves prisoners of peasant ignorance and superstition, came with traditional hatreds and suspicions of one another, and they did not lose these feelings quickly in the United States. All of these conditions contributed to the widespread intolerance and bigotry that flourished in the United States during the late nineteenth and well into the twentieth centuries.

PSEUDOSCIENTIFIC RACISM

Pseudoscientific racism provided the intellectual foundation for the nation's intolerance. New immigrants were measured by Anglo-Saxon standards. One sociologist enunciated the views of many Americans when he described the immigrants to the United States. Northern Europeans, he believed, were most desirable because they possessed—and surpassed everyone else in—"innate ethical endowment." Southern and eastern Europeans, on the other hand, were "beaten men of beaten breeds," and some of them clearly belonged in "skins, in wattled huts at the close of the Great Ice Age."

Such ideas found wide acceptance. As a result there was not

a region or section in the United States that did not detest the minority peoples in its midst, nor were there any states where blacks or immigrants could feel secure. Throughout the nation the only major difference was which group would bear the brunt of local prejudice. Usually the largest minority in an area attracted the most unfavorable attention, but even small groups failed to escape the widespread bigotry.

Despite the viciousness and muddled thinking that characterized the assessments of immigrants, the bigotry was even more intense when directed against racial minorities, especially black Americans. Whites stereotyped blacks in newspapers, speeches, and on the stage as lazy, shiftless, and childlike, as beasts and rapists. They called blacks "niggers," "darkies," and "coons." Politician Tom Watson of Georgia, who early in his career courted black votes, later wrote that the black man has "no comprehension of virtue, honesty, truth, gratitude and principle." And he insisted that the white South had to "lynch him occasionally, and flog him now and then, to keep him from blaspheming the Almighty, by his conduct, on account of his smell and his color." A few racists likened blacks to apes and scarcely considered them as human beings at all. One book, entitled *The Negro A Beast*, had wide circulation in the early twentieth century.

A variety of "learned" opinions buttressed such diatribes. Blacks allegedly ranked lowest on a "scale" of human worth, falling below the southern and eastern Europeans. Proponents of the Darwinian notions popular in the late nineteenth century, who saw life as a jungle where the fittest survived, claimed that blacks were losing out in the competition among races, and some even thought that blacks were moving backward into a morass of vice and immorality. At the very least, the argument ran, the racially inferior blacks had to be ruled by whites. Even many of the people who demanded better treatment for black Americans believed that they were innately inferior beings.

Old-stock Americans did not universally succumb to the dominant ethnic ideologies of the era. Presidents Grover Cleveland, William Howard Taft, and Woodrow Wilson, who may or may

Cover for a piece of sheet music, 1899. (*State Historical Society of Wisconsin*)

not have harbored similar views, nevertheless vetoed immigration-restriction legislation that discriminated against southern and eastern Europeans. In Wilson's case, at least, his veto marked a reversal of a position enunciated in earlier years when he indicated that many of the newer immigrants consisted of "multitudes of men of lowest class from the south of Italy, and men of the meaner sort out of Hungary and Poland, men out of the ranks where there was neither skill nor energy nor any initiative of quick intelligence. . . . The Chinese were more to be desired, as workmen if not as citizens, than most of the coarse crew that came crowding in every year at the eastern ports."

Not until World War I did anti-immigrant feeling have enough strength to curb immigration. Various reformers cautioned against slurring foreigners and urged acceptance of pluralism. Some helped organize the Immigrants' Protective League while others, like Jane Addams, lived and worked in the urban ethnic neighborhoods. Probably the major reason for the failure of immigration restriction prior to the 1920s was economic; the nation had a seemingly endless need for the labor the newcomers brought. When workers began to saturate the industrial employment market, and the fears of further immigration became overwhelming, legislation to restrict European and Asian entry into the United States was passed.

As for blacks, few whites after 1890 could be found to speak in their behalf. Racial demagogy peaked around the turn of the century and its expressions pervaded even the highest levels of government. In 1902 Alabama's United States senator, John T. Morgan, ranted on the Senate floor about how "negro suffrage . . . has been one unbroken line of political, social, and industrial obstruction to progress, and a constant disturbance of the peace in a vast region of the United States." Senator Francis G. Newlands of Nevada, born in Natchez, Mississippi, and reared in southern Illinois, offered specific suggestions for change. At the Democratic National Convention in 1912 he called for the repeal of the Fifteenth Amendment to the Constitution, which forbids the denial or abridgment of the vote "on account of race, color, or previous condition of servitude," and asked for a national prohibition against black suffrage. Even President Theodore Roosevelt expressed shallow and bigoted opinions. In 1906 he wrote to one correspondent: "Now as to the Negroes! I entirely agree with you that as a race and in the mass [they] are altogether inferior to the whites."

Some reformers challenged these outbursts. In 1905, when a South Carolina psychologist concluded that the IQ test proved innate black inferiority, Oswald Garrison Villard, editor of the *New York Evening Post*, disapproved and debunked his findings. Some liberal whites, like Mary White Ovington, defended the black man's right to vote. Along with others, she tried to help blacks in organizations like the Urban League, founded in 1911, which had a social work approach. More militant whites joined with blacks and founded the NAACP in 1909.

TRIUMPH OF JIM CROWISM

These voices against bigotry were a minority, however, after the 1880s. The prevalent views, along with the weariness most Americans felt about the crusade to help the freedman, helped put an end to Radical Reconstruction in the South in 1877. However, the overthrow of Southern Radical Republicans did not bring an immediate end to all of the achievements of Reconstruction. But by the 1890s a torrent of racism engulfed Southern blacks. Almost every area of human contact became subject to state and municipal legislation segregating the races. Collectively known as "Jim Crow" laws, this legislation proliferated throughout the region. First, "grandfather clauses" (which allowed men to vote if their grandfathers had been eligible to vote), literacy tests, poll taxes, and white primaries were instituted to eliminate blacks from the electoral process. Then communities segregated railroads, streetcars, schools, steamboats, restrooms, drinking fountains, and other public facilities and enacted ordinances requiring separate neighborhoods.

Lynching, or at least the threat of it, was the most brutal method of chastising the blacks. This incredible means of dispensing "justice" occurred in several regions of the country but most frequently in the South. Whites and Asians were also left dangling from trees, but overwhelmingly more blacks than others were victimized. By the late nineteenth century Southern lynchings averaged more than two per week, although most took place during the warm months between April and October. On occasion large mobs witnessed the hangings and torturings of helpless blacks, some of whom were even burned alive. In 1893 a few men gouged out the eyes of a black man with a hot poker before setting fire to him; in 1921, after a particularly vicious group burned a black male, the onlookers waited for the fire to subside before scrambling for the man's bones, which they took as souvenirs.

For a number of angry Americans, individual assaults did not suffice. Many an attack included large groups of people. Between the 1870s and 1890s the Chinese in the West suffered from massive outbursts in Los Angeles, San Francisco, Seattle, Reno, and Denver. Of the last, one Chinese scholar lecturing in Chicago observed, "If a single American was treated in China as were the victims of the anti-Chinese riots at Denver, the United States would send 100,000 missionaries to civilize the heathen." Greeks were beaten in Nebraska and Slavs endured similar assaults in Utah. Italians were gunned down or strung up in places as diverse as Florida, Colorado, and Illinois. One incident, which had international repercussions, resulted in the lynching of eleven Italians in New Orleans in 1891 after a local jury had acquitted them of murder.

Despite widespread antipathy toward immigrants, the worst demonstrations were aimed at the blacks. In Atlanta in 1906, newspaper suggestions that some black men had raped white women set off one of the bloodiest racial assaults since the massacre at Wounded Knee in 1890. Black migration also triggered demonstrations in the North. The Great Migration, between 1910 and 1920, sent over 500,000 blacks from the South to Northern cities, frequently to be used by employers to break unions and keep down wages. Competition between blacks and whites for housing and recreational facilities also caused trouble. In 1917, in East St. Louis, Illinois, tension between black and white workers erupted into a full-scale race riot. Two years later a similar outburst rocked the nation's capital, and in July 1919 Chicagoans witnessed an even bloodier episode. Chicago had experienced decades of racial tensions before the Great Migration heightened the competition for jobs and homes, and even before the riot blacks who purchased or rented housing in white areas were the targets of bomb throwers. The Chicago riot itself began when whites threw rocks at a black youth who swam across the supposed line separating the "white" from the "black" swimming area of the city's beaches. When the youth drowned, violence erupted into a race war and the city experienced a week of terror and bloodshed; 23 whites and 25 blacks died and over 500 persons were injured before the state militia restored order.

TREATMENT OF INDIANS

The nation's oldest minority, the Indians, experienced no race riots only because few of them lived close to large numbers of whites. Despite this the tribesmen suffered from violence and bigotry during the nineteenth century. The decades after the Civil War saw the federal government accelerate its policy of racial segregation by forcing the last Western tribes onto ever-contracting reservations. Then, whenever the restless tribesmen fled from their captivity, columns of blue-clad troops rode after them in pursuit. Thus the violence against Indians seemed to come from the government rather than individual citizens, but this was not so. Widespread civilian antipathy toward Indians made it impossible for any government policy to help them, and army campigns resulted from the popular hatred of Indians.

Particularly in the West whites considered the tribesmen as pests at best and as mortal enemies at worst. One Nevada news-paperman claimed that the only way to end Indian hostilities was through the "total extermination of every redskin from the [Canadian] to the Mexican frontier." Several years later another Western spokesman claimed that the life of a single pioneer was worth more than hundreds "of the best red devils that ever scalped a white person." Yet another editor recommended welcoming the Indians when they asked for peace and then slaughtering them "as though they were as many nests of rat-tlesnakes." With such views prevalent throughout the West, it is not surprising that the white population generally welcomed violence against their Indian neighbors.

When military actions against the tribes ended late in the nineteenth century, the government continued its efforts to acculturate the Indians, and education played a major role in this process. Beginning in 1870, the government earmarked funds specifically for Indian education, and reservation and boarding schools competed for money and the chance to "civilize" their charges. From the late 1890s to the 1930s thousands of Indian children were legally kidnaped and forced to attend school far from home. When their parents could not pay for their transportation home during vacations, the youngsters remained at school. The government curriculum, designed to eradicate all signs of Indianness, made no concession to the children's cultures. As a general policy the school's staff cut off the boys' long hair, punished children for speaking their native languages, and replaced their clothes with ill-fitting hand-me-downs. Bureau of Indian Affairs' employees cooperated with zealous Christian missionaries to prohibit the children from holding tribal dances or ceremonies, which they considered pagan rites that had to be abolished.

Stifling regulation of all aspects of student life turned the schools into virtual prisons. Continuing shortages of funds led superintendents to cut their costs, often by reducing the food budget for the children. A major investigation showed that the schools fed their charges at a per capita cost of 12¢ to 14¢ a day at a time when the army spent 52¢ per day for each soldier's food. At the same time, the field matrons who worked with the children encouraged the students to consume dairy products. Unfortunately some of the Indian children suffered stomach disorders because they had trouble digesting the milk and cheese. The effort to alter their diets caused another serious problem, ill health: many dairy cattle then carried tuberculosis, which spread quickly throughout the Indian schools. The problem became so bad that even government officials admitted widespread malaise among the children. According to investigators, "malnutrition was evident. They [the children] were indolent and when they had a chance to play, they merely sat about on the ground showing no exuberance of healthy youth." The poor diet and crowded living conditions spread disease, and only when the authorities feared that a child was dying would they voluntarily send him or her back to the reservation.

Despite these circumstances, not all of the students looked back on their school days with anger. Some remembered the friendships they made with members of other tribes and residents of other reservations. This led to a growing pan-Indian movement a few years later. The academic training and vocational skills they received pleased others, while their participation in athletic events, marching bands, and military-style units brought satisfaction as well. By the turn of the century graduates of schools such as Carlisle and Hampton secured permanent jobs as a part of the growing Indian service bureaucracy. Although a small number of them worked for the government and a few even went to college, most Indian school students returned home, often with few skills for that environment. Certainly the use of education to weaken tribal cultures succeeded, and only rarely did the schools offer anything to replace the values they tried to destroy. Yet they did prepare a group of young Indians for leadership roles.

Physical brutality also took its toll. At the Ogalala boarding school near Pine Ridge, South Dakota, two runaway boys were captured, returned, and beaten. "Their heads were shaved, though it was winter. One of the boys had a ball and chain locked onto his leg and was locked to the bed at night." There were tales of other cruelties. One Bureau employee reported having seen Indian children "thrown in cellars under the building. . . . I have seen their shoes taken away from them and they then [were] forced to walk through the snow to the barn to help milk. I have seen them whipped with a hemp rope, also a water hose."

For those who remained at home the situation was also bad. Few reservations included good farmland, even if the Indians

Tom Torlino, a Navajo, photographed about 1886. (*Arizona Historical Society*)

had chosen to till their acreage, and religious beliefs about Mother Earth prevented many from farming. For those who tried, however, poor soil, repeated droughts, and crop failures were discouraging. With no economic base and little opportunity for employment, the reservations became pens of misery and despair. By the 1920s most Indians lived in dirt-floored shacks or tents with no water or plumbing and little heat. Usually the entire family ate, sat, and slept in a single room with

Tom Torlino after three years at the Carlisle Indian School. (*Arizona Historical Society*)

only a table, a couple of boxes for chairs, and a single bed. Their food consisted of whatever rations they got from the agency office, a few vegetables they raised, and fruit berries they gathered. Often dogs and horses had to be eaten to prevent starvation.

By the early decades of the twentieth century the position of Indians seemed hopeless. Using almost any standard of measure—family income, infant mortality, life expectancy, unemployment, alcoholism, or suicide—American Indians stood firmly mired at the bottom of the social and economic ladder. Whether by accident or by design, most Indian tribes had ceased to function or had been reduced to ineffectiveness. As their culture disappeared Indian despair mounted, but they tried to retain control of their reservations and lives. Beginning as early as 1878, when Congress created the agency police, young men seeking relief from enforced inactivity volunteered to serve as policemen and army scouts. Both positions incorporated the traditional duties of a warrior, and both brought some cultural satisfaction. On the other hand, Indian police had to serve as cultural change models by wearing white men's clothing, cutting their hair, and having only one wife. Present on at least forty-six reservations, these men enforced the Bureau of Indian Affairs' agent's will, which often pitted them against others of the tribe. When Congress established the Courts of Indian Offenses to deal with outlawed religious ceremonies and dances, healers and medicine men, and plural marriage, some leaders served as judges. This brought those who sought to control the pace and direction of accommodation to the white demands into conflict with traditionalists, who opposed any cultural transformation of Indian society.

By the 1880s some Indians turned to pan-Indian rather than tribal or reservation efforts to improve their situation. On the Southern Plains the Native American church evolved out of a new combination of peyote use and Christian practices and ideas. Peyote, a cactus fruit long used in the Southwest to produce visions among its users, fit well into the long-held practices of inducing dreams through fasting. By the 1890s ritual use of peyote had spread through many Oklahoma tribes; a decade later it appeared in the Missouri and Mississippi valleys too. The new religion merged Indian and Christian beliefs reaching beyond any single tribe or reservation. Although actively opposed by the Bureau of Indian Affairs and by Christian missionaries, adherents persisted; in 1918 groups in Oklahoma incorporated the Native American church, which continues to unify Indian people today.

Off-reservation Indians took some initiatives too. By 1900 many young Indians had met young people from other tribes at the boarding schools. They came to realize that they shared difficulties, and a growing sense of Indianness began to replace local identities. A small group of college-educated people called for a national organization to speak for all tribes, and in 1911 they founded the Society of American Indians. Although divided over goals and methods, prominent Indians such as Carlos Montezuma, Gertrude Bonnin, Thomas L. Sloan, and Charles Eastmen worked to bring tribal difficulties to public notice.

Little would have been done to improve the situation had not the public become involved. In 1922 a major congressional fight erupted over the Bursum Pueblo Land Bill, which sought to strip the New Mexico tribes of most of their remaining lands. This focused public attention on the plight of the Indians. Alarmed humanitarians awoke to the desperate conditions on the reservations and demands for change became widespread. Long-established groups such as the Indian Rights Association, as well as the newly organized American Indian Defense Association, began a muckraking campaign against the federal government—and in particular the Bureau of Indian Affairs. Articles blasting incompetent and dishonest bureaucrats appeared in the *New York Times*, *The Nation*, *Good Housekeeping* magazine, and the *Literary Digest* in the East as well as *Sunset* magazine in the West. These publications described the Indians as being "shamelessly and openly robbed" by local officials who seemed to consider Indian property as "legitimate game."

The government took two actions. It appointed a Committee of One Hundred to investigate and make recommendations. Then in 1924 Congress passed, and President Calvin Coolidge signed, the Indian Citizenship Bill. This act gave all Indians full citizenship in theory but not in fact. The BIA still regulated many areas of Indians' lives, and both federal and local laws prevented tribesmen from voting in public elections or from legally buying alcoholic beverages. The Committee of One Hundred called for a further investigation, and in 1928 the Institute for Government Research published the Merriam Report. This documented in painful detail what reformers had only suspected about wretched conditions on the reservations and at the Bureau schools. More importantly, it questioned the entire twentieth-century effort to force assimilation on the Indians.

The crisis of the Great Depression gave the nation a chance to overhaul long-range policies toward the Indians. In 1933 President Franklin D. Roosevelt appointed John Collier, long a vociferous advocate of Indian rights, as the new commissioner of Indian affairs. The next year Collier lobbied successfully for the passage of the Indian Reorganization Act, or the Wheeler–Howard Act. Under this law the government encouraged Indians to reconstruct their tribes, adopt tribal constitutions, elect their own leaders, and form tribal corporations to work for economic progress. Proposed as a return to traditional Indian ways, the idea of elected leaders ran counter to existing Indian practices, and many objected strenuously. Nevertheless, fifty-eight tribes chose to follow this new path that same year, and most of the tribal governments existing today got their start under the 1934 Reorganization Act. At least for a time, after two centuries of trying to destroy Indian societies and to force tribal people into the national mainstream, the government accepted the idea that the tribesmen did not have to surrender their unique cultures to be loyal Americans.

ATTITUDES TOWARD ASIANS

While the Indians had been placed on barren reservations, other groups in the West, needed for their labor, had to be housed among members of the dominant community. The Chinese experience in the West created too much interracial friction to encourage further emigration. In fact, the riots and vocal hostility of the 1870s had resulted in the United States Congress curbing Chinese immigration in 1882. Nevertheless, Caucasians still shunned the menial tasks the Chinese had performed, and so other Asians were encouraged to replace them. The newcomers, first the Japanese and later the Filipinos, ultimately received no better treatment from the Westerners than the Chinese had.

Nativists repeatedly insisted that the Japanese workers lowered the American standard of living and that they could not be assimilated into American life because they were an alien race with inferior customs. At first the warning about Japanese immigrants attracted little support, but by 1900 the situation in California changed. Newspapers carrying headlines like "Brown Man an Evil in the Public Schools" and "The Yellow Peril— How the Japanese Crowd Out the White Race" fanned public hysteria. In 1905 anti-Japanese agitators met to form the Asiatic Exclusion League. This group drew its support from labor organizations and patriotic societies because it insisted that Japanese workers labored for lower wages and were undesirable citizens. In addition, League spokesmen warned that the growing power of Japan in the Pacific was a threat to American security. Some racists claimed that Japanese immigrants might be agents of a dangerous foreign power.

Opposition to the Japanese led to an international incident in 1906 when the San Francisco School Board announced that it was going to segregate Japanese schoolchildren, who numbered fewer than one hundred. The personal intervention of President Theodore Roosevelt and negotiations with Japan led to a rescinding of the order and the "Gentlemen's Agreement," which limited emigration from Japan. As the immigration subsided, anti-Japanese opposition declined somewhat in California, although the legislature did enact laws to prohibit immigrant Japanese from owning land, and politicians and patriots continually assailed them. Social and economic discrimination also persisted.

To some extent hostility toward Asian minorities shifted to the Filipinos, who replaced the Japanese as agricultural workers, especially during the 1920s. Although not American citizens, Filipinos could immigrate freely to the United States because they lived in an American possession. Their arrival in Hawaii and California led to antagonism, discrimination, and even violence in those places. Patriotic and labor groups said they took jobs from Americans and demanded their exclusion. In 1934 Congress settled the issue by passing a law that granted an immigration quota of fifty per year to the Philippine Islands until independence was to be achieved ten years later. In 1946 the Philippines became self-governing and its citizens were then subject to American immigration laws.

ATTITUDES TOWARD EUROPEANS

European immigrants, who constituted by far the largest numbers of minorities in America, also encountered much hostility in the United States. In general, however—although there certainly were exceptions—they received better treatment than Asians, Mexicans, blacks, and Indians. As the Europeans assimilated into American society and adopted American cultural mores as their own, they became indistinguishable from other whites. But until the assimilating process had eradicated their foreign ways, they did not enjoy the privileges of equal status.

Germans and Scandinavians, greeted at times with much suspicion, gradually received more cordial treatment, although World War I resulted in a torret of abuse directed at the Germans. The Irish, on the other hand, had a much more difficult time as many Americans continued to dislike them. One commonly used textbook in the nineteenth century warned that unless this country curbed immigration, the United States would become "the common sewer of Ireland."

The coming of the southern and eastern Europeans after the 1880s somewhat muted the prejudices toward the earlier immigrants, now seen in some quarters as substantial citizens, frugal, hard-working, industrious, and capable of assimilation into American society. The venom heaped on Jews, Italians, Greeks, and other southern and eastern Europeans rivaled the worst epithets borne by the Irish decades before them. The Italians, dismissed as "the Chinese of Europe," became the symbol of those southern and eastern Europeans who spoke no English and who

"blotted the native landscape." The poorest and worst neighborhoods in Chicago were described as teeming "with negroes, Jews
of the lowest class, and 'dagoes,' which term, as everyone knows,
is applied indiscriminately to Italians, Sicilians, Corsicans, and
Greeks." Called "wop" or "Dago" or "Guinea," the Italian was
assumed to be a criminal and an inferior being not fit to associate with "white" Americans. In many areas of the South Italian-
American children had to attend the segregated black schools,
and a common saying on the New York docks was, "One white
man is as good as two or three Italians." Other Europeans met
similar hostility. The Greeks were awarded the sobriquet "the
scum of Europe." A California restaurateur summarized his
feelings toward them in a pithy advertisement: "John's Res-
taurant. Pure American. No Rats. No Greeks."

Europeans were sometimes blamed for the ills and conflicts of
the cities and rapid industrialization. When strikes and labor–
management disagreements led to violence in the late nineteenth
century, old-stock Americans said that foreigners were bringing
radical and alien ideas to America and that the immigrants, not
working conditions, caused trouble. Following the assassination
of President William McKinley, Congress banned anarchists.
While blaming foreigners for labor problems, Americans also
said that the newcomers supported corrupt political machines in
the nation's growing cities. Some reformers understood that immigrants voted for the machines because the bosses helped their
adjustment to the new land, but other Americans equated mass
immigration with political corruption and insisted that urban
crime would not subside until immigration was curbed.

INTERETHNIC CONFLICT

With all of this rancor displayed toward ethnic groups, one
might assume that the minorities would have banded together
to protect themselves. Just the opposite occurred. Immigrants of
different backgrounds shunned one another, and often this behavior led to friction and hostility. Sometimes rivalries emerged

because competing groups sought the same jobs; at other times they were due to historical squabbles brought from Europe or served as a way for foreigners to take on the coloration of "real" Americans. Also important, however, was the fact that America so brutalized the immigrants in the lower classes that one of the few ways for them to vent their frustrations was to attack another group.

Of the early immigrants, the Irish seemed to have had great difficulty with almost everyone else with whom they came in contact. At first they even looked on Irish from different sections of the old country with malice, and American observers regarded them as "involved in continual internecine strife." Rivalries of "Corkonians," "Far-Downs," and "Connaught-Men" (representing different counties in Ireland) often produced bloody brawls. Later they abandoned such quarrels, joined together, and battled Czechs, French Canadians, Greeks, Poles, Italians, and Jews.

The Germans divided not only along religious lines between Catholics and Protestants but according to regional backgrounds as well. High Germans dissociated themselves from Low Germans, Swabians shunned Bavarians, Württembergers disliked Prussians, and so it went. Together the Germans snickered at the Poles and sneered at the "wops." In one Nebraska county there remained until the 1950s an "iron curtain" separating Germans from Danes.

The Czechs got on with the Germans but not with the Magyars, Italians, or Irish. They frequently attributed personal misfortunes to the antagonism from the Irish that they incurred in Chicago. The Czechs and Slovaks, who united to push for their own country in Europe, still were not completely at home with one another in America. Among the Slovaks themselves, Catholics and Lutherans kept their distance; both remained wary of the secularists. Croatians and Serbs in the United States engaged in numerous bouts of name-calling and fist-fighting when circumstances brought them together. In the Pennsylvania mines Hungarians, Swedes, Italians, and Irishmen bat-

tled one another; in cities all over America there was little intermingling among the residents of the many "Greektowns,"
"Corktowns" (Irish), "Dutchtowns" (German), "Dago Hills,"
or "Sauerkraut Rows."

In many communities the Greeks from Crete had to be separated from mainland Greeks and both of them from Italians,
Turks, and Slavs. Finns did not get on with Swedes or Montenegrins, while in some sections of the United States French and
German barroom brawls became major concerns to the local
populace. Like the Irish, the Poles had a reputation for being
"constant troublemakers." They fought everyone they came
near, including Italians, Syrians, Greeks, Slovaks, and Czechs,
and they despised the Jews.

RELIGIOUS BIGOTRY

Anti-Semitism, in fact, was the one prejudice common to most
of the European immigrants, and it surfaced among Americans
as well. Jews long resident in the United States also harbored
animosity toward their brethren from eastern Europe. The older
American Jewish community, originally populated by emigrants
from the Iberian peninsula and central Europe, feared the entry of the strange-garbed Orthodox Jews. American Jews worried that with the arrival of co-religionists from Russia, Poland,
and Rumania the latent anti-Semitism in this country would
erupt, and events proved them to be correct. Once the eastern
Europeans arrived, however, the Americanized Jews did everything they could to ease their adjustment to the New World.
They set up numerous educational and charitable institutions
and provided community leadership in affairs touching Jews in
general. The gentile majority, on the other hand, responded to
the influx by increasing its discriminatory practices, barring
Jews from clubs and resorts, from jobs and certain residential
areas. Most vicious, however, was the frequent harassment from
street thugs and bullies who beat up Jewish children, pulled old
men's beards, and hurled epithets at Jews in general. This hos-

A demonstration by the Ku Klux Klan in Beckley, West Virginia. The re-
vived Klan reached a peak of membership, estimated by some at around
four million, in the early 1920s. (*Library of Congress*)

tility toward Jews prevailed among Protestants and Catholics,
old-line Americans, and immigrants.

Antipathy toward Jews was never as virulent or as well organized in the United States as antagonism to Roman Catholics.
The death of the Know-Nothing party in the 1850s resulted
in decades of unorganized opposition to them, but in 1887 a
new anti-Catholic group, the American Protective Association
(APA), was formed in Clinton, Iowa. Dedicated to preserving
public schools and aiming to eliminate Catholics from what it
perceived as their growing "political control" of the nation, the
APA won the support of more than two and one-half million
Protestant Americans, mostly in the Midwest and the Rocky
Mountain states. It reached the zenith of its power during the

terrible depression years of 1893–94 and then, as one historian
of the movement writes, died after 1896 "for no apparent reason
other than that the times were not ripe for it to flourish." The
demise of the APA, however, did not mean the end of anti-
Catholicism; it waxed especially strong in the areas where the
largest numbers of Catholics lived, as well as in the Southern
and Midwestern "Bible belts," where Baptist and Methodist
fundamentalists dwelled and where frustrated politicians, like
Tom Watson of Georgia, stirred rabble enmities. Watson conducted an anti-Catholic crusade in his newspaper, the *Jeffersonian*, from 1910 to 1917. He considered the Roman Catholic
hierarchy "the Deadliest Menace to Our Liberties and Our
Civilization" and characterized the Roman Catholic religion as
a "jackassical faith." Thanks in part to Watson's outrageous
diatribes, a new Ku Klux Klan formed in Georgia in 1915. During the next decade it went on to become one of the most powerful anti-Catholic, as well as antiforeign, organizations in the
history of the country.

WORLD WAR I

In addition to Watson's fulminations and the Klan's bigotry,
World War I unleashed still more ethnic tensions. President
Woodrow Wilson asked Americans to remain neutral, but nat-
urally, with so many allegiances to the Old World and its con-
stituent peoples, they did not. Ethnic Americans had ties to
those they left behind in Europe and they tried to help compatriots there. But once the United States entered the war in 1917,
Americans were encouraged to view anyone or anything that
smacked of Germany and Germans with great distrust. The war
lasted less than two years, but the nativist feelings aroused
during the conflagration did not die quickly. Americanization
drives during the war turned into antiforeign debaucheries; and
after the war ended proponents for immigration restriction had
won enough support to get legislation through Congress.

IMMIGRATION RESTRICTION

It was not only the wartime hysteria that led to a rejection of America's historic policy of free immigration from Europe; nevertheless, growing xenophobia on the eve of the war gave Congress the impetus necessary to override President Wilson's second veto of a literacy bill in 1917. This act, which excluded from the United States those over age 16 unable to read a short passage in English or another language, was designed to keep out southern and eastern Europeans. The triumph of the Bolsheviks in Russia created pressures for additional restrictions, for Americans feared that foreign radicals would attempt to carry the revolution to America. Furthermore, anti-Semitism and anti-Catholicism were especially strong in the 1920s, and those who believed that southern and eastern Europeans were inferior and undesirable found increased support. American workers also worried that a flood of immigrants would depress their wages and take their jobs.

The time was now right for a drastic change in immigration policy. In 1921, and again in 1924, Congress passed laws to help curb the influx from abroad. In the first bill each European nation was allowed a quota equal to 3 percent of that country's total in the American population in 1910. Three years later the legislators reduced the figure to 2 percent and the base year to 1890. thereby favoring members of ethnic groups that had arrived before that date. The 1924 act excluded further Asian immigration and provided for the establishment of a commission to set permanent quotas. In 1929 a new immigration policy went into effect. Each European group was apportioned a percentage in relation to its total population in the United States in 1920 as well as to an overall annual immigrant ceiling of 153,714. The legislation had been designed to favor northern Europeans; consequently the British, the Germans, and the Irish received more than 65 percent of the allotted places.

Immigration restriction cut the flow of unskilled labor to America, but the nation's economy no longer needed so many

"You can't come in. The quota for 1620 is full."

Cartoonist's view of the national origins quota. By Hendrik W. Van Loon. From the *Survey*, 1924.

unskilled workers for its mines and mills. Even before the 1920s white-collar employment had grown faster than blue-collar, and many of the new clerical jobs were taken by women rather than immigrant males. Of course the nation still needed some unskilled and low-paid workers for agricultural, manufacturing, and service industries, but rural native whites, and, after 1910, blacks, Mexicans, and Filipinos, were available. During periods of labor shortages, such as World War II, special arrangements were made to recruit Mexicans. In more recent years many illegal immigrants, mostly from Latin America, have arrived to take low-paying jobs.

Whereas restriction drastically reduced immigration, it neither ended nor curbed American prejudices. The period between the end of World War I and the end of World War II witnessed some of the most blatant discrimination ever seen in the United States. Part of the prejudice remained as a carryover from the Americanization drives inaugurated during World War I; part was aggravated by the propaganda of the Ku Klux Klan and other leaders of bigotry like Henry Ford in the 1920s and Father Charles Coughlin of Detroit in the 1930s; and part no doubt must be attributed to the economic woes that visited most Americans in the 1920s, and especially the 1930s. But we also must emphasize that discrimination and hostility to minorities existed among the rich as well as the poor, the educated as well as the ill-informed, the old-line Americans as well as the recent immigrants. Although we can attribute some of the bigotry to religious teachings, education or the lack thereof, frustration with life in general, and economic deprivation, we cannot ignore the prevalent American view that had existed for centuries: America should remain a white, Anglo-Saxon, Protestant nation and all other people must either assimilate or be relegated to a permanently inferior status.

THE MEXICAN EXPERIENCE

During the height of American nativism in the 1920s hundreds of thousands of Mexicans migrated to the American West to take menial positions in agriculture and on the railroads. They met a fate similar to that of the Asians with one major exception—there was no significant movement to exclude them. In fact, great efforts were made by Southwestern growers and railroad magnates to prevent any quota restrictions against Latin Americans because their labor was in such demand. Agricultural production could not expand without the Mexican field hands, and the Western railroads found Mexicans to be ideal replacements for Greeks, Poles, Italians, Japanese, and other former menials who were now moving up the economic ladder. Once again, however, just as with other groups, economic needs did not lead to tolerance or social acceptance. Mexicans, even as they worked long hours every day, were condemned as immoral, irresponsible, and lazy "greasers" who had to be kept in their place.

By 1930 Mexicans constituted the largest minority in California and the second largest in Texas. Many residents of the Golden State believed, in the words of one educator, that they were "a menace to the health and morals of the rest of the community." In Texas, however, which was peopled by Southerners with strong attitudes about the races, Mexicans suffered more than in any other state. Theaters segregated them, food shops refused them service, and many public facilities barred their presence. One Texan called them "dirty as hogs"; another concluded, "They're just a dumb-bell people. . . . They drink too much, fight too much."

ECONOMIC DEPRESSION AND INCREASED TENSIONS

During the depression decade of the 1930s many Mexicans could not get jobs while others were fired to make room for non–Mexican Americans such as the refugees escaping the poverty of the Dust Bowl in Kansas and Oklahoma. As a result, a mass exodus occurred with the encouragement and financial support of both the Mexican and local American governments. The returning flow to Mexico in the 1930s was much greater than the traffic north.

For people who were unable or unwilling to return to the countries whence they came, the depression years were particularly difficult. As in the past, rampant job discrimination continued against Catholics and Jews. With a surplus of labor, employers could specify "WPX" (the acronym for white Protestant Christian) in job orders to employment agencies and in advertisements. Statistics on employment barriers against white groups are difficult to find, but some are available for Jews. In Minneapolis more than 60 percent of the city's retail and manufacturing concerns refused to hire Jews, and this figure may have been representative of the nation as a whole.

The end of World War I had inaugurated a period of hostility and discrimination against Jews that intensified through the mid-1940s. In the 1920s colleges and professional schools established Jewish quotas, Ku Klux Klan chapters spread hate, and Henry Ford started a campaign alleging a Jewish plot to establish a world dictatorship. Los Angeles, where Jews had participated in civic and political life until the early 1920s, systematically excluded them from elective office and leadership in community and cultural affairs despite their dominant position in the Hollywood film industry. In the 1930s Detroit's Father Charles Coughlin succeeded Henry Ford as the nation's best-known anti-Semite. Not until World War II, when the federal government importuned the archbishop of Detroit to silence the bigoted priest because his ravings were detrimental to the war effort, did the church curtail Coughlin's diatribes. But in Boston, where according to one writer the Roman Catholic church "could do more than any other single agency or institution" to curb attacks on Jews, the church did little. Boston toughs regularily beat up Jews, desecrated their cemeteries, and destroyed their property. One organization tallied 611 anti-Jewish incidents in Boston during the years 1942–43, and it took a New York City newspaper exposé to force the governor of Massachusetts to appoint a committee to investigate the charges.

The attacks on Jews, vicious as they were, did not compare to the difficulties encountered by some other groups during World War II. Blacks made economic gains during the war due to the labor shortage but still encountered prejudice and discrimination when they worked in the nation's defense plants and sought better housing. Nor did the traditional segregation and discrimination policies of the armed forces end, in spite of the need for manpower. In 1943 both Harlem and Detroit experienced ugly riots. In Detroit white workers resented the black arrivals and were egged on by white supremacists who assailed blacks. Tensions over jobs, housing, and amusement areas led to a riot in June when whites and blacks battled on Belle Isle, a recreational spot. Whites then attacked blacks in the ghetto and blacks in turn fought back. Before federal troops restored order, twenty-five blacks and nine whites were dead.

Mexican Americans were also the victims of injustice and rioting during the war. Seventeen Mexican youths were unjustifiably arrested in Los Angeles in 1942 and nine of them were convicted of murder by a bigoted prosecuting attorney, judge, and jury. It took two years before a state court of appeals overturned the conviction for lack of sufficient evidence, but in the meantime the Mexican-American youths had spent two years in San Quentin prison. Sailors rioting at Los Angeles in 1943 focused their wrath on Mexican Americans they met in what later became known as the "Zoot-Suit" riots, named for the mode of dress many of the Mexican-American youths favored. The worst atrocity during the war years, however, was perpetuated against West Coast citizens and aliens of Japanese ancestry, whom the government rounded up and sent to relocation centers simply because of their ancestry.

"CONCENTRATION CAMPS U.S.A."

The experience of the Japanese on the West Coast is one of the sorrier chapters in American minority group history. Despite the fact that the Japanese were frugal, careful, and excellent workers who initiated no "social problems," racial antipathy conditioned American responses to them. Alien land laws curtailed their opportunities for purchasing property in the West, and business firms refused to hire them in any but menial positions. Their scholastic attainments were quite high but highly educated Japanese Americans were often doomed to a lifetime of selling fruits from sidewalk stands or working for other Japanese businessmen. The law that supposedly protected all Americans worked against those of Japanese ancestry. On San Francisco streets those who tried to defend themselves from wanton assaults were arrested for disturbing the peace. An Arizona vegetable farmer summarized the feelings of many Americans when he said, "One person of Japanese descent was worse than one thousand rattlesnakes."

The accumulated venom toward Japanese Americans, who accounted for only 2 percent of the West Coast's population in 1940, broke loose after the Japanese attacked Pearl Harbor in December 1941. Although the nation had been drifting toward war in 1940 and 1941, the government had made no plans for military control of civilians, nor did the FBI have an overall internal-security plan. Once the war began, however, and while it was going badly for the United States in the early days, a demand arose for internment of Japanese Americans.

Californians feared sabotage by West Coast Japanese Americans, and the state attorney general expressed the belief that the fact that no sabotage had occurred did not mean the Japanese Americans were not still plotting! Many thought something should be done about the Japanese-American "menace," and in April 1942, in seeming violation of all constitutional guarantees, the federal government rounded up 110,000 Americans of Japanese ancestry on the West Coast and sent them to "relocation centers," or "concentration camps," as many critics labeled them. They left their homes and most of their possessions behind, and after the war the government paid them only a fraction of what their property had been worth. The rationale for isolating these Americans was, according to the army commanding general on the West Coast, that "the Japanese race is an enemy race and while many second and third generation Japanese born on United States soil, possessed of United States citizenship, have become 'Americanized,' the racial strains are undiluted."

The areas selected for the camps were in the bleakest parts of California, Arkansas, and the Western states. One evacuee recalled her first experience in Utah:

Japanese Americans, young and old, awaiting removal from their West Coast homes to the relocation camps during World War II. From the War Relocation Authority. (*National Archives*)

As I stepped on the ground, the dust came up in my face. This was Topaz! We had a hard time to find our home for the barracks were all alike. Topaz looked so big, so enormous to us. It made me feel like an ant. The dust gets in our hair. Every place we go we cannot escape the dust. Inside of our houses, in the laundry, in the latrines, in the mess halls, dust and more dust everywhere.

The other camps were not much better and some were worse. Another woman told of her camp: "We had to shower in the horses' showers, and the floors were filthy."

The Japanese Americans remained locked up for more than two years until finally in 1945, the government released them. In the interim many of the internees left the camps to take specific jobs where labor shortages existed; those eligible for the armed forces could enlist and many did. The Japanese-American 442nd Combat Team compiled an outstanding record fighting in Italy. In intense and bloody fighting the unit suffered heavy casualties and won over 18,000 individual decorations for valor. After the camps closed in 1945 the internees scattered to different parts of the United States; a few moved to Asia, but most returned to California to begin life anew.

The devastating psychological effects of interment left lifetime scars. Many of those who had been in the camps refused to talk about what had happened to them behind barbed-wire fences—even with their children and close friends. Then, in the 1970s, a movement began for the United States government to make amends—if any, indeed, could be made—for what had been done to the Japanese Americans during World War II. The efforts culminated in the summer of 1988 when Congress passed legislation offering some financial restitution (about $20,000 per person) to the survivors and their immediate families, along with a formal apology from the government for what it had done to these people.

The end of World War II marked the close of one of the most intense periods of American bigotry. Afterward, with the continuation of wartime prosperity and the end of wartime pressures, some changes occurred. States passed antidiscrimination statutes, schools and employers lessened their quotas and tried to change established patterns, and the federal government began to act to end discriminatory practices. The changes away from traditional prejudice and Anglo dominance marked a major shift in historic ethnic relations in America toward a growing tolerance and a greater acceptance of pluralism.

9

New Immigration and
the Ethnic Shape
of Contemporary America
(1941–1990)

DURING THE PAST FIFTY YEARS both the role and the status of American minorities have altered. Peoples already here saw changes that they perhaps had never expected to witness. To the surprise of almost all Americans alive in 1940, the flow of immigrants to this country not only accelerated over the pace of the 1930s but its nature and character differed as well. Formerly most Americans had European roots; in the 1970s and 1980s, however, over 75 percent of the newcomers traced their ancestry to Latin America and Asia. In the past, minorities were despised groups who were expected to know their place at the bottom rungs of society; today we not only encourage immigrants and minorities to avail themselves of opportunities to move ahead in American society but governments at every level have programs and agencies to help them do so. Moreover, whereas pre–World War II immigrants were told to forget their backgrounds and Americanize as quickly as possible, today everyone is encouraged to respect and glorify ancestral traditions and make them part of their lives as Americans. How these changes came about and what new policies and programs the United States inaugurated in the past half century will be the focus of this chapter.

World War II, with its need for military manpower and increased production, changed an economically depressed nation into one desperately seeking more hands. Those who had been underemployed got a chance to utilize their skills; those who had been unemployed found jobs; and those who sought expanded opportunities in other sections of the country were encouraged to do so. The war reduced the number of emigrants from Europe and American immigration laws almost totally barred people from Asia; thus the new menial workers had to be obtained elsewhere. Defense plants in cities like Los Angeles and Detroit recruited the Mexicans in their midst and sought blacks from the rural South (although 55 of the 185 war plants in the Detroit area hired virtually no blacks), while agricultural growers in 21 states, mostly in the South and West, induced the federal government to recruit Mexican nationals to handle the increased workload. At the same time the descendants of Europeans found greater opportunity as skilled workers in defense plants, in private businesses, and in the lower ranks of the American corporate world. The war, in fact, acted as the catalyst that pushed the children and grandchildren of early-twentieth-century immigrants into the mainstream of American society.

Wartime prosperity continued in the United States even after the conflict ended. In general the labor force was upgraded, with proportionately more skilled workers needed. Professionals and managerial personnel also found greater opportunities than they had had during the earlier age of rapid industrialization. As a result returning servicemen, encouraged by new career possibilities and the GI Bill of Rights, which helped them go to college, either acquired more education and went into the ranks of corporate America or, if they moved into blue-collar jobs, received credit for seniority based on their military service. These factors helped many climb from the lowest levels on the economic ladder, leaving menial jobs to be filled in manufacturing and the expanding service industries. Women had been heavily recruited during the early 1940s, when an estimated six million

left their homes to work for the war effort. Afterward many
returned home but soon they moved back into the labor market,
usually in low-paying, low-status jobs. In many cases they became clerks or secretaries in the nation's offices. Also, as in the
war years, the lowest level positions often went to blacks leaving
Southern farms, Mexican migrants, both legal and illegal, and
to a new group, the Puerto Ricans, who as American citizens
could take a flight from San Juan to New York City and start a
new life for themselves.

SOUTHERNERS MOVE NORTH

Rural blacks eagerly moved to the Northern and Western industrial regions. During World War II the booming defense industries lured them to the bustling cities of Philadelphia, New
York, Chicago, Detroit, and Los Angeles. Factory work paid better than farm labor and urban ghettos, despicable as they were,
nevertheless provided better shelter than rural shacks. When the
war ended the blacks remained in the North, and because job
opportunities continued to be good, relatives and friends soon
joined them.

Moreover, after 1940, the mechanization of Southern agriculture started uprooting farm labor. Demographically speaking,
it resulted in the greatest displacement of one segment of the
population—farmers—in the history of the nation: 20 million
Americans, a figure comparable in scope to the 30 million immigrants who entered the United States between 1880 and 1930,
were dislocated in the thirty years between 1940 and 1970.
About 16 million of these people were white; 4 million were
black. Planters simply tore down the shacks of their tenants as
the tractor, bulldozer, and cotton picker forced poor blacks and
whites alike off the farms and into the cities throughout the
nation. Mississippi had nearly 300,000 farms in 1940, but only
72,000 thirty years later. Moving offered the only choice these
people had; they were too poor to buy machines. Not even legislation helped; the New Deal farm subsidies of the 1930s went

mostly to the larger landholders. The federal minimum wage law of 1966 finally set a dollar an hour for some farm workers, but it simply speeded agricultural mechanization. As one tenant put it, "At first, the machines started throwin' people off the plantation and after the wage law came along that made plantation owners buy more machines and put more people off." From a peak in the 1920s when nearly one million black farmers owned 15 million acres of Southern land, in 1988 only 30,000 blacks still farmed in the region. Lamented one black grower in Arkansas, "We're just like dry ground in the wind: we're all going to blow away."

Overall the movement of blacks was striking. Over 1.5 million left the South during the 1940s and, although the rate slowed after 1950, more than 2.5 million more left between 1950 and 1970. The statistics on blacks in Boston and Philadelphia, two representative Northern cities, tell the tale.

By the late 1980s some Northern cities, like Newark, New Jersey, and Gary, Indiana, claimed black majorities. Blacks continued to migrate in the early 1970s and 1980s, especially to Western cities like Los Angeles and Long Beach, California. But in recent years more of them have been returning to the South than are venturing above the Mason–Dixon line. They have not been trying their hand at farming, however, but have been seeking jobs and homes in the area's rapidly growing urban centers like Dallas, Houston, Atlanta, and Birmingham. By the 1980s, moreover, cities like Atlanta, New Orleans, and Birmingham claimed black majorities.

Table 9.1

BLACKS IN TWO NORTHERN CITIES

	Number of Blacks			Percentage of Blacks in Total Population		
	1940	1970	1980	1940	1970	1980
Boston	23,679	104,596	126,673	3.1	16.3	22.5
Philadelphia	250,000	653,000	638,230	13.1	33.6	37.6

The movement south was in part a response to the decreasing number of jobs available in the North and increased economic growth in the South. These opportunities were a testimonial to the accomplishments of the civil rights movements of the 1960s, which will be discussed in the next chapter. In 1910 blacks were less urbanized than whites, but by the mid-1980s they were more so. Moreover, whereas 90 percent of black Americans lived in the Southern states in 1910, by 1990 about half lived in other regions.

Mechanization and poverty in rural areas were color-blind. Although rural poverty afflicted proportionately more black than white farmers, numerically more poor whites in the South were driven off the land. As did the blacks, these descendants of the old-stock English and Scotch-Irish also went north and west to defense plants during World War II and afterward moved into the automobile factories of Detroit, the rubber plants of Akron, and the many industries of Chicago, Kansas City, and Los Angeles. Many from the Appalachians lost their jobs as the coal mines shut down or utilized machines instead of men. Miners then left in search of employment elsewhere. Yet they did not always go to the big cities the way most blacks did; frequently they found places in smaller communities nearer their homes. Nor did they face the same discrimination in jobs or housing as did black migrants.

Some blacks and whites leaving Southern farms and mining regions found jobs in the growing cities and industries of the South. After the Civil War, proponents of a New South had argued that the former Confederacy should industrialize, diversify its agriculture, and build cities. Although Southerners did see a burst of industrialization and urbanization after 1880, at the time of the Great Depression of the 1930s the South remained an overwhelmingly rural region, still heavily tied to cotton and poorer than the rest of the nation.

After 1940, however, the American South at long last began to modernize at a fast pace. New industries sprang up, diversification and mechanization came to agriculture, and cities grew rapidly. By 1960 Atlanta, Dallas, and Houston, to name only three, were among the nation's major urban areas. The 1970 census reported that about three of every four Americans lived in an urban or suburban region, but in the South only two of three did. Thus a gap in urbanization still existed but it was nearly closed by 1990. Urban and industrial growth also enabled the South to close the income gap. Although Southerners were more apt to be poor than people elsewhere, wages had become more nearly equal. Traditionally wages had been about one-third less in the South than in the North, but the 1970 census indicated that incomes in the South were less than 20 percent below the national averages. By 1987 the gap was narrowed. Whereas the national median family income was $30,863, the figure for the South was $28,250.

To modernize, the South needed labor. During the late nineteenth century white Southerners had failed in their attempts to attract European immigrants, and the South remained essentially a land of old-stock Americans and blacks. So the industries of the region finally turned to their natural source of labor, displaced black and poor white farmers eager to move into the cities in search of jobs. As Southern cities began to offer more to blacks, many remained in the region. The modern South was even able to attract outside workers, and during the 1960s it made a net gain of population through migration. Many blacks still left, but trained and skilled workers sought opportunities there.

THE *BRACEROS*

With so many people leaving the farms and rural communities during and after World War II, there was a serious lack of agricultural labor, especially in Texas and the Southwest. As a result, the United States and Mexico signed an agreement in 1942 that allowed for the temporary entry of Mexican nationals into America. The Mexican government screened the laborers and then the American government placed them on farms, in fields, or in other enterprises where the need seemed the great-est. The workers also received transportation to their jobs, food, shelter, and medical care. Usually they earned substandard wages, although even those sums were greater than the men could have made at home. The agreements, intended to be of short duration, were extended, with periodic interruptions, through 1964. Over the years almost five million *braceros,* as these temporary workers were called, came to the United States. Although many growers resented having to pay the Mexicans first 30¢, then 50¢ an hour for their labor, the *braceros* rarely earned more than $500 a year.

More important than the *braceros* in Southwestern agricul-ture, however, were the illegal immigrants, dubbed "wetbacks," whose numbers probably exceeded five million after the 1940s. The *bracero* program may have inadvertently stimulated the "wetbacks." Many of those who came illegally had wanted to be *braceros* but their government did not include them. They knew, however, that work existed in the United States and they were desperate for it. Rural Mexicans were so poor, and there was so little opportunity for them at home, that they willingly took any means necessary to work in the United States. Ameri-can argibusiness interests, on the other hand, welcomed the cheap and illegal migrants. They could pay them even less than *braceros* earned, and since the workers could not complain about conditions without fear of being arrested and deported, the growers' profits soared. It is generally acknowledged that after World War II the "wetbacks" were the single and most impor-tant labor source for farmers in the Southwest. Some of the most unscrupulous employers allowed the "wetbacks" to work until just before payday and then informed the immigration officials of their presence. The migrants were deported to Mexico having labored hard but without any pay.

The influx of *braceros* and "wetbacks" who worked for low wages may be partially responsible for the exodus of many rural Mexican Americans to the cities. This migration began during World War II and has continued ever since. Moreover,

Attempt to smuggle illegal aliens in the back of a camper. The number of illegal aliens coming to America increased throughout the 1970s and early 1980s. Many walked across the Mexican border, but some, like this group, were smuggled into the country in trucks and cars and even campers. (*Immigration and Naturalization Service*)

many legal Mexican immigrants have gone directly to urban areas during the past thirty years. In 1989 an estimated 80 to 85 percent of the Mexican-American population lived in cities, with about one third of them centered in the metropolitan regions around Los Angeles, San Francisco, San Antonio, and El Paso. During the early 1940s they found jobs in various defense plants, later moving into garment factories, auto plants, and the building trades. They also obtained civil service appointments at all levels of government as another means of advancement. A minority of the Mexicans, or Chicanos, as some members of the younger generation prefer to be called, even moved to Midwestern farms, foundries, and factories. Since 1965 groups of them have appeared in Illinois, Michigan, Ohio, Indiana, Wisconsin, Missouri, Iowa, and Kansas.

FILLING THE EAST COAST LABOR VACUUM

On the East Coast black migrants from the South, American citizens from Puerto Rico, and European and Caribbean immigrants filled the unskilled labor vacuum, especially after the end of World War II. Of these groups the Puerto Ricans attracted the most attention because they came in such large numbers and appeared to be introducing a new ingredient to New York City's ethnic mix. More than one million arrived on the mainland from 1940 to 1970, and during the 1940s and 1950s more than 95 percent went directly to New York City. Because they were poor, spoke little or no English, and could obtain only the most menial positions in hotels, restaurants, hospitals, and light manufacturing industries, many New Yorkers regarded them as another despicable and dirty immigrant group. They resembled the immigrants of previous generations except for two characteristics: they were American citizens and they were of mixed color. Some were light skinned, others were extremely dark, and many were in between. On the mainland those who were lighter found adjustment somewhat easier than those regarded as "niggers."

POSTWAR REFUGEES

After the war the arrival of European immigrants to the United States ostensibly caused less fuss than had the coming of people from those same groups in earlier years. Few people publicly denounced the survivors of World War II who sought admission to the United States outside of the quota limits, but at the same time Congress moved slowly before making any special effort to assist those Europeans displaced by the war. When Congress finally did act, in 1948, the legislation passed specifically favored individuals of German origin and discriminated against eastern European Jews. In 1950, after Israel had become an independent nation and had opened its doors to all the Jews in the European displaced-persons camps, Congress amended the 1948 act and eliminated most of its discriminatory and administratively cumbersome provisions. As a result of the two Displaced Persons acts about 400,000 Europeans, mostly Germans, Balts, Poles, and Jews, arrived in the United States. When broken down according to religious affiliation, 47 percent of these people were Roman Catholic, 35 percent Protestant and Greek Orthodox, and 18 percent Jewish.

The United States government also made special provisions for individuals and groups whom the Congress and the president regarded as victims of "Communist tyranny." Following the abortive Hungarian Revolution of 1956, the United States admitted roughly 40,000 Magyars, many of whom settled among other Hungarians in New Jersey, Cleveland, or New York City. The two largest groups of political refugees were the Indochinese, who numbered almost one million entrants between 1975 and 1990, and the nearly 900,000 persons who came from Cuba. After Fidel Castro assumed power on Cuba in 1959, over 5 percent of the island's population, mostly the literate, educated, and the rich, accepted the welcome mat put out by the United States. Most of the exiles settled in and around Miami, Florida, with others going to the New York City area. There were some Cubans, however, in practically every section of the country.

Cuban refugees arriving in the 1960s were of relatively high social and economic status, and because of their marketable skills their adjustment to American society came quickly. By 1990 they constituted the majority of Miami's population and were well represented in business and professional positions. They even became bank presidents and began the Trade Fair of the Americas, which quickly attracted all Latin American nations as a showpiece for international trade. In 1985 the city of Miami elected Xavier Suarez as its first Cuban-American mayor.

The Cuban exodus of 1980 from the port of Mariel to Florida was somewhat different. When Castro announced that all who wanted to leave the island could do so, about 130,000 left by boat. Unlike the earlier refugees, these Cubans were of working-class background, and the presence of several thousand criminals and mentally ill persons among them caused considerable apprehension in the United States. The immigration authorities deemed several thousand inadmissible under immigration laws and interned them in American prisons. Hundreds of others later were convicted of crimes and found themselves serving sentences in American jails.

At first Cuba refused to take back these unfortunate persons, but finally in late 1987 the United States and Cuba reached an agreement on returning those in American jails or detention centers. Faced with the prospect of deportation to Cuba, several thousand inmates of the federal penitentiary in Atlanta and the immigration detention center at Oakdale, Louisiana, rioted and seized hostages; the Oakdale facility was virtually destroyed. After days of negotiation and promises of a careful review of individual cases, the rioters released their hostages and returned to custody.

The *Marielitos'* uprising in November 1987 was certainly one of the most sensational episodes involving post–World War II refugees, but most European newcomers had entered with less fanfare. After the failure of an uprising in Czechoslovakia in 1968, the United States admitted several thousand Czechs. Thousands of Polish emigrés found asylum here in the 1980s. From the Soviet Union, Armenians and Jews, numbering over 100,000, entered this country during the 1970s and 1980s. The main area of Soviet Jewish settlement was in the Brighton Beach section of Brooklyn, New York, while Armenians were more likely to head for California, especially Los Angeles, where in 1990 an estimated 200,000 of them resided. In the city's Hollywood section, two dozen churches and twelve Armenian schools helped bind that community together. In the early 1980s, as relations between the United States and the Soviet Union cooled, emigration from Russia dropped radically. In 1986 authorities allowed fewer than 1,000 Jews to emigrate, but the figure topped 8,000 the next year after United States–Soviet relations improved, and in 1989 our State Department permitted 25,000 Armenians and Jews to enter this country.

THE NEWEST ASIAN IMMIGRANTS

In 1965 Congress changed the basic American immigration law and eliminated ethnic origin as a criterion for admittance to the United States. The government gave preferential treatment to people with close relatives already here as well as to those whose occupational skills were in demand. The new policy began a major shift in historic immigration patterns and also substantially increased the numbers and variety of newcomers. From 1968, when the new law went into effect, through 1990 about ten million people arrived in the United States. Four million came in the 1970s; and another six million entered in the next decade. Most of these newcomers hailed from Asia, Mexico and the Caribbean, and other Latin American countries. Europe, which for centuries had provided most of the newest Americans, accounted for only 10 percent of the arrivals by the late 1980s. Clearly the nature of the recent migrations was changing the ethnic shape of contemporary America. Unless Congress radically alters existing statutes, current trends will continue into the twenty-first century.

In the mid-1970s almost one third of the immigrants entering the United States came from Asia, and by the 1980s that figure exceeded 40 percent. In 1985 over five million Asian Americans resided in this country and that number was expected to surpass seven million by 1990. Included among these people are Chinese and Japanese Americans, as well as sizable communities of Koreans, Filipinos, Laotians, Kampucheans (Cambodians), Vietnamese, and people from India. Just like the migrants of yesteryear, they scattered around the nation, but like other post–World War II newcomers, they found homes in California, New York, and Illinois. Los Angeles has already replaced New York City as the major port of entry, but New York and Chicago still get a disproportionately large number of foreigners. Unlike previous waves of immigrants from Europe, many of the Asians are well educated and many open their own businesses shortly after arrival. Large numbers of physicians and nurses have arrived from the Philippines and India, while Koreans have opened small shops in Los Angeles, New York City, and elsewhere. In New York City alone it has been estimated that 75 percent of the fruit-and-vegetable stores are owned by Koreans; whole families work long hours to keep themselves going and build a better life for themselves and their children in the future.

Although most of the Asians in this country entered by using the family unification provision of the 1965 immigration act, the circumstances which allowed the Vietnamese, Kampuchean, and Laotian refugees of the 1970s to enter the United States were quite different. Several waves of these unfortunate people, numbering perhaps one million in the 1970s and 1980s, arrived after the fall of the American-backed government in South Vietnam. The first group of approximately 140,000 left in 1975; several thousand more emigrated in subsequent periods. Then, in 1978, a new crisis developed in Vietnam and soon enveloped neighboring Kampuchea and Laos. Hundreds of thousands of refugees fled across the border to Thailand or escaped by boat to neighboring Southeast Asian nations. Many were victimized at sea by pirates, and others found themselves living in squalid refugee camps. In response, the United States began to take in large numbers of "boat people" and other stranded emigrants after 1978. The number admitted after the mid-1980s declined, but about 30,000 or so were still being received as refugees annually in the late 1980s.

The 1975 refugees, many of whom were Roman Catholic and well educated, were brought to military enclaves like Camp Chafee, Arkansas, and Camp Pendleton, California, while a variety of private organizations helped the government find them jobs and homes. Federal surveys have indicated that the heads of households among the first Vietnamese refugees were

Table 9.2

IMMIGRANTS, BY COUNTRY OF BIRTH: 1961 TO 1986

(In thousands, for fiscal years ending in year shown)

Country of Birth	1961–1970, total	1971–1980, total	1981–1985, total	1986
All countries	3,321.7	4,493.3	2,864.4	601.7
Europe*	1,238.6	801.3	321.8	62.5
Austria	13.7	4.7	1.9	.5
Belgium	8.5	4.0	2.6	.6
Czechoslovakia	21.4	10.2	5.1	1.1
Denmark	11.8	4.5	2.5	.6
Finland	5.8	3.4	1.6	.3
France	34.3	17.8	10.1	2.5
Germany	200.0	66.0	34.5	7.1
Greece	90.2	93.7	16.3	2.5
Hungary	17.3	11.6	3.7	1.0
Ireland	42.4	14.1	5.6	1.8
Italy	206.7	130.1	17.8	3.1
Netherlands	27.8	10.7	5.6	1.3
Norway	16.4	4.0	1.9	.4
Poland	73.3	43.6	36.3	8.5
Portugal	79.3	104.5	21.4	3.8
Rumania	14.9	17.5	16.8	5.2
Soviet Union**	15.7	43.2	39.5	2.6
Spain	30.5	30.0	7.6	1.6
Sweden	16.7	6.3	4.7	1.1
Switzerland	16.3	6.6	3.2	.7
United Kingdom	230.5	123.5	71.7	13.7
Yugoslavia	46.2	42.1	8.1	2.0
Asia*	445.3	1,633.8	1,376.3	268.2
Cambodia	1.2	8.4	70.1	13.5
China: Mainland } Taiwan	96.7	202.5	180.9	{ 25.1 13.4
Hong Kong	25.6	47.5	25.7	5.0
India	31.2	176.8	119.7	26.2
Iran	10.4	46.2	62.5	16.5
Iraq	6.4	23.4	12.9	1.3
Israel	12.9	26.6	16.3	3.8
Japan	38.5	47.9	20.0	4.0
Jordan	14.0	29.6	14.9	3.1
Korea	35.8	272.0	166.0	35.8
Laos	.1	22.6	97.4	7.8
Lebanon	7.5	33.8	17.0	4.0

Table 9.2 (Continued)

Country of Birth	1961–1970, total	1971–1980, total	1981–1985, total	1986
Pakistan	4.9	31.2	25.8	6.0
Philippines	101.5	360.2	221.2	52.6
Thailand	5.0	44.1	26.3	6.2
Turkey	6.8	18.6	11.4	1.8
Vietnam	4.6	179.7	234.8	30.0
North America*	1,351.1	1,645.0	835.7	207.7
Canada	286.7	114.8	55.6	11.0
Mexico	443.3	637.2	335.2	66.5
Caribbean*	519.5	759.8	371.6	101.6
Barbados	9.4	20.9	9.4	1.6
Cuba	256.8	276.8	58.9	33.1
Dominican Republic	94.1	148.0	104.6	26.2
Haiti	37.5	58.7	43.9	12.7
Jamaica	71.0	142.0	100.5	19.6
Trinidad and Tobago	24.6	61.8	17.0	2.9
Central America*	97.7	132.4	123.1	28.4
El Salvador	15.0	34.4	42.9	10.9
Guatemala	15.4	25.6	19.9	5.2
Nicaragua	10.1	13.0	14.3	2.8
Panama	18.4	22.7	15.4	2.2
South America*	228.3	284.4	184.0	41.9
Argentina	42.1	25.1	10.2	2.2
Brazil	20.5	13.7	8.7	2.3
Colombia	70.3	77.6	51.6	11.4
Ecuador	37.0	50.2	22.2	4.5
Guyana	7.1	47.5	42.7	10.4
Peru	18.6	29.1	21.8	4.9
Africa	39.3	91.5	77.0	17.5
Egypt	17.2	25.5	14.2	3.0
Australia	9.9	14.3	6.6	1.4
New Zealand	3.7	5.3	3.2	.6
Other countries	5.5	17.7	9.8	1.9

* Includes countries not shown separately.
** Europe and Asia.
Source: U.S. Immigration and Naturalization Service, *Statistical Yearbook*, annual; and releases.

fairly well educated, with a significant proportion having attended college and possessing skills that could be put to productive use in the American economy.

But many Asians who arrived after 1978, including the Cambodians and Laotians, had horrible experiences in escaping Indochina and were less well educated than the Vietnamese. They were reported to be having difficulty in their new land, and in the late 1980s a number of these families still relied on government welfare programs for support. Indochinese women seemed to be having a particularly hard time. They came from a culture so different from that in the United States that they were depressed by the immigrant experience. A refugee official working among the Hmong (Laotian) people noted that these newcomers had never encountered checkbooks, birth control pills, or modern freeways filled with autos. He concluded, "This is like Disneyland to them. It's like going to Mars and starting all over again."

THE LATIN AMERICANS

Like the Asians, the Latin Americans have surfaced in recent decades as a significant component in American immigration statistics. From 1950 through 1990 Mexico furnished almost two million immigrants to this country—more than the total number of newcomers from any other nation in that period. While these people were not necessarily the poorest Mexicans, they came to escape a bleak future in their own land, where there were too few jobs to support the rapidly growing population. (Even in the United States the Mexican birth rate is exceedingly high. From 1983 to 1985 there was an 11 percent increase in the Hispanic birth rate in the United States compared to a 3 percent increase for non-Hispanics. All told, 17 percent of the newborns in 1985 were Hispanics and two thirds of those children had Mexican mothers.) With little education and few skills, most found jobs in the garment factories of Los Angeles as well as in hotels and motels in the Southwest, and in a variety of low-paying service jobs wherever they went. Their impact on cities like San Diego, Los Angeles, Houston, San Antonio, Denver, Tucson, and Chicago was great. Signs announcing "aqui se habla español" appeared in numerous shop windows, but in many sections it simply did not have to be articulated.

Other groups of Latin Americans who faced acute poverty at home and migrated north included Dominicans, Haitians, and Colombians, who could be found throughout the United States. The bulk of them, however, located in the New York City area. There Creole- and French-speaking Haitians joined English-speaking people from Trinidad, Barbados, and Jamaica. After 1965 these immigrants moved to New York City in large numbers. The 1980 census counted 300,000 non-Hispanic people from the Caribbean in the city, and their numbers appeared to be growing rapidly. In 1988, one New York City official estimated that 6,000 to 8,000 Caribbean businesses were operating in the city.

Among the Hispanic Caribbean migrants, Dominicans comprised the largest element, about 150,000 in New York City alone, and perhaps a similar number scattered elsewhere. An estimated 80,000 Colombians gravitated to the Jackson Heights section of Queens. Central Americans, particularly from El Salvador, lived on Long Island. Together these immigrants, along with Puerto Ricans, now give a distinct Caribbean and Latin flavor to New York City, which also is known for its Asian, black, Irish, Jewish, and Italian ethos.

This Hispanic influence is not confined to the East, however. About twenty million people of Latin ancestry, a third of whom were not in this country in 1980, reside in the United States. Although a huge majority of them are of Mexican heritage and reside in the Southwest, other groups of Mexicans, as well as Dominicans, Puerto Ricans, and Cubans, have formed ethnic enclaves in the South and Midwest. Nine states have a strong Hispanic influence; Table 9.3 lists them and indicates the percentage of Hispanics in their population.

Table 9.3

HISPANICS AS PERCENTAGES OF STATE POPULATION

New Mexico	37.8%
Texas	25.5
California	23.0
Arizona	15.3
New York	11.9
Florida	9.9
Colorado	9.7
New Jersey	8.0
Illinois	6.2

Source: U.S. Census Bureau, 1986 figures.

RENEWED NATIVISM

The presence of so many new immigrants caused apprehension among those Americans who had arrived before World War II. While overt bigotry declined after 1945 and Congress and the president lifted some of the more restrictive features of our laws, uneasiness about immigration continued. In the 1970s and 1980s, the Civil Rights Commission and the media recorded numerous incidents of violence and interethnic friction. In Michigan, Dearborn's Fordson High School, where 40 percent of the school's 1,755 students were Arab Americans, conflicts continually arose. Bathroom graffiti included ugly slogans like "Kill the Arabs" and "Death to America." A minor fight in the cafeteria in 1984 brought both the police and negative publicity for the school.

The Mariel Cubans received much attention because of the criminals within the group, but other immigrants were singled out as undesirable as well. Some Americans even attributed the nation's serious drug problem to foreigners in our midst. Police and public officials noted that Colombians, Chinese, and other immigrants were involved in the drug trade, and they urged a crackdown on immigrant criminals. For a brief period in the mid-1980s, Haitians were seen by INS officials as likely carriers of AIDS and hence undesirable newcomers.

In the past various restrictionist groups had claimed that certain people were unassimilable. This charge reappeared in the 1980s and seemed especially directed at Hispanics. In 1981 Senator Alan Simpson of Wyoming insisted that "a substantial proportion of these new persons and their descendants do not assimilate into our society. . . . If language and cultural separation rise above a certain level, the unity and political stability of our nation will—in time—be seriously eroded."

Simpson and others believed that bilingual programs were not effective. They opposed electoral ballots in a foreign language, which were mandated by federal law, and they insisted that educational programs in other than the English language fostered segregation. Yet in most states not enough bilingual teachers could be found to help those immigrants who wanted to learn English. In the 1980s, however, an organization called U.S. English emerged with the purpose of making English the official language of the United States, which seems superfluous since English always has been this country's language. A number of states considered and passed such a proposition, but nowhere was the controversy so heated as in California with its large number of Mexican and Asian Americans. Hispanic leaders called the proposition "racist in character," but California voters approved it by a two-to-one margin in 1986.

The meaning of officially sanctioning the English language was left unclear. Two years later, the Los Angeles School Board approved a master plan for an expansion of bilingual programs and specifically provided for the teaching of most courses in the students' own language until they mastered English. The school board had its eye on perhaps the nation's most diverse student body, where over eighty languages were spoken by the city's schoolchildren. Of the 600,000 pupils in the schools, 163,000 were reported to speak little or no English. About 90 percent of these students were Spanish speaking, with Koreans, Cantonese, Vietnamese, Kampucheans, and Armenians constituting the minorities. Critics attacked the proposal as retarding assimilation, but its defenders responded, "It's clear now that academic progress must continue while students learn English. It's not enough to become English proficient but to fall behind in content."

The debates over assimilation and bilingualism will no doubt continue, but these were not the only aspects about immigrants troubling Americans. When the United States ended the *bracero* program and enacted a new immigration law in 1965, the number of undocumented or illegal entrants, which had been relatively low to that point, started increasing. By the 1970s undocumented immigration had become a national issue and it remained so in the next decade as well.

NEW IMMIGRANTS AND REVISED POLICIES

The immigration act of 1965 had opened the door for increased immigration, but those wanting to emigrate to the United States were far greater in number than visa slots available for them. South of the United States stood Mexico, a poor country with a host of economic problems. Because of these economic conditions, and because Mexico had the same number of slots as all countries after 1978 (20,000 annually excluding immediate family members of American citizens), thousands of Mexicans entered the United States illegally. By the late 1970s the Immigration and Naturalization Service (INS) patrols were catching over one million persons, mostly Mexican, attempting to cross without documents along the 1,900-mile United States–Mexico border annually. Other individuals entered the United States as students or visitors and stayed on when their visas expired. These included Israelis, Filipinos, Chinese, and a host of others.

One new group illustrating the diversity of the undocumented population appeared on the East Coast in the 1980s: the Irish. Prolonged economic difficulties influenced many of Ireland's educated young people to leave. One Irish publisher observed, "This country has denied a young generation of their right to dream in Ireland, and over 100,000 have now hawked their dream to America like millions of Irish before them."

Another growing influx of undocumented immigrants fleeing poverty and bloody civil wars came from Central American countries like El Salvador, Guatemala, and Nicaragua. As political refugees they sought sanctuary on the basis of international law and the 1980 Refugee Act, which granted political asylum to those who had fled from lands where their freedom might be threatened or where, based on race, religion, nationality, social association, or political opinions, their lives might be in jeopardy. The Reagan administration considered most of these individuals to be fleeing from economic rather than politically life-threatening causes and hence would not approve their presence in the United States. Some Nicaraguans, claiming to be refugees from Communism, were accepted.

As conditions deteriorated and violence remained common in the late 1980s, a growing number of Central Americans sought refuge in the United States. They traveled mainly from Nicaragua, but also from Guatemala and El Salvador, through Mexico and across the southern border of the United States. Once on American territory, they applied for asylum as political refugees. With visions of thousands of asylum seekers coming to the United States, the immigration authorities insisted that they must stay at their entry point in Texas and refused them work permits while their cases were pending. In early 1989 a federal judge nullified these rulings and granted the refugees permission to leave. Many did so, heading for the Miami area, the home of so many Cuban, Haitian, and Nicaraguan refugees.

Florida politicians did not want this latest immigrant influx. Bob Graham, a U.S. senator from Florida, declared: "Florida has suffered enough. We've been strained to the breaking point of crisis immigration. The current system is out of control and unfair to Florida." Miami officials did not have adequate housing for these latest newcomers, so some Central Americans found themselves living in tents in the city's baseball and football stadiums.

Friendly groups seeking to assist the refugees used the courts to delay their departures. Church leaders, especially in the

Southwest, were among those who founded a movement to give sanctuary to Central Americans in churches. Members of the sanctuary movement interpreted the law to favor those whose lives were in danger, but their position conflicted with the positions taken by the State Department and the INS. Two celebrated cases developed in Arizona and New Mexico with apparently different results, although the nuances of the law differed in each situation. In 1985 in Tucson, federal government officials successfully challenged church leaders who had illegally smuggled refugees into this country. The defendants received suspended sentences as the courts upheld the official position of the Reagan administration. However, circumstances in New Mexico in 1988 were different, and those prosecuted for providing sanctuary were found innocent on the grounds that the former governor of the state, Toney Anaya, had proclaimed New Mexico a sanctuary state in 1986, and the defendants acted on the belief that the governor's edict in effect legalized their decision to provide assistance to political refugees.

Whether claiming to be refugees or simply seeking economic opportunities, the growing number of undocumented aliens was perceived to be an economic burden. Political leaders said these people took jobs from Americans or used public facilities such as schools or hospitals, and hence were economically harmful to the United States. But experts and politicians could not agree on the effects these immigrants had in the United States, nor could they devise a plan to halt the flow.

After much debate and considerable compromise Congress finally enacted the Simpson–Rodino Act of 1986. One provision made it unlawful to knowingly hire undocumented aliens, thus removing the incentive—finding employment—for those entering illegally. A second clause granted amnesty for those who had arrived without proper papers before 1982 and had lived here since that time. A third aspect, which granted legal status for several hundred thousand who had worked illegally in agriculture, was a concession to growers, who claimed that without undocumented workers they could not harvest their crops.

Beginning in May 1987, the government gave eligible undocumented immigrants one year to apply for amnesty in order to become legal resident aliens and eventually United States citizens. About 1.6 million did so, a figure less than that predicted by INS authorities. The turnout was good in Los Angeles and Houston, but poor in New York City. As expected, the largest group was Mexicans. The claims of the vast majority of these persons appeared to be valid, but no one knew what would happen to those who had arrived illegally after 1982.

The sanctions against employers hiring undocumented aliens were just beginning in 1988, so the effectiveness of that part of the law cannot yet be determined. Amid reports that many undocumented aliens were leaving, employers complained that they could no longer find eager workers, but at the Mexican–American border hundreds of thousands of persons were still trying in 1988 to cross the barriers. Only the future will tell how effective the law will be in keeping out undocumented immigrants.

THE OTHER ETHNIC GROUPS

With attention focused on the most visibly different minorities, people often ignore the fact that groups of Europeans are still arriving in the United States. Statistics tell us that Greeks, Germans, Poles, Italians, and Irish are the most numerous, frequently settling, unnoticed, in the big cities. A 1988 news item reminded us not only of their presence but of how similar their experiences are to those who reached the United States earlier. An analysis of their impact appeared in regard to the rebirth of the ethnic newspaper. Not since the 1920s have there been as many new dailies aimed at immigrants. In New York City, for example, there are at least a dozen foreign-language dailies, not to mention three or four times that number appearing weekly or irregularly. In contrast, there are only four major English-language papers that New Yorkers can purchase.

The ethnic papers bear names like the *Irish Echo*, the *Polish*

Daily News, and the *Korean Herald;* no one needs to be told who reads them. But the *United Journal* appears in Chinese, *Il Progresso* is in Italian, and *El Diario* is printed in Spanish. Some of the newspapers have as few as eight pages; others as many as sixty. Circulation varies, but the *Polish Daily News* prints more than 20,000 copies a day and in the 1980s grew from eight to sixteen pages an issue. The newspapers serve newcomers who have not yet become assimilated, and their numbers reflect the increasing tide of immigrants to our shores. Even though statistics on immigration exist, exact figures are always hard to come by. The growth of the ethnic press tells us, however, that there is a hungry audience for the kind of information presented. And while it is true that Asians and people from the Caribbean make up most of the newcomers to the United States in the most recent past, New York City has carefully noted the significant presence of people from Ireland and Poland as well.

We should not overlook some of the smaller regional groups such as the Swiss and other Europeans in southeastern Ohio, the Portuguese in Massachusetts and Rhode Island, the Basques in Idaho, Oregon, and Nevada, the Cajuns in southwestern Louisiana, and the Middle Easterners in and around Detroit, Washington, D.C., Jacksonville, Florida, and Brooklyn, New York. Residents of these communities are aware of the ethnic heritage of their neighbors and in most cases take pride in the cosmopolitan atmosphere that different peoples living together provide. The Basques, who were best known as sheepmen in the Great Basin, now occupy positions in every level of society. Boise, Idaho, is still the most populous of the Basque communities in the West, but the group also exerts an important influence in eastern Oregon and northern Nevada. The Cajuns of southwestern Louisiana are the French-Catholic descendants of the French exiles from Acadia, Canada, who made their way south in 1755. There are rich Cajuns and poor ones and estimates place their population at anywhere from 500,000 to 1,000,000 people. Most of them are not "pure" in the sense of having had no admixture of ethnic strains: over the centuries they have intermarried with Germans, Britons, Italians, Spaniards, and other peoples. Today, however, anyone who considers himself a Cajun is one. The modern Cajuns try to preserve their own French patois, which they view as the basic ingredient for their culture. "If the language dies," one observer has explained, "the days are numbered for jambalaya, crawfish pie, and filé gumbo, for the *boucherie de campagne,* for feast days and festivals, for quarterhorse races, cock fights, and *jolies* blondes, and finally, when the assimilation is finished, for the very *joie de vivre* that sets these people apart and makes them special."

Immigrants from the Middle East, too, have been coming to the United States since the late nineteenth century, but their numbers have increased markedly since the passage of the 1965 act. Since the end of World War II, over 300,000 Arabs emigrated to America. Middle Easterners include Chaldeans, or Christians from Iraq; Palestinian Moslems, Yemenis, Egyptians, Syrians, and Lebanese, many of whom have been in the United States for two or more generations.

This mostly Arab immigration came in several waves after World War II. From 1948 until 1966, many Arabs were uprooted by the conflict between Israel and its Arab neighbors, and some eventually emigrated to the United States. Government figures recorded only a few thousand Palestinian immigrants in this period, but thousands of others came by way of Arab nations such as Jordan and Syria. Unlike the pre–World War II Arab immigrants who were Christians, these exiles were mostly Moslems.

A second wave from the Middle East entered from 1967 to 1985, in response to new Arab–Israeli battles, a bitter civil war in Lebanon, and the Iran–Iraq conflict. Many were Palestinians, though their countries of origin were listed as Jordan, Syria, Lebanon, and the Persian Gulf countries. Some experts believe that as many as 200,000 Palestinians have come to the United States since 1945. Like many other Third World immigrants, many are well-educated professional people. A prominent Middle East journal reported in 1983 that as many as half of all Arab science and engineering Ph.D.s had left the Arab world, many to emigrate to the United States.

Although a majority of the Middle Eastern emigrés were Moslems, a considerable number were Christians. These included Egyptian Copts, who settled in California and New Jersey, and Chaldean immigrants from Iraq. The center of Chaldean settlement is Detroit, with other communities in Washington, D.C., and Jacksonville, Florida. Chaldeans are unique among immigrants to America. About 70 percent are bilingual and speak English, and many are professionals. In Detroit they are frequently associated with groceries and milk and ice cream distributorships. Ironically, many of the Christian Chaldeans who left Iraq because they were afraid they would lose their identity among Moslems have settled in or near Detroit, the center for Arabic-speaking people in America.

In Detroit they encountered, among other Arabs, Yemenis. Yemeni immigrants are mostly men who sought jobs in the automobile industry as temporary workers, intending to return someday to Yemen. When the motor industry experienced unemployment in the 1970s and 1980s, many of these Yemeni workers found unskilled jobs in restaurants or as seafarers on the Great Lakes. They also opened shops to serve their fellow workers.

Only about twenty thousand immigrants from Iran entered the United States before the Islamic Revolution of 1979. However, after that upheaval emigration increased. From 1982 to 1985 over eleven thousand Iranians alone received asylum in the United States; thousands of others entered as regular immigrants. These included some Iranian students already in the United States and thousands of religious minorities—Jews, Christians, and Bahais—who feared for their fate in the new Islamic society.

One of the reasons that little is known about the Arab community in the United States is that unlike other groups of newcomers, past and present, it prefers anonymity and assimilation to ethnic cohesion. But this is changing. Journalist Gregory Orfalea has explored the unique nature of this phenomenon in his book *Before the Flames: A Quest for the History of Arab Americans,* which may help induce other investigators and scholars to expand our knowledge of this group. Moreover, relatively new Arab-American organizations like the American-Arab Anti-Discrimination Committee now protest ethnic slurs on their group and try to present the Arab viewpoint concerning events in the Middle East.

NATIVE AMERICAN MIGRATION

Like other minority groups, the Indians moved to the cities during the twentieth century. Veterans of World War I and a few thousand other reservation dwellers who had job skills began moving into the towns and cities of eastern Oklahoma during the 1920s. This migration continued during the Depression as the Bureau of Indian Affairs (BIA) increased its off-reservation employment efforts. World War II brought a marked upsurge in the Indian movement away from the reservations as an estimated 150,000 Native Americans joined the military, took defense industry jobs, or found other employment. Shortly after the war a terrible blizzard in the Southwest brought the federal government into the process of off-reservation migration on a large scale. In 1948 the BIA opened placement offices in Denver, Los Angeles, and Salt Lake City for Navajo young people. Within a few years this modest effort expanded into the relocation program, a part of Congress's policy of terminating its involvement in Indian affairs. The idea was to cut federal expenditures by getting people off the reservations and into the cities. By the 1960s twelve cities, including Los Angeles, Chicago, and Minneapolis, had relocation centers, and about 200,000 Indians left their reservations as part of this program. This migration produced a dramatic shift in Indian population. In 1950 only about 56,000 Indians lived in urban areas, but by 1980 that number had surpassed 740,000. Although many experienced major social and economic difficulties in the cities, by 1980 the census bureau reported that over half of the nearly 1.4 million Indians lived off the reservations.

For people from rural or small-town backgrounds, life in the major urban centers proved difficult at best. In theory the BIA job training and placement programs would ease their transition from reservation to city, and for some this happened. For others, city life proved impersonal, crowded, noisy, and unsatisfying. As a result many despondent, lonely, or unemployed Indians returned home after a few months in town. Rarely did they have the education or economic skills to compete successfully. Of the thousands who remained or returned to the cities for another try, many encountered the same problems as blacks or Spanish-speaking people—lack of housing, bad schools, high crime rates, and low-paying jobs. In addition, however, the tribal people suffered from a sense of personal alienation and a loss of the family and community ties many had treasured while on the reservation.

PROSPERITY AND MOBILITY

Most Indians, Mexican Americans, Puerto Ricans, and blacks have experienced great difficulties in overcoming prejudice and making sufficient social and economic progress to allow them to move comfortably in the dominant society. As a result, they have formed many organizations, especially since 1945, to improve their positions. This story, with its successes and failures, will be treated in the next chapter.

But for so many of the other groups who came to America, social and economic status have steadily improved over generations. Some immigrants were already making progress when the Depression of the 1930s devastated many families and groups. World War II then ended unemployment and afterward economic prosperity continued. Even Asians, who had been victimized by depression as well as racial prejudice, found wider opportunities. Economic growth slowed in the 1970s, with its high rate of unemployment and inflation, but in general the rate of economic progress in the period after World War II was high and brought many opportunities for whites and Asian Americans. Plant expansion, especially in the South, Southwest, and West, in such industries as textiles, chemicals, aeronautics, food processing, and oil created many new jobs. Yet the growth of the blue-collar work force lagged and by the 1960s more Americans were working in white-collar jobs than in blue-collar ones. Beginning during the New Deal and continuing after 1941, increased governmental employment in teaching, social work, and bureaucracies was also noticeable; by the 1970s about one sixth of all employed people worked for various government agencies.

The children and grandchildren of the immigrants saw these opportunities, and they also realized that education was necessary for mobility. So they flocked to the schools and especially to the growing colleges and universities. By the 1970s over 40 percent of the college-age population was attending some institution of higher education, and many of these students were the descendants of the new immigrants. By the 1980s groups like the Jews and Japanese sent about 90 percent of their children to college. Others, like the Italians and Poles, lagged behind. In 1969 the United States government reported that only 5.9 percent of Italian Americans aged 35 and over had completed college, compared to the national average of 9.8 percent. Among Polish Americans the figure was 7.2 percent. Yet it was clear in the 1970s and 1980s that the descendants of these ethnic minorities were flocking to the colleges and universities in larger numbers, determined to get an education and a better job.

The rising standard of living of the white ethnic groups and their movement into the higher-status occupations of teacher, manager, lawyer, doctor, scientist, and the like, began to change the ethnic basis of the occupational structure of post–World War II America. Yet the changes came slowly and the descendants of European immigrants, although better off than blacks and Spanish-speaking minorities, were by no means proportionately represented in all American occupations. Catholics were overrepresented in the blue-collar jobs, as trade unionists, and among the ranks of the lower white-collar jobs. Jews were twice as likely to be professionals as were other Americans, but at the top of the business world, in the large corporations that dominated American manufacturing and in the large banks, financial institutions, and law firms, WASPs still predominated. Only slowly and very recently did the doors at the top open. One could find a Jewish, Italian, or Polish name among the elite, but the breakthroughs were just beginning in the 1970s.

The decline of ethnic prejudice and increased opportunities for minorities continued into the 1980s. In the world of business, banks, investment houses, and law firms began to hire Jews, Italians, and other persons of southern and eastern European background. Various scholarly studies demonstrated that hiring and promotion were steadily moving in the direction of merit rather than WASP privilege. Prejudice by no means disappeared, but the trend was clear.

As white ethnic groups improved their educations and jobs, they began to move out of their urban enclaves. Just as the rapid industrialization of America in the half-century after the end of the Civil War was accompanied by the growth of cities, so the economic changes of the last half-century have been characterized by the suburbanization of the nation. Ethnic neighborhoods of course did not dissolve instantly or even in a matter of a few years; but in the late 1940s, and in some cities even earlier, one could see the beginnings of movement out of the ghettos and into the better urban residences and newer suburban ones. Older ethnic communities had changed drastically by the 1970s and the suburbs of the 1940s and 1950s had mushroomed. So great was the movement out of the cities that by 1970 more Americans lived in suburbia than in the cities.

The increased incomes of Americans made it possible for them to buy the new homes on Long Island, the shores of Lake Erie and Lake Michigan, or in the sprawling towns of greater Los Angeles. But changes in government policy, economy, and technology also helped disperse the populace. Through the Veterans'

Administration loan program and agencies like the New Deal Federal Housing Administration, the government stimulated the housing industry. The federal government also aided by enacting legislation in 1956 inaugurating the interstate highway system, which poured billions of dollars into urban–suburban roads. The automobile was a key factor in the suburbanization of America, for it enabled people to live and work in new areas and spawned the sprawling industrial parks and shopping malls.

Much of the movement to the suburbs may be attributed to the flight of middle-class white people, who did not want to live near the poorer minorities then moving into the older urban neighborhoods. Blacks and Puerto Ricans, for example, replaced southern and eastern Europeans in the ghettos of the Eastern and Midwestern cities while blacks, Mexicans, and newer arrivals from Asia found their homes in older neighborhoods on the West Coast. Some cities, like Los Angeles, almost defy categorization. The city is cosmopolitan in housing large contingents of Midwestern, Southern, and Eastern Americans and also numerous colonies of almost every European, Latin American, and Asian group that can be found in the country. Like New York City and Chicago of an earlier day, Los Angeles is perhaps the most popular immigrant city of our own era. It attracts the newcomers because of its spectacular economic growth since 1940, because of its climate, and because greater proportions of recent arrivals have come from Asia and Latin America. In 1970 the Commissioner of Immigration reported that in the previous year 50 percent of all the Mexican immigrants, 13 percent of the Canadians, 39 percent of the Filipinos, 36 percent of the Chinese, 18 percent of the Koreans, 16 percent of the Indians from Asia, and 20 percent of the Portuguese immigrants chose to settle in California.

RETAINING ETHNIC TIES

At the same time that newer elements jointed American society, older groups engaged in the dual process of moving away from and yet trying to retain their ethnic heritage. Many older immigrants, frequently their children, and sometimes the grandchildren could still be found in decaying urban neighborhoods across the United States. Some lacked the financial means to move; for others a strong sense of ethnic identity kept their communities alive as the people there preferred to live and work among others of similar background. The forces for assimilation had not overwhelmed the residents, especially the older ones, and the familiar shops, churches, clubs, and streets provided welcome signs and sources of comfort amid the pressures of a mass society. As one retired Polish auto worker, who had reached the United States in 1913, said of Hamtramck, Michigan, "You feel better here. I know every stone in the sidewalk. I could go to Florida, but everything would be strange. You feel at home here."

Those left behind in the older neighborhoods were less likely to be assimilated into the mainstream of American society. Thus the process of assimilation and movement, like the process of adjustment for the immigrants, was by no means an even one. The older colonial peoples were largely assimilated by the early nineteenth century, and the Dutch, English, Scots, Welsh, Scotch-Irish, and Germans who came after the Napoleonic Wars lost most of their national heritage before the 1870s. Although many of the first and second generation of the post-1840 mass immigration waves had lived in ghettos, which sometimes contained inhabitants of diverse backgrounds, they associated with and married their own peoples. Hence the Germans, Irish, and Scandinavians retained much of their heritage well into the twentieth century. Yet they too began to merge with one another, especially after World War I. For some this was a gradual process of the children and grandchildren going through the schools and finding jobs, homes, and even friends and mates outside their own groups. For others, such as the Irish, it took generations of struggle to obtain respectability and acceptance into American life. Nevertheless, by 1960 men of Irish extraction were well represented in the executive levels of major American corporations and John F. Kennedy, a descendant of Irish immigrants, won election to the White House.

Another indication of the change in immigrant culture and movement into the mainstream was the decline of the immigrant church. The churches, once the keystone of community involvement, disappeared gradually among European immigrants, except for a few in decaying areas of some cities. The nationality parochial schools have mostly been supplanted by strictly religious ones. Moreover, both the Jewish and Catholic religions have become more modern and ecumenical, less intolerant and defensive, and more Americanized.

In many areas, of course, signs of ethnic consciousness remained unmistakable among both those in the cities and those who had moved to the suburbs. Many Irish of Boston, Chicago, and elsewhere still remained in the cities and retained a strong sense of community. As late as the mid-1970s public demonstrations in Boston let the world see how strongly these communities felt about merging the neighborhood schools with black ones. In 1961 the Maine cities of Brunswick and Lewiston still contained French-Canadian majorities and one could find Scandinavian settlements in Midwestern cities like Chicago, St. Paul, and Minneapolis. Large colonies of Norwegians, Greeks, and Armenians are housed in cities like New York, Chicago, and Seattle. In Pittsburgh's Squirrel Hill district eastern European Jews and their descendants still retain the flavor of an identifiable urban ethnic enclave, while in the "Polish Hill" section of the same city residents rejected a Model Cities proposal in 1968 because they specifically did not want to "rejuvenate" their neighborhood.

Many of those who have moved away from their ethnic neighborhoods and who are indistinguishable to outsiders by their work, dress, or manner still retain an attachment to their heritage. They join societies like the Sons of Norway Lodges, the Japanese American Citizens League, or the American Jewish Committee. To census interviewers they proudly announce, as did 4.2 million Americans in 1969, that they are "ethnically

Polish." They promote ethnic festivals and celebrations, more perhaps as a reminder of days gone by than because of a strong present commitment. Every year Denver holds an Oktoberfest; Basques meet for a weekend in Elko, Nevada; Hungarians have their harvest festivals; Swiss Americans enjoy *Bundesfeier;* and Greeks orchestrate local festivities across the country. In the early 1970s New York City changed the name of one of the streets where Italians hold an annual San Gennaro festival from Mulberry to Via San Gennaro. Many Americans still celebrate St. Patrick's Day. In Savannah, Georgia, the city closes its schools on March 17, the local dairy puts out mint-flavored milk, and restaurants offer green whipped cream, green drinking water, and green beer. About half of Savannah's 120,000 people turn out for the annual St. Patrick's Day parade, which is second in size only to that of New York City.

American Indians are also involved in the celebration of their traditions. Many who live on or near the reservations, as well as those residing in the Indian communities in the larger cities, now strive openly to retain their Indian ways. In the past, isolation from the rest of society, particularly for the reservation dwellers, made this easy, but since the mid-1960s young Indians have overcome earlier feelings of inferiority about their culture. Thus from places as varied as the small Stockbridge community in central Wisconsin and the sprawling Navajo reservation in Arizona to Indian settlements in Los Angeles and Baltimore, the stress is now on cultural pride. In language, art, handicraft skills, medicine, and religious practices this determination to retain much of the old Indian way is growing. In major cities Indian cultural centers now offer tribal language classes or a place to learn music, dancing, or traditional lore. In many ways these cultural centers serve the same purposes a German-American club might in any large city. The Native American church also provides cross-tribal bonds for Indian people throughout the country. Indians now share their cultural pride with the rest of society through regional powwows and rodeos as well as a professional dance group and the work of artisans who offer a wide variety of regional styles and traditions.

ETHNIC GROUPS AND POLITICS

Descendants of various ethnic groups also like to see signs recognizing their accomplishments, their status, and their worth. One of the most common of these is political recognition. In the late nineteenth and early twentieth centuries, the Irish had a stronghold on most of the urban political machines. After World War II noticeable changes occurred. The Italians became the single largest voting bloc in Rhode Island and promptly elected the nation's first governor, and then United States senator, of Italian origin. Buffalo, New York, chose the first mayor of Polish heritage in 1949, and Maine sent another man of Polish extraction, Edmund Muskie, first to the governorship and then to the United States Senate in the 1950s. Throughout the 1950s and 1960s Italians received what they considered their political due: the mayoralty of New York City, governorships in Massachusetts and the state of Washington, and appointments to the cabinet of the president of the United States in 1962 and 1969. President John F. Kennedy also appointed a man of Polish heritage to his cabinet, while Ronald Reagan named the first Hispanic.

Since World War II the ethnically "balanced ticket" has become a political necessity in many states, reflecting the strength of the groups that live there. One story, possibly apocryphal but nevertheless reflecting the thoughts of so many politicos, circulated in 1962 concerning the desperate need of John Bailey, the Democratic political "boss" in Connecticut, for a Polish-speaking Catholic candidate to run as congressman-at-large. Legend has it that in interviewing prospective nominees Bailey asked each only three questions: (1) Are you Polish? (2) Are you Catholic? and (3) Do you speak Polish? He finally settled on Bernard F. Grabowski after eliminating another possibility, Frank Kowalski. The ethnically identifiable name is crucial, of course. Once Bailey came up with Elizabeth Zdunczyk as a candidate for Connecticut's secretary of state. She was of Irish ancestry but had married a man of Polish extraction, and as the politicos said, "the last name was what counted." In 1972 the first Cuban American received appointment as a commissioner on Miami's City Commission. The *New York Times* reported the "local power brokers [thought] that for the purpose of racial balance there ought to be a 'Cuban seat' on Miami's City Commission. The existence of a 'black seat' and a 'Jewish seat' on different elective bodies [in the city] had been taken for granted for many years." In 1975 one political observer found eighteen Jews, eleven Italians, seven Irish, four blacks, two Puerto Ricans, and one "other" on the forty-three–person New York City Council. The "other," Robert F. Wagner, III, son of a former mayor and grandson of a United States senator, was listed as being of "German, English, and Irish" background.

In some areas what is demanded is recognition regardless of balance. From 1925 through 1976 every governor of Minnesota (Christianson, Olson, Benson, Stassen, Thye, Youngdahl, Anderson) was of Scandinavian background. When Wendell R. Anderson resigned in December 1976 to take the seat Walter Mondale, the vice president–elect, had vacated in the United States Senate, he was replaced by Rudolph G. Perpich, son of a Croatian immigrant. Perpich regarded his elevation to the governorship as a political Horatio Alger story. He recalled that he was so much a part of an ethnic community in his earliest years that he spoke no English when he entered kindergarten in 1933.

Ethnic entrants into the political arena usually received a good deal of press attention, particularly in the 1980s. In 1982 Mario Cuomo became the first Italian American to be elected governor of New York; and when Walter Mondale, the Democratic candidate for president in 1984, picked a running mate, he selected an Italian-American congresswoman, Geraldine Ferraro. Two years later the voters of Maryland sent a Polish American, Barbara Mikulski, to the United States Senate. Jewish Americans have won election to the United States Senate from states with relatively small Jewish populations such as Ohio and Nevada.

The career of Michael J. Dukakis epitomizes the rise of descendants of southern European immigrants. Dukakis's Greek grandparents were shepherds and farmers. His father, Panos, immigrated to America in 1915 at the age of sixteen. Like so many Greek immigrants, he arrived with little money but a great desire to achieve success in America, eventually becoming a physician. His mother, Euterpe, landed in the United States at the age of nine. She attended Bates College in Maine and became a teacher. Their son, Michael, chose politics. In 1974 Dukakis won election as governor of Massachusetts, and in 1988 he took the Democratic party's nomination for the presidency. Greek Americans swelled with pride during the Dukakis campaign and donated a considerable amount of money to promote his candidacy. Declared one New Jersey resident, "It sounds corney because I'm Greek, but I hope [Dukakis] does the Greek people proud." Yet non-Greek ethnics expressed pride as well. As a New York congressman remarked, "We're all the sons or grandsons" of immigrants, "so there is a sense of pride in Dukakis as a first-generation American, even if he's not one of your own." Dukakis symbolized another trend in contemporary ethnic America: intermarriage. His wife, Kitty, is Jewish.

Japanese Americans, formerly one of the most despised of American minorities, found political acceptance after World War II. As memories of the war years faded, and as the second-generation Japanese Americans grew up and turned to politics, they won victories in Hawaii, where they comprised about 30 percent of the electorate, and in California, the state of historic hostility to these people. Hawaii sent Japanese Americans to the United States Senate and the House of Representatives, and California in 1976 elected a Japanese American, S. I. Hayakawa, as U.S. senator. In 1988 both Hawaiian senators were Americans of Japanese descent.

In closing this section we are reminded of the French expression which, roughly translated, means "the more things change the more they remain the same." Even as our country matures and older generations of immigrants blend in and assimilate with others in this country, waves of foreigners are always on the horizon to redo what others have done before them and suffer the consequences of being the new kids on the block. Individual friendliness can be found throughout the United States, but suspicions of what the future portends because of the arrival of one group or another continue as the descendants of the earlier immigrants and current minorities forget the receptions and treatment of their forebears and themselves. Bigotry and xenophobia wax and wane—what changes are the groups of victims and the assumptions Americans make about them. But, as we said at the beginning of this chapter, there is one major difference in immigrant and minority treatment and reception. And that is that both our government and most members of society, despite their prejudices, are committed to helping the newcomers "make it" in America in a way that had not been true before 1965. We say that we want the minorities to be "like us" and retain their heritage as well. A paradox? Of course. Only the future will tell if such opposite goals are both compatible and obtainable.

10

The Struggle for Equality
(1945–1990)

AFTER WORLD WAR II the Jews, Irish, Italians, Asians, and others who had been scorned, excluded, and victimized by prejudice found bigotry declining in this country. The growth of tolerance, however, neither brought about a cultural utopia where all groups enjoyed equal respect nor meant that the nation had at long last achieved an immigrant melting pot. Nevertheless, the bigotry so characteristic of American group relations lost some of its intensity. Economic prosperity, higher levels of education, lessening insecurities and tensions among religious bodies, growing contacts between various peoples, and the long efforts of those who had struggled to bring equality to America all helped to account for the developing acceptance of others to a greater degree than had been customary in the past. No doubt the fact that the descendants of so many immigrants had become Americanized helped to increase toleration, because they no longer seemed so different.

Before the middle of the 1960s, however, a majority of Americans did not or would not publicly support programs designed to ensure equal rights for all citizens. California abolished legal school segregation in 1947; Arizona granted Indians the right to vote in 1948; and in 1952 Asian immigrants became eligible for citizenship. In a dramatic and significant move in 1945, the Brooklyn Dodgers baseball team broke the color line in major league baseball by signing Jackie Robinson to a contract. But these actions seemed quite sufficient to most Americans in the 1940s and early 1950s, and discrimination continued, although not always in as crude a form as existed in the 1920s and 1930s. Robinson, for example, could not stay in all of the hotels that white teammates were booked into around the country. Detroit had over six hundred Jewish teachers in its school system but no Jewish principals. In California Mexicans could no longer be forced to go to separate schools, but Anglo attitudes did not seem to change. A graduate student who attended a seminar concerning Mexican-American problems acknowledged at its conclusion: "I've had a very entertaining experience, but as far as I am concerned they are still dirty, stupid, and dumb." On the national level President Harry S. Truman urged Congress to pass civil rights legislation that would ban discrimination on interstate transportation facilities, provide federal penalties for lynching, outlaw the poll tax, and otherwise protect the black minority in this country, but the legislators failed to consider these proposals seriously.

Groups like the NAACP, B'nai B'rith's Anti-Defamation League, and the Japanese American Citizens League challenged discrimination in the courts, lobbied for laws prohibiting distinctions among people solely because of race, religion, or national origin, and brought pressure on the media for favorable images of diverse minorities. At the same time, social scientists refuted the notion that one group was inherently superior to another. Yet progress came slowly. For a number of minorities, especially the blacks, Indians, and Mexicans, the changes that occurred demonstrated how much longer a road they had to travel than did the descendants of the European and Asian immigrants of another era.

THE DEPRIVED MINORITIES

Although the Asian and European immigrants and their descendants make up the largest percentage of ethnic groups receiving political recognition, in recent decades blacks and Hispanics have become the most visible of the minority groups. In fact, the term *ethnic minority* has often been used to denote blacks, Mexican Americans, and Puerto Ricans rather than any specific Caucasians, who are sometimes called *white ethnics*. The three former groups, along with the Indians, have constituted the most deprived ethnic members in American society. There is hardly a major Northern or Western urban area without its black and/or Spanish-speaking ghetto.

When earlier groups moved they abandoned the buildings to the poorer, newer immigrants, blacks, and Hispanics. For these people ghetto living brought innumerable deprivations. To begin with most of the housing left to the blacks and Latin Americans was old and run-down. Although residences in the United States generally improved during the building boom after World War II, blacks and recent immigrants lived in inferior dwellings, and in many inner-city wards blight is common. Rat-infested buildings, falling plaster, broken windows, malfunctioning heating, and poor maintenance are characteristic of black and Spanish-speaking urban areas. Children who eat the paint in the older buildings contract lead poisoning. Neither building codes nor their enforcement, which is often unreliable, is able to arrest the urban decay.

In the 1930s the federal government embarked on programs to improve the nation's housing. Since then the Federal Housing Administration and the Veterans' Administration have aided millions in purchasing their own homes. Unfortunately, the vast majority of these houses were constructed in suburbs and many were too expensive for the poorest minorities. Those blacks and Hispanics who could afford their purchase encountered discrimination from banks, mortgage companies, or real-

The Biddle Alley district of the black ghetto of Baltimore, 1910. (*State Historical Society of Wisconsin*)

tors, and for many years the federal government tacitly allowed these practices.

Slum-clearance programs, sometimes called urban renewal, had a more direct impact on the nation's ghettos. Beginning modestly in the 1930s, the federal bulldozer tore down many old, decaying neighborhoods and replaced them with public housing projects. But it also cleared the way for expressways and municipal projects like New York City's Lincoln Center. Moreover, in many of the razed areas there arose expensive apartments, priced well beyond the means of the urban poor. Hence the various programs were sometimes known as "Negro removal." After the 1949 urban renewal bill was passed the

The black ghetto of Milwaukee, 1968–1969. (*Milwaukee Journal, State Historical Society of Wisconsin*)

federal government tore down more housing for the poor than it built.

The ghetto-dwelling black and Spanish-speaking Americans also suffered from poor health, high crime rates, and drug addiction. Blacks did make gains in health in the 1940s and 1950s, but they still used fewer medical services than whites did and visited physicians and dentists less frequently. Living in areas such as the rural South, migrant camps, or the inner cities, where treatment facilities were lacking or usually inferior, blacks and Hispanic Americans were at a disadvantage. Better facilities existed in the cities than in rural America, but in the cities medical care often cost too much for the poor.

If receiving adequate medical care was a problem, so, too, was crime. The incidence of assaults was more frequent in the inner-city black and Spanish-speaking neighborhoods than elsewhere.

Increasing police patrols failed to halt the growth of crime, and the presence of the police, important as they were for fighting crime, proved a source of difficulty. Relations between these ethnic minorities and the police in many neighborhoods were fraught with misunderstandings and conflicts. Charges of police brutality and the breakdown of communications between the police and the community triggered more than one riot in the 1960s. Related to crime was narcotics addiction. Like the indexes of crime, drug addiction was higher in the ghettos than in other neighborhoods.

The problems facing the urban poor were multifaceted and in turn closely related to economics and racism. So many of the difficulties—poor housing, poor health, higher crime rates—were generally common to people with little money. Certainly blacks and Spanish-speaking Americans made some economic progress after 1940, but they still suffered from lack of money.

Not all black and Spanish-speaking poor lived in the cities. In the rural South, black families struggled to make a decent living while migrant workers—Mexican Americans in the Southwest and Puerto Ricans and blacks in the East—were among the nation's most indigent families.

Of course, not all blacks and Hispanics were impoverished; many had pulled themselves into the middle class. Among the Spanish-speaking minorities the Cubans were perhaps the most successful. Although they arrived in America with little and frequently at first had to live on welfare benefits, they made rapid strides in the years after their arrival. They moved quickly up the economic ladder in the Miami region and became proprietors of shops, construction workers, and even successful bankers. The second generation was quick to learn in schools and pursued education with great enthusiasm. A number of Mexican-American families in California, New Mexico, and elsewhere in the Southwest also prospered and lead lives similar to those of other middle- and upper-class Americans. The same, of course, is true for many Puerto Ricans. Among the blacks a substantial middle class has emerged since World War

II. In the South, for example, only 2 percent of the black families earned $15,000 a year or more in 1964, while a decade later 13 percent did. In the same period the number of black families earning $10,000 a year or more increased from 9 to 31 percent. Despite these figures, however, there were substantially more blacks and Hispanic Americans living in want than there were living prosperously on the eve of the civil rights movement of the 1960s.

TOWARD CIVIL RIGHTS

In spite of these modest gains, blacks—and later Hispanics and American Indians—took to the streets, the courts, and the halls of Congress and state legislatures to win their rights. The conflicts escalated in the 1950s and gained steam in the 1960s, making that decade an era of struggle for equality.

Black Americans had protested against discrimination and segregation long before then. At the turn of the century they mounted local boycotts against segregated schools and Southern transportation facilities, but these efforts failed. The National Association for the Advancement of Colored People (NAACP), founded in 1909, was active from its first days fighting racism. The Association lobbied for an antilynching bill in Congress during the 1920s and 1930s but failed to get the legislators' votes or presidential support. Blacks won some gains during the New Deal, but not a civil rights program. During World War II, however, they threatened public protests. A. Philip Randolph, head of the Brotherhood of Sleeping Car Porters, warned Franklin D. Roosevelt that he would lead a massive March on Washington unless presidential action was taken to prevent discrimination in the nation's defense industries. Roosevelt, fearing wartime disunity, ordered the creation of a Fair Employment Practices Commission (FEPC) to prevent job discrimination. The FEPC, however, lacked real power and therefore its effectiveness was limited.

In the 1940s, and even before, some white Americans had

become more receptive to the concept of equality. Sociologists, anthropologists, and psychologists increasingly stressed the role of environment—the schools, the home, the neighborhood, and racial discrimination—in explaining differences in IQ tests and academic achievement. Historians also rediscovered the black past, in both Africa and the United States, and noted the many contributions that blacks had made to the growth of America. These notions, which slowly made their way into the media, the schools, popular journals, and political and religious rhetoric, were perhaps best exemplified in Gunnar Myrdal's *An American Dilemma* (1944). In this classic study the author painted a picture of blacks caught in a vicious circle. Whites used black poverty to argue that blacks were inferior and therefore justified fewer opportunities for them, which in turn guaranteed continued poverty. Books like *An American Dilemma* demonstrated that the effects of segregation and poverty were devastating, but most white Americans neither realized how outrageous conditions for blacks were nor had any intention of doing much about them.

To achieve racial equality blacks fought zealously in the courts, in the political arena, and ultimately in the streets. Much of their effort was directed at the federal government, and they attempted to utilize the government to win equality. This was a practical strategy because in the twentieth century the federal government's power had grown steadily and it exerted immense influence on American society. Various reform groups had sought to use federal power to achieve their ends, beginning with farmers during the Populist upheavals of the late nineteenth century. The Populists were largely unsuccessful, but the Progressives did enact some laws aimed at dealing with the social problems of the modern industrial and urban society. Social reform was out of fashion during the 1920s, but when the nation plunged into a prolonged depression after that decade's relative prosperity, many eyes looked again to the nation's capitol for action. Little wonder that they did so; state, local, and private sources of relief were drying up and about one quarter of all workers were out of work when Franklin Roosevelt took the oath of office on March 4, 1933. Not only were the lines of the unemployed long and business conditions horrendous, but the banking system had come to standstill.

Roosevelt's New Deal enacted many measures aimed at economic recovery and relief. The banks were closed, then helped; businesses, homeowners, and farmers were subsidized; and state and local communities were aided with their relief problems. The federal government also employed many of the jobless in constructing schools, roads, parks, and various public buildings. But the New Deal did not stop at recovery and relief; it attempted to reform the social and economic system. The stock market was regulated by the Securities Exchange Commission, and other businesses were brought under some degree of federal control. The Wagner Act gave labor the right to organize; the Social Security system inaugurated old-age pensions and unemployment insurance; and the Fair Labor Standards Act established minimum wages and outlawed child labor.

The power of the federal government was awesome during World War II, when it mobilized the nation to fight the Axis powers. After the war the government, with its large military budget and growing social programs, continued its involvement with the economy. Many groups thus turned to Washington for subsidies and regulation. And so did blacks.

Black Americans had benefited from the New Deal relief programs, although the Roosevelt administration did not seriously tackle the problems of racial discrimination and segregation. But black Americans after the war saw that federal power could be used to help them, and they had special reasons for seeking to enlist it in their cause. The federal government had destroyed slavery, and during the Reconstruction period it was federal power that attempted briefly, and ultimately unsuccessfully, to bring racial equality to the South. After the failure of Reconstruction it was the state and local governments that segregated blacks and discriminated against them. Consequently, many black leaders came to believe that the federal government could be used to destroy racism.

The NAACP concentrated on lobbying and legal action. In a series of cases the Association persuaded the federal courts to outlaw discriminatory election procedures and ban segregated schools, housing, transportation facilities, and recreational areas. The most significant as well as the most famous of the many victories was the school desegregation case, *Brown* vs. *Board of Education* (1954), in which the United States Supreme Court declared the "separate-but-equal" facilities in public schools inherently unequal and therefore in violation of the Fourteenth Amendment to the Constitution, which guarantees each citizen "equal protection of the laws."

The importance of the *Brown* vs. *Board of Education* ruling cannot be overstated, but it had little meaning until enforced. The Court had urged desegregation with "all deliberate speed," but ten years later few Southern schools had complied.

School desegregation, furthermore, was only one, albeit an important one, of the changes necessary on the road to social and economic equality. A. Philip Randolph's announced March on Washington had demonstrated the power of a threat of disruptive action, but in 1955 the arrest of a black woman in Montgomery, Alabama, for refusing to relinquish her bus seat to a white man, afforded the opportunity to use coercive measures constructively and pointed the way to a new strategy combating racism. A newcomer to the community, the Reverend Martin Luther King, Jr., led in galvanizing the blacks and organizing a boycott of all of Montgomery's public buses. After a year the protest succeeded, the city's buses were desegregated, and King became a hero in the civil rights movement. The Montgomery bus boycott also resulted in the organization of the Southern Christian Leadership Conference (SCLC) and King's rise to national prominence.

In the spring of 1960 black students continued the process of nonviolent demonstrations against segregation when they staged

Civil rights pickets in Florida, August 1960. (*CORE, State Historical Society of Wisconsin*)

sit-ins at lunch counters throughout the South. They maintained that they would sit peacefully until served at food outlets that catered only to whites. As the sit-ins spread, and as demonstrators were arrested, Southern college students formed the Student Non-Violent Coordinating Committee (SNCC) to coordinate their activities. The sit-ins captured the imagination of the black community even more than had the bus boycott, and thus began a decade of intense activity to desegregate America.

Through the 1960s blacks held demonstrations against existing inequalities. In 1961 college youths went on integrated buses, popularly known as "Freedom Rides," to protest segregated facilities in interstate transportation. Their actions resulted in violence from Southern whites and national media coverage. More and more people began to believe federal legislation was necessary to prevent outbursts of violence during peaceful demonstrations: the protesters had to be protected! White Southern wrath came to the fore again in May 1963 when, with massive demonstrations, SNCC and King protested segregation in Birmingham, Alabama. The local police responded with firehoses, sharp-fanged German shepherds, and arrests of peaceful participants. As a result of police and popular brutality in Birmingham, which the news media publicized nationally, President John F. Kennedy went before Congress to demand the passage of stringent federal legislation to protect the rights of all Americans. Civil rights laws had been enacted in 1957 and 1960, but their provisions were limited. Congress did not immediately respond to the president's request, but after Kennedy's assassination, and under the forceful prodding of President Lyndon B. Johnson, it enacted the 1964 Civil Rights Act. This law banned discrimination in public accommodations, created a federal fair employment practices agency, protected the right of all adult Americans to vote, and gave the executive branch the power to cut off funds to state and local agencies that practiced racial discrimination.

Desegregation of public accommodations was an issue most white Northerners could support. Public places in the North had generally been open to blacks since the 1940s, and in many cases before that, and the brutal way in which white Southerners resisted integration shocked many other Americans. The specter of firehoses and dogs being turned loose on blacks was especially appalling. Liberal churches and the labor unions had already begun to support desegregation before the Birmingham incident. Together with other interested activists they joined the blacks in a massive March on Washington in August 1963 to urge federal action; collectively they threw their weight behind the movement for the new Civil Rights Act of 1964.

The new law did not end racial discrimination, for there still remained the issue of enforcement. Gradually, however, the South integrated public facilities, although some communities chose to close their beaches or swimming pools rather than accommodate both races together. Yet blacks still had to face the problems of poor housing, inadequate employment opportunities, and lack of political power.

Voting registration drives, spearheaded by SNCC and SCLC and supported by white liberals, led to an increase in black suffrage. Actually the number of Southern blacks exercising the franchise had grown considerably since the end of World War II. But the proportion voting in the mid-1960s in Alabama, Mississippi, Louisiana, Georgia, and South Carolina was considerably less than it was for whites. Direct federal intervention was required to ensure minority suffrage. Some blacks concentrated on community action while others tried to work through the Democratic party and Congress. Martin Luther King, Jr., dramatized the problem at Selma, Alabama, in 1965, and once again Congress responded by passing a more effective voting rights law.

Ultimately the civil rights movement changed the South, but civil rights laws did little for residents of Northern cities. For them there was the War on Poverty of the 1960s. Programs like Model Cities, Job Corps Training, Operation Head Start, and the various activities of the Office of Economic Opportunity aimed to help the nation's poor—and since blacks made up a disproportionate share of this group, they stood to benefit. The effects of the War on Poverty were limited, however, and some programs were phased out in the 1970s, casualties of inadequate funding and the war in Vietnam. But other governmental policies, such as the Social Security program, with its expanded benefits, the Veterans' Administration programs, the Food Stamp program, and welfare, all aided lower-income blacks. These programs grew in the late 1960s and 1970s, even during the administrations of Richard Nixon and Gerald Ford, who were not sympathetic to the notion of a "war" on poverty. During the last year of Ford's presidency the federal government spent more than $400 billion dollars, over half of it in programs for human resources.

The Reagan administration wanted to cut or eliminate many of these programs, but Congress resisted. As a result, although there were cuts in appropriations for low-income families' educational, housing, and nutritional needs, the federal government still provided many benefits as the Reagan years came to an end.

In addition to developing federal programs to aid poor blacks, the government also tried to put its own house in order, but the results were often mixed. One of the first federal institutions to act, the military, began to desegregate during the Truman administration. The Korean and Vietnam wars hastened the process, and the military desegregated faster than many other institutions in American society. Yet problems remained. In the post-Vietnam volunteer army of the 1970s about one quarter of those in service were black, whereas only 6 percent of the officers were. One black major complained, "Folks talk about the new, modern Army but black men still get lousy efficiency reports because they're black, they still get jobs that are not exactly career-enhancing. In order to be competitive you have to do twice as well, have to be a 'super spade.' " While complaints about promotions and assignments were uttered by black soldiers, racial tension in the 1960s and 1970s occasionally erupted into violence on army posts and at sea. In the late 1970s and 1980s the army embarked on race relations programs to improve conditions and to promote blacks more rapidly. For example, under the Carter administration the secretary of the army, Clifford L. Alexander, was black. Even the best efforts to create harmony had limitations. One soldier noted, "You can be the best of buddies with someone during the day, but when it's nighttime, forget it. I've been to parties where a guy I've worked with has even refused to introduce me to his wife."

THE MOVEMENT FOR BLACK POWER

Neither the federal government nor its programs eliminated poverty. Consequently many blacks began to lose faith in the legalistic and nonviolent approach to solving their problems.

Those living in the ghettos wanted something more immediate and concrete. The civil rights legislation of the 1960s may have ensured Martin Luther King, Jr., accommodations at any Holiday Inn in America and given voting rights to blacks who had never before exercised the franchise, but the laws did not feed the hungry, educate the poor, or provide jobs for the unemployed. At the Democratic party's national convention in 1964, furthermore, the majority refused to seat the black representatives who had been elected in Mississippi and instead recognized the group that had been chosen by a "lilywhite" gathering in the state. That single action, combined with previous experiences with white liberals who tried to "uplift" Southern blacks by taking over "tasks, conversations, meetings, and publicity that should have been handled by Negroes," convinced many to reject the goal of desegregation; they now insisted on equality with the preservation of black culture and values under the guidance of black leadership. Certainly, too, black leaders were aware of the racial stirrings in Africa and the rise of Third World consciousness in the 1960s. Some blacks were also aware of the role of black nationalism and black culture in American history, from the back-to-Africa movements of the nineteenth century to the literary movement known as the Harlem Renaissance and the political and economic programs of Marcus Garvey in the 1920s. Stokely Carmichael, the leader of SNCC, perhaps expressed the group's views best when he said that what was needed was "Black Power." The expression signified different things to different blacks, but it conveyed to all of them what they wanted but lacked—power!

Many white liberals thereafter either became preoccupied with the Vietnamese war or lost interest in the civil rights movement because they did not feel at home with burgeoning black nationalism. White ethnic minorities, who had sympathized with some of the civil rights goals, increasingly felt threatened by people who wanted absolute equality in housing, schooling, jobs, and leadership positions in society. Thus just at the moment of its greatest legislative achievements, in the mid-1960s, the civil rights movement began to disintegrate. Old-line civil rights groups like the National Urban League and the NAACP continued their activities, but the main thrust of the movement was blunted by the end of the decade.

Militants took over SNCC and the Congress of Racial Equality (CORE), an interracial group founded in the 1940s, but these two organizations were very weak and had few followers. A more important group was the Nation of Islam, a black religious body that rejected Christianity and looked to the Middle East instead for inspiration. Founded in the 1930s, the Nation grew slowly at first, then became stronger in the 1960s under the leadership of Elijah Muhammad and the dynamic Malcolm X. Malcolm broke with the Black Muslims, as the followers of the Nation were called, and began an independent movement before he was assassinated in 1964. The Nation did not have a large following, but it proved effective in ghetto work among lower-class blacks. It emphasized strict moral conduct and the building of an economic foundation in the black community. The nationalist groups lacked massive numbers, but they signified the weakening of civil rights approaches and the divisions of opinion within the black community. Other manifestations of nationalism included cultural emphasis on African history and Afro-American music and arts, and a desire for separation among black students on college campuses. Some nationalists were more directly political and urged the building of a black power base in the cities and rural South. Although the Muslims had talked of resisting whites with violence and saw the white man as the devil, they later modified their line.

More radical were the Black Panthers, a small revolutionary organization that urged a Marxist approach. Individual blacks also called for violence against whites and guerrilla warfare in the cities. Some organized themselves in unusual associations. One, the Revolutionary Action Movement, had two of its members convicted for conspiracy to murder NAACP leader Roy Wilkins and Whitney Young of the National Urban League. Calls for revolutionary resistance and warfare, like appeals to nationalism, were not new, and like their forerunners, they did not have large organizations to back them. But the anger and despair of these appeals struck a responsive chord in the 1960s.

As the civil rights movement failed to achieve equality, as the expectations of blacks rose, and as hopes became shattered dreams, anger and frustration increased in the nation's racial ghettos. On August 11, 1965, during a Los Angeles heat wave, a highway patrolman arrested a black youth for speeding and being intoxicated. A bystander was mistakenly struck by the police and a young woman, accused erroneously of spitting on the police, was dragged to the middle of the street. Although an angry mob gathered, it merely stoned the police car as the officers left the scene; but thereafter, until early morning, sporadic acts of vandalism and rock-throwing took place. The next day community leaders met with neighborhood residents in an attempt to calm the situation and prevent further flare-ups. During these efforts at reconciliation a few outbursts began again. Crowds grew larger and meaner and incidents became more numerous and violent. Within two days there was a full-fledged riot. For five days blacks hurled firebombs at buildings, threw rocks at cars, and looted and burned white-owned property in the Watts ghetto. Once the riot spread, the police lost control. The city requested assistance from the National Guard, which came and finally quelled the demonstrations, but not before thirty-four persons were killed and an estimated $35 million in property had been damaged.

The white majority in the United States deplored the rioting, the vandalism, and the killings, but some blacks basked in the sunshine of regained pride. The black author of a narrative about the Folsom, California, prison described the ecstasy with which the men from Watts received the news of the riots. Those prisoners who came from the Watts district in Los Angeles had been ashamed of their background because the term *Watts* had been synonymous with "hayseed" or "country bumpkin." It was used as a "put-down" in the same way that a city slicker might slight a country boy. But after the explosion at Watts the men who came from that district were proud of how their brothers had lashed out at "whitey." "Baby," fellow prisoner Eldridge Cleaver recalled one of them saying,

> they walking in fours and kicking in doors; dropping Reds and busting heads; drinking wine and committing crime; shooting and looting; high-siding and low-riding; setting fires and slashing tires; turning over cars and burning down bars; making [police chief] Parker mad and making me glad; putting an end to that "go slow" crap and putting sweet Watts on the map—my black ass is in Folsom this morning but my black heart is in Watts!

There were other riots that year, and still more in 1966, 1967, and 1968 after the assassination of Martin Luther King, Jr., in a Memphis motel. The riots in the summer of 1967 were especially destructive. Those in Newark claimed twenty-three lives; all but two victims were black. About the same number died in upheavals in Detroit, where the damage cost an estimated $50 million. All of the riots served notice that the blacks were fed up with gradualism and that "go slow crap." No longer would they accept abuse from white Americans. In 1967 H. Rap Brown, a spokesman for one of the more militant black organizations, warned, "America, you'd better repent and straighten up or we'll burn you down."

Partly in response to the uprisings and partly because of the pressure of the civil rights movement, economic discrimination began to wane. American business firms not only started hiring blacks for executive and professional positions but they also embarked on affirmative action campaigns seeking out talented members of minority groups to occupy positions that they would never have considered them for only a few years earlier. Those who because of centuries of discrimination had not been trained and educated still had rough going after the riots, but for the young people who had marketable skills new doors sprang open. In New York City the public university system embarked on a program of "open enrollment" for all local high school graduates and remedial assistance was added to the curriculum to give aid to those who needed it. Thousands took advantage of this new opportunity, but not everyone could overcome the severity of his or her educational handicaps. What was most important, however, was that progress toward significant change had really begun.

As the 1980s came to an end it was obvious that the civil rights movement, the riots of the 1960s, and the black power movement had failed to achieve racial equality in the United States. A group of scholars comparing the situation in 1988 to that of 1968 agreed that a mixed picture emerged. Another panel, sponsored by the Commission on Minority Participation in Education and American Life, reached a similar but more pessimistic conclusion. This commission, which included former presidents Jimmy Carter and Gerald R. Ford among a group of distinguished citizens, stated, "America is moving backward— not forward—in its efforts to achieve the full participation of minority citizens in the life and prosperity of the nation."

At the same time, it was clear to many observers that fundamental changes had occurred since the 1950s. By the 1980s legal discrimination in Southern public facilities had been overturned: blacks could ride where they pleased on buses, trains, and airplanes, use public parks, and gain entrance to restaurants, movie houses, hotels, motels, and other such facilities. Blacks were also serving on juries and as attorneys in Southern courts.

Moreover, in the 1970s the pace of desegregation of Southern school districts increased. By the 1980s schools were more desegregated there than they were in the North. A basic problem, North and South, was that the white exodus from the central cities in large numbers in post–World War II America left behind overwhelmingly minority neighborhoods and schools.

Black Americans were thus segregated in the cities and in the suburbs as well. Only about 5 percent of suburban populations were black in 1980, but in some cases these communities became racially segregated. The situation was especially slow to change in large cities. After comparing census data from 1970 to 1980, two researchers concluded, "Blacks are still frozen out of the

American dream. . . . Despite the advent of fair-housing legislation, more tolerant white racial attitudes, and a growing black
middle class with income sufficient to promote residential mobility, the segregation of blacks in large cities has hardly changed."
Nor did the situation appear to change radically in the 1980s.
Unless the nation decided to integrate suburban and urban
schools, desegregation in education would be hard to achieve.
And even then, in some Northern and Southern cities, white
parents elected to send their children to private rather than public schools, thereby ensuring little contact with minorities.

One key to racial equality was economics, the finding and
holding of desirable, well-paying jobs. Professional sports and
entertainment provided one avenue for black mobility for a tiny
group. In professional baseball, football, and especially basket-
ball blacks achieved success on the field, but this was not carried
over to jobs as coaches and managers and in the front offices. In
1988 only one professional baseball team, the Baltimore Orioles,
had a black manager and the National Football League, with
blacks constituting nearly 40 percent of the players, had no
black head coach.

The new black middle class, aided by more tolerant racial attitudes and affirmative action programs, also found jobs in areas
largely barred before in universities, corporations, and especially
the federal government. Many state and local governments, in
response to growing black voting power, also expanded their
hiring programs. From 1970 to 1986 the proportion of black
families earning over $35,000 annually grew at a faster rate
than did similar white families. However, the gap still existed:
in 1986 only 21 percent of black families earned more than
$35,000, whereas 42 percent of white families did.

Working-class employment also opened up in the 1960s. One
could see a growing number of construction jobs filled by black
workers, and in factories and the service industries new opportunities beckoned.

Yet for all these economic gains, there was another side. The
black unemployment rate consistently remained double that of

whites, and young male adults without good educations faced a particularly distressing job market. Large cities reported up to 40 percent of these men out of work in the 1980s. One black teenager, supposedly "optimistic by nature" according to those who knew him, wearily reported that his search for a job sometimes got him down: "I hear 'no, no, no' so much I wonder if I'm ever gonna hear 'yes.' "

In 1987, some 33.1 percent of black families lived below the government's poverty line compared to 10.5 percent of white families. Especially crucial for the black poor is the economic plight of women and the structure of the black family. Most black families are stable two-parent households. Yet a higher proportion of black families than white are headed by women, and the percentage of female-headed households has grown steadily since 1940. Fourteen percent of white families were headed by women in 1986, compared to 42 percent of black families. Black female-headed families are likely to have young children, yet the mother does not have adequate day-care facilities so she can work to support her family. Even when she does find a job, a black woman faces the double burden of discrimination on account of both sex and race. On the average, black women earn only 75 percent of what white women earn, as they frequently hold unskilled, low-paying jobs. Many females do not choose to work, or cannot because of their young children. Hence they have to live on welfare payments, particularly the Aid to Dependent Children program of the federal government. Welfare benefits are higher in the urban North than in the South, but even in Northern cities this program does not provide enough for a decent standard of living. The problem of the female-headed household is especially acute, and a growing proportion of those blacks living in poverty are members of such families. Nearly two thirds of all black families living in poverty in the late 1980s were headed by women.

Children from broken families are especially at a disadvantage. An absent father and a working mother can provide little supervision, and youngsters are left to the education of the streets. They frequently drop out of school, resort to hustling, crime, prostitution, and drugs, or otherwise run afoul of the law. Illegitimacy, although not carrying the same stigma as in the white middle-class communities, is as high as 50 percent in some inner-city areas. The offspring in turn are raised in similar circumstances. Indeed, a cycle for the poor is common; the children of poor blacks are prime candidates to remain in poverty.

One of the goals of black Americans is to increase the chances of success for their children, especially through the educational system. The gap between education for majority and minority youngsters decreased after World War II. For the very young, government programs have made it more likely that blacks rather than poor whites would be found in preschool programs. Although the disparity in expenditures for black and white schools narrowed, ghetto facilities still face chronic problems. Government expenditures do not guarantee equality, and the quality of instruction in schools with many minority group students is still inferior to that of the prosperous suburbs. Some students drop further behind the longer they stay in school. Thus middle-class black children as well as those of the working class face educational problems.

In higher education, black students were less than 5 percent of the total enrollment in 1960. During the next two decades increased numbers and larger percentages attended colleges and universities. By 1980 they constituted about 10 percent of the total, and they made up about 11 percent of college freshmen. However, they were less likely than whites to graduate, and they were more likely to be found in two-year community colleges. Moreover, in the 1980s black educational progress appeared to be stalled and even slipping. By the end of the 1980s the proportion of all students in higher education who were black dropped to just under 9 percent. Decreases were recorded not only in colleges but in professional schools, where fewer than 5 percent of the students were black.

Perhaps nowhere were the signs of black successes and failures more visible than in politics. Before the civil rights move-

Table 10.1
NUMBER OF BLACKS HOLDING POLITICAL OFFICE

Office	1970	1988
U.S. Representatives	10	23
Mayors	48	303
State legislators		
Senators	31	89
Representatives	137	311

ment few blacks in the Deep South were registered to vote, and in the North their impact on political life was small. Black voters and politicians recorded sharp gains after that, and even Southern white political leaders courted them in the 1980s. Table 10.1 indicates changes between 1970 and 1988. Among the cities that have elected black mayors are Philadelphia, Atlanta, Los Angeles, Chicago, and Newark. Moreover, the Reverend Jesse Jackson's campaigns for the Democratic presidential nomination in 1984 and 1988 caught the public's imagination. In 1984 he appeared to be a novelty, but in 1988 he ran second behind Governor Michael Dukakis, polling as many as 20 to 30 percent of the white voters in some states.

In spite of this progress and the emergence of numerous political leaders, black Americans were still substantially underrepresented politically. No black sat in the United States Senate, nor did one serve as governor of any of the nation's fifty states. Black politicians had come a long way from 1945 but still had far to go in the 1990s.

Many black leaders and organizations such as the NAACP and the National Urban League, as well as many white liberals, placed much of the blame for the persistence of poverty, failing black college attendance, and high unemployment on the administration of Ronald Reagan. They pointed to the president's successful budget cuts, which affected low-income college students. In addition, they noted that President Reagan had pushed for cuts in job training, housing, and other programs intended to help the poor.

Certainly the Reagan administration demonstrated little concern for low-income groups. The president himself had never indicated much support for civil rights legislation and his Justice Department was hostile to affirmative action programs. Reagan vetoed a civil rights bill in 1988, affecting funds for education, and had appointed people with narrow vision to the Civil Rights Commission, the United States Supreme Court, and lower federal courts. President Jimmy Carter had given 37 of his 258 judicial appointments to blacks, but Reagan's 367 appointments to the federal bench included only 6 blacks. The problem, contended an assistant attorney general in 1988, was that black judges were too liberal and there was not even "a respectively small pool" of black lawyers who shared the president's philosophy of "judicial restraint."

THE HISPANICS

While much of the nation's attention focused on the difficulties of American blacks, groups of young Mexican Americans were stirring. The militants believed that they should develop their own culture in the United States and coexist with everyone else on an equal basis. No large subgroup has ever done this before and there was little reason to believe that Chicanos would be uniquely successful in their effort. The major problems for the Mexican Americans revolve around bread-and-butter issues: satisfying jobs, higher incomes, and good educational facilities for children. The 1974 report of the United States Civil Rights Commission on the education of Mexican-American children in the Southwest (Arizona, California, Colorado, New Mexico, and Texas) concluded that facilities for them were poorer than for Anglos, that their teachers ought to have more practical training for dealing with minority children, and that a pressing need for bilingual classes existed. The Commission's study was important for focusing on the plight of the Mexican Americans, many of whom believe that current federal programs have been directed toward the welfare of urban blacks.

They are not far off in their evaluations. Not until the middle of the 1960s, in fact, did the national media, centered in New York and Washington, pay much attention to the condition of the Mexican Americans in the Southwest, and as a result this group considered itself "the most overlooked minority in the United States." The Southwestern militants, however, regarded "the social issues that beset the Chicano [as] far worse than those which triggered the American Revolution."

Mexican Americans had not received the recognition they felt they deserved largely because they lacked strong, visible associations and leadership. Hence they did not have the political clout or ability to attract media attention that such groups as the NAACP, the American Jewish Committee, and the Irish-American–dominated Catholic church already possessed. This has changed, and between 1965 and 1990 more than two hundred defense and political groups like the United Farm Workers, the League of United Latin American Citizens, and the Mexican American Political Association came to the fore. These new organizations demand redress for the decades of social and economic inequality, encourage pride in ancestry and culture, and provide indigenous leadership. One Chicano poet captured the spirit of the movement when he wrote:

> Thus far
> The image of my people
> Comes from gringo hands. . . .
> Now must be the time to change,
> And with my forming hands, create my real self,
> I shape the clay,
> My clay,
> Upon the wheel and begin.
> And the clenched fist I use
> To mash and crush the gringo's vision
> Of what I should be. . . .

The first major Mexican-American effort to obtain justice, as well as national attention, can be traced to 1965 and César Chávez's crusade, *La Huelga*. Chávez led a grape pickers' strike in California and a subsequent national boycott of grapes that

lasted five years before reaching a partially successful conclusion. The national prominence Chávez achieved far exceeded
the monetary benefits to the workers, for never before had any
Mexican American received such recognition. As a result Chávez stood as both symbol and inspiration to all Chicanos in their
quest for social justice. In New Mexico, Reies López Tijerina
organized the *Alianza Federal de Mercedes* in 1963 to regain
Mexican-American lands that he claimed had been "stolen" in
1848, when the United States acquired the territory from Mexico. José Angel Guitiérrez established *La Raza Unida* party in
southwest Texas in 1970 because he realized that the only way
for Chicanos to achieve social and economic improvement was
by gaining political control of their counties. In Colorado, Rudolph "Corky" Gonzales promoted his Crusade for Justice with
the intention of improving social and economic opportunities for
all Mexican Americans.

Through the efforts of these emerging leaders, by the late
1960s Chicanos had developed a keen sense of group awareness
and the term *La Raza* connoted their dedication to promoting
the Mexican-American culture, welfare, and lifestyle on a par
with that of the Anglos. *La Causa*, the term used to denote the
need for overall advancement of Chicanos, seems in effect to
have been translated into traditional ethnic goals of recognition
and opportunity.

Puerto Ricans, located mainly in the New York City area, are
the poorest Hispanic group. By the end of the 1980s over 40 percent of the city's Puerto Ricans lived below the poverty level.
They have high rates of unemployment, poor standards of health
care, and they live in inadequate housing. While they made
gains in the 1950s and 1960s, conditions did not improve much
after 1970, and they found themselves at the bottom of the economic ladder in 1990. Some mainland Puerto Ricans returned
to Puerto Rico after 1970, but economic conditions there were
not good either.

Like the Chicanos, they have organized to secure a share of
government programs in housing, education, health, and jobs.

For example, in New York City during the late 1960s a Puerto Rican youth group, the Young Lords, took over a neighborhood church to demonstrate the need for a free children's breakfast program. Another organization, the Puerto Rican Association for Community Affairs, began ASPIRA to encourage young Puerto Ricans to continue their education, but it had only limited success. Because they are American citizens, Puerto Ricans are eligible to vote, but they have yet to win their proportional share of New York City's political offices, which would give them more say in receiving government benefits.

Hispanic protest combined with more sympathetic non-Hispanic attitudes to produce some changes in the 1960s. Civil rights legislation, welfare and poverty programs, and affirmative action activities included Hispanics as well as blacks. As a result, educated Mexican Americans and Puerto Ricans found better jobs and more opportunities politically. Moreover, the emerging Hispanic middle class was less likely than the black middle class to be residentially segregated.

In 1988 a Hispanic organization claimed that 3,360 Hispanics were serving in elected public offices, and that this number had grown over 100 percent in a decade. New Mexico, with its historic tradition of Hispanic political participation, topped the list with the most state legislators. But the Mexican Americans were also winning elections in states like Colorado, Texas, and California. Two of their rising political leaders were Frederico Peña, mayor of Denver, and Henry Cisneros, former mayor of San Antonio, both of whom were receiving national attention.

Yet Hispanics, like blacks, were underrepresented in the nation's legislative and administrative bodies. In part this was due to the fact that, except for Puerto Ricans, many were new immigrants, not citizens, and hence were not voters. In part, too, Hispanic Americans were divided and did not always see eye to eye on political issues and candidates. Cubans, who were emerging as a major force in Florida, tended to be strongly anti-Communist and Republican, whereas Puerto Ricans and Mexican Americans usually voted Democratic.

320 THE STRUGGLE FOR EQUALITY

Although the Hispanic middle class was growing, at the end of the 1980s, nearly 30 percent of all Hispanics lived below the federal government's poverty line, and the median family income of Puerto Ricans was less than half that of Americans of European origin. Mexican Americans did better, but they still lagged considerably behind national averages.

For those living in poverty, housing was crowded and run-down, drugs common, and violence and crime constant reminders of their plight. Poor barrio dwellers complained that neither the police nor city officials responded to their grievances. A New York City commission on Hispanic concerns reported in 1986 that the city's health care system dealt with "Hispanic needs on a patch-work basis," and that city agencies "seem to substitute public relations for real efforts to meet or even measure the needs of the Hispanic community."

One key to economic success is education. Educated Hispanics did about as well as similarly educated non-Hispanics. Thus educators and Hispanic leaders found cause for alarm in the continued high dropout rates among Hispanic youth. Even Hispanic students with good grades from middle-class families have school dropout rates two to three times that of their non-Hispanic peers. Although low teacher expectations, minimal school district financial expenditures, and some language problems cannot be ignored, group cultural values also contribute to this condition. In many families—and among several ethnic groups—athletic prowess ranks higher than academic accomplishment. Of course this is not true for every group and even among Hispanics, middle-class Cubans seem to have the same retention rates as middle-class whites. Students of Puerto Rican and Mexican-American backgrounds, however, appear to have less interest in pursuing scholastic endeavors. One University of Wisconsin professor, Dr. Ricardo R. Fernandez, opined, "It defies what we know. Hispanics are not behaving the way whites and blacks are."

Exploration of cultural ethos often reveals that different ethnic groups have unique values and habits. Unfortunately, many well-meaning middle-class Americans assume that all peoples recognize the importance of education, the work ethic, and devotion to duty that we often associate with the first Puritans and the Germans who predominated among immigrants to the United States in the nineteenth century. That is simply untrue and shows a lack of respect for the goals and visions of different groups. When it comes to education we do not know exactly why members of some ethnic heritages are more avid and successful learners than others, but we can always speculate. Mayor Henry Cisneros of San Antonio, however—himself a Harvard graduate—suggested in 1988 why many Mexican Americans might not be as geared to scholastic pursuits as individuals from some other cultural heritages such as the Asians and the Jews: "Hispanics are predominantly poor. They come from rural areas where there's no tradition of higher education, and their social patterns and mores are a disincentive. Fathers are very protective of their daughters and don't want them to leave home. The males are supposed to go to work to help the family or into the military."

To overcome such problems, school districts experimented with programs to help Hispanic students remain in school, and colleges and universities in the 1980s actively recruited them. These efforts succeeded. In 1986 the U.S. Department of Education reported that Hispanic enrollment in higher education was 624,000, up from 384,000 a decade before. Yet the percentage of Hispanics in these institutions lagged considerably behind that of non-Hispanic whites. Because American society's better jobs increasingly depend on education, many Americans worried for the economic future of Hispanic Americans.

THE INDIANS

Along with blacks and Spanish-speaking Americans, Indians also struggled for equality. World War II had a major impact on them; about 25,000 men left the reservations to serve in the armed forces and another 50,000, mostly young men, left to work in defense industries. When these people returned to their homes they brought new ideas with them. Unhappy veterans criticized the BIA for meddling and in particular objected to the ban on alcohol, which remained federal law until 1953. The young men looked at some tribal matters from a perspective that differed from that of reservation leaders, thus causing friction. The experience of leaving the reservation, traveling, and occasionally meeting other Indians fostered a broader outlook, and a growing pan-Indian movement took hold after the war. Groups such as the National Congress of American Indians held meetings at which representatives from dozens of tribes met and discussed mutual problems, thus helping to reduce some intertribal differences while convincing many that Indians needed to cooperate with one another to survive.

By the late 1940s serious objections by whites to the New Deal program of encouraging Indians to preserve their distinct cultures had reappeared. Indeed, in 1950 the government launched a new program—termination—designed to eliminate itself from the Indian business. Despite the objections of skeptics, who claimed that private lumber and mining interests hoped to get their hands on Indian-held resources, Congress passed several termination bills that cut tribes loose from federal supervision. Only about 10,000 Indians received this treatment before a chorus of criticism forced the bureaucrats into a hasty retreat. Many of those terminated encountered disaster. The Menominee of Wisconsin saw much of their tribal land sold to outsiders while their medical and educational benefits were curtailed sharply. The Klamath in Oregon came close to losing most of their vast timber holdings before the federal government altered its policy. Proponents of termination claimed it would put the Indian on an equal footing with the rest of society. Unfortunately, for many this meant being handed over to the tender mercies of state and local officials, traditional enemies of Indian interests. In 1958 the Secretary of the Interior halted termination, and by 1970 the policy had been repudiated.

Meanwhile, the members of tribes unaffected by the termination controversy worked to combine traditional ways with new ideas and practices learned from the rest of American society. The Papago tribe, which lives on a sprawling reservation in the southern Arizona desert, offers a good example of this. Many Papago live in small villages scattered widely across the reservation without a nearby store or even electricity. They support themselves by raising livestock, hunting, harvesting cactus fruit, and weaving and selling baskets to tourists. Most of those who leave get nonskilled or semiskilled jobs in nearby Arizona communities.

While life in the desert is rigorous, it is not impossible, and the Papago have adapted such items as pickup trucks and television sets to their way of life. Their housing is a good example of the blending of cultures, as the tribesmen live in mud-and-stick and adobe dwellings as well as modern, government-financed homes. Medical practices also show of how the Indians have merged elements of their culture with those of white society. In addition to treatment from tribal medicine men and singers, some Papago receive care from lightly trained community health representatives or even may go to the outpatient clinics or hospitals staffed by the doctors and nurses of the Public Health Service.

Despite the continuing pressures on the Papago to shed their traditional ways, a dramatic shift in the opposite direction took place during the 1980s. This effort brought a sharply increased sense of cultural pride and tribal identity, even among the young, educated, and off-reservation Papago. On the reservation the tribal schools now give bilingual instruction, so that for the first time in a generation or more Indian children are being taught their own language and history. This new cultural pride has brought some disagreement within the tribe too. The young and vigorous leaders persuaded their followers to drop the Spanish name Papago and return to using their aboriginal name, the Tohono O'odham Nation. Although this causes discomfort to some tribal members, these young people are clearly more aware of their traditional culture, beliefs, and practices than any of their predecessors during the past half-century.

Historically, groups intending to help tribesmen were usually composed of whites, but this changed abruptly after midcentury. In 1961 a number of young, educated, and articulate Indians organized the National Indian Youth Council (NIYC), which they hoped could speak for all Indians rather than taking the more tribally oriented approach of earlier associations. Recognizing the successes of militant black civil rights demonstrations, the NIYC gained national publicity in 1964 by staging a "fish-in" in Washington state to remind the public of special Indian treaty rights that state and local actions tended to weaken or destroy. Lapel buttons and bumper stickers calling for "Red Power" and reminding whites that "Custer Died for Your Sins" appeared to show the increasing strength of Indian commitment to this movement.

Responding to growing public support, Congress passed the 1968 Civil Rights Act, which contained a so-called Indian Bill of Rights. This was meant to protect individual tribesmen from any exercise of arbitrary power by either white or tribal officials, but it tended to disrupt and displace tribal laws and customs. Soon it brought sharp disagreements on reservations between the elected tribal governments and those who disapproved of electing officials and preferred a return to the hereditary leadership of the past. In late 1969 Indian frustration with government unresponsiveness led to the seizure of Alcatraz Island in San Francisco Bay. Claiming "the Rock" as unoccupied federal territory and thus subject to use by the Indians under the Sioux treaty of 1868, the militants hoped to turn the island into a pan-Indian cultural center. In 1971, however, the government forced them to leave.

The militants became increasingly active as other civil rights groups seemed to achieve their goals. In 1972 members of the radical American Indian Movement (AIM) occupied the offices of the Bureau of Indian Affairs in Washington, D.C. After some days they departed peacefully, but only after "trashing" the offices and stealing or ruining many tribal records. In other widely scattered sit-ins Indians demonstrated from New Mexico to Maine. Their most spectacular activity, however, was the 1973 occupation of Wounded Knee, South Dakota. A carefully staged media event that depended on both the immense popularity of Dee Brown's best-selling *Bury My Heart at Wounded Knee* and extensive television news coverage, the occupation thrust AIM leaders Dennis Banks and Russell Means into national head-lines. Although the organization failed to achieve its stated goals of overthrowing the elected tribal leaders at the Pine Ridge, South Dakota, reservation or obtaining recognition for the tribes as independent nations within the general society, this should not obscure Indians' real discontent during the 1970s.

There is much debate as to whether AIM represented what most Indians wanted, but clearly through it militant leaders mobilized men and women from tribes across the country in at least a semblance of cohesion. During the 1970s a generation of college-educated Indians moved into positions of leadership in both the tribes and the BIA. They used their education and or-ganizational skills to focus public attention on Indian problems and to exploit the guilt of many Americans, while at the same time defending traditional Indian culture and tribal aspirations. They encouraged the tribes to assume control of their own schools, and in many places Indian children now receive in-struction in bilingual classes.

The tribes have moved aggressively to use education to help themselves improve their standard of living. Under provisions of federal legislation passed during the 1970s tribal governments now routinely contract to operate their own schools, much as cit-ies and school districts do. The long-term impact of Indian edu-cational initiatives remains unclear, but both the tribes and the BIA have greatly increased spending for schools. For the BIA-operated schools the results as of 1990 remain unsatisfactory. According to their own figures the average achievement test scores for Indian children in both the second and sixth grades remain mired at only the 21st percentile of children nationally.

That figure, however, represents only schools operated by the government, not by the tribes, and so it does not provide a complete picture.

If one looks at higher education, the picture seems a bit brighter. Between 1968 and 1979 nineteen tribally controlled colleges have been organized. Current enrollment stands at about 5,000 Indian students. Only a few of these fledgling institutions have more than 300 students, so the impact of tribally sponsored higher education remains modest. Most Indian students who attend colleges or universities do so in publicly supported institutions, where their enrollments have increased from 78,000 in 1978 to an estimated 90,000 by 1986. Most of the students are women, and they usually attend public two-year institutions. Even with tribal schools and colleges and the training received at public schools, Indians still have less education per capita than any other significant minority in American society.

Various tribes have succeeded in obtaining or retaining traditional lands and resources, too. In 1965 the people of Taos Pueblo, New Mexico, won a cash settlement from the Indian Claims Commission for having lost their sacred Blue Lake to the United States Forest Service. They rejected the money and continued to press for the return of the lake and surrounding forest area. In 1971 they succeeded as the Nixon administration supported legislation for that purpose. That same year the federal government negotiated the Alaska Native Claims Settlement, which awarded 40,000,000 acres of land to the Indians, Aleuts, and Eskimo people of Alaska. The controversy over who got what land and how to best use the resources there continues, even though the agreement was a major step in getting a secure tribal title to the lands in question.

Civil rights and tribal self-determination have been slow in coming for some Indian groups. Many tribes retain a continuing "special relationship" to the federal government because of nineteenth-century treaty rights. Others faced discrimination because of federal regulations. For example, the so-called Five Civilized Tribes of Oklahoma could not elect their own leaders between 1906 and 1970, when the government relented and stopped appointing tribal executives. Unreasonable and uneven law enforcement, particularly in urban areas and in small towns near the reservations, caused frequent trouble. Much of the early activity of AIM resulted from police heavyhandedness in dealing with urban Indian people. The case of Raymond Yellow Thunder, who was beaten to death by a mob in Gordon, Nebraska, during the early 1970s, brought the issue to national attention. Although eventually two men were convicted of manslaughter, the issue persists.

Because of growing awareness and ethnic pride, Indian groups long thought to have disappeared have emerged and now demand recognition as legal entities. Particularly strong in the East, their movement led the Indians to launch damage claims against both state and federal authorities for compensation for lost lands and for reinstatement as tribes with treaty rights. The first such group to draw major national attention was the Maine Passamaquoddy. In 1975 they won a judgment against the Interior Department and since then have negotiated a settlement worth $81.5 million. Perhaps as important as the cash settlement was their achievement of federal recognition as a tribe. Their suit and similar actions by other Indian groups led the BIA to establish a new office to deal with this issue. In 1978 the BIA announced the first guidelines for the process of gaining tribal recognition, and since then 111 groups have applied for tribal status. Of these, by 1988 only 11 had been successful, while the claims of an equal number were rejected. Most of the remaining groups are somewhere in the process; how many will be recognized as legal tribes is difficult to predict.

Since the late 1940s Indian people have grown in numbers, visibility, and competence in dealing with the rest of American society. Yet despite increased education, better health care, and the shift of more than half of them off the reservation, the tribal people have not achieved an equal position in the general society. By any measure, as a group Indians rank at the bottom of the list of economic, social, and health indicators. Their continuing insistence that they be allowed to retain parts of their aboriginal culture continues to trouble many other Americans, and the general public gives few indications that it is willing to accept tribal differences with any enthusiasm. This is perhaps best illustrated by President Ronald Reagan's remarks about Indians during the March 1988 summit meetings in Moscow. Speaking to students at Moscow University, he said, "Maybe we [the U.S. government] made a mistake in trying to maintain Indian cultures. Maybe we should not have humored them [Indians] in wanting to stay in that kind of primitive lifestyle." This comment brought sharp criticism from Indian rights groups, but the public paid little attention. Few other Americans accepted the Indians' complaints as justified, and the story dropped from the news quickly. Certainly by the end of 1989 few Indians feel that they have been treated equally or fairly by the rest of society.

THE WHITE ETHNIC GROUPS

The dramatic protests made by Indians, blacks, and Spanish-speaking minorities frequently antagonized the children and grandchildren of the southern and eastern European immigrants from another era. By the end of the 1960s the descendants of Slavs, Italians, and other groups believed that their problems were neglected and that they too needed social programs to aid their movement into the middle class (or, conversely, that they had received no governmental largesse and therefore no one else should).

White ethnic groups particularly objected because the liberal establishment in universities, foundations, and the federal administration had seemingly ignored them while condemning bigotry against Indians, blacks, and Spanish-speaking Americans. These white ethnic minorities resented the racial integration that was being forced on their neighborhoods by government bureaucrats and courts while the "limousine liberals" lived in homogeneous middle-class communities or exclusive residences and sent their children to high-priced private or fancy suburban schools. In an impassioned defense of the white ethnic minorities who felt that their interests were being shunted aside while they themselves were being condemned, Barbara Mikulski, a Polish-American woman later elected to the Senate, described the United States as a

> sizzling cauldron for the ethnic American who feels that he has been politically extorted by both government and private enterprise. The ethnic American is sick of being stereotyped as a racist and dullard by phony white liberals, pseudo-black militants and patronizing bureaucrats. He pays the bill for every major government program and gets nothing or little in the way of return. Tricked by the political rhetoric of the illusionary funding for black-oriented social programs, he turns his anger to race—when he himself is the victim of class prejudice. He has worked hard all of his life to become a "good American"; he and his sons have fought on every battlefield—then he is made fun of because he likes the flag.

Banding together in groups like the Italian American Civil Rights League, the Portuguese Congress in America, and a variety of other organizations based on nationality and religion, these whites demanded more governmental sensitivity to their concerns and a larger share of the benefits. The Italian American Civil Rights League, for example, staged rallies and protested against the alleged slurs made by the FBI and television stations concerning ties between the Italian-American community and organized crime. The League lost much of its vitality after its leader, Joseph Columbo, was shot in 1970, but other groups made similar demands. The Polish American Congress sued the American Broadcasting Company because the network refused to allow its representatives equal time on the air to respond to four jokes on one of its shows that the group believed constituted "personal attacks on the character, intelligence, hygiene or appearance" of Americans of Polish descent. The Congress of Italian American Organizations, formed in 1965, argued that "the government is blatantly insensitive to the needs of the Italian-American community," and its director declared, "We are going to fight for our share of the pie."

Jews, who had formerly been aligned with liberal causes, now feared that their hard-won gains of previous decades were endangered. Because many Jews had qualified for professional and executive positions, they interpreted affirmative action as a euphemism for the quota system and, particularly in the contracting economy of the 1970s, as discrimination against them. Hence Norman Podhoretz, editor of the prominent American Jewish monthly *Commentary*, spoke out vigorously against a changed American policy that seemed to be ignoring whites and favoring blacks. He wrote that Jews should start questioning public policies and asking themselves, "Is it good for the Jews? That is to say, I think that Jews must once again begin to look at proposals and policies from the point of view of the Jewish interest, and must once again begin to ask what the consequences, if any, of any proposals or policy are likely to be so far as the Jewish position is concerned."

The heavy emphasis in American society during the 1960s and 1970s on helping members of the more noticeable minority groups "uplift" themselves and develop pride in their heritages also stimulated the descendants of European and Asian immigrants to demand equal attention to their own pasts. As a result, Congress enacted the Ethnic Heritage Act of 1973, which funded programs designed to enhance the image of numerous American subgroups. In addition, a growing number of books, like Michael Novak's *The Rise of the Unmeltable Ethnics* and Irving Howe's *World of Our Fathers*, celebrated the cultures and values of the immigrant groups of yesteryear. As usual, academic institutions responded with alacrity. A survey by the United States Office of Education found that in the 1973 academic year, 135 colleges and universities offered 315 courses concerning the ethnicity of white groups, including many in the area of Jewish-, Italian-, Greek-, Basque-, and Polish-American studies.

The renewed assertion of ethnic pride and identity in the

1970s appeared to have faded by the 1980s. To be sure, migrants from one section of the country to another often seek out the Swedish-American Club, the Greek association, or some other ethnic or religious organization as a way of meeting people and helping ease the transition to a new community, but otherwise most Americans of foreign ancestry are more anxious to blend into the dominant society and to be regarded as "Americans" than they are in trying to remain "ethnic." While they retain certain foods and festivals for culinary or nostalgic satisfaction, they do not want to revert to an isolated ethnic experience. Educated people in the United States can no more go back to a ghetto culture than "Eliza Doolittle" in Shaw's *Pygmalion* could go back to being a flower girl after "Professor Henry Higgins" trained her for another station in life.

The institutions of society—the schools, the media, and especially television—promote an American culture that only the most secluded can escape. The propaganda agencies of the government, the civil rights legislation of the 1960s, and the United States Supreme Court decisions demanding "equal protection of the laws" have combined to accelerate the pace of Americanization, the ending of discriminatory treatment, and the accordance of respect to all individuals regardless of heritage. Ironically, this improved treatment hastens the cultural breakdown of white ghettos rather than cementing them. Minorities stick together most closely in times of stress and during threats to group identity. With greater acceptance of variety by the dominant community, the gradual disappearance of white minority cultures seems likely for all except the few groups, like the Amish, who voluntarily isolate themselves from the rest of society.

The assimilation of so many descendants of the European immigrants should not lead one to conclude that America lacked ethnic diversity as the 1980s came to an end. Many of the twelve million or so immigrants who arrived after the enactment of the 1965 immigration act had middle-class aspirations and wished to join the mainstream of American society. But like so many millions of immigrants before them, they still retained much of their culture, as the Greeks and Colombians of New York City and the Koreans of Los Angeles demonstrated. The civil rights movement had opened doors for many blacks, but others remained trapped in the nation's urban ghettos with little hope. Although Spanish-speaking people had been emigrating for a long time, they too were often segregated from American life. The nation's oldest and poorest group, the Indians, also kept distinct cultures. Many moved to the cities in search of jobs, but they were not necessarily welcomed there, and for those left behind on the reservations, there was poverty and isolation. Thus whatever path the American society and economy followed, and whatever the role of various ethnic groups in determining this direction, it appeared that cultural diversity would be part of the future as it had been part of the past.

Afterword

As AMERICANS CELEBRATED THE BICENTENNIAL of the Constitution and looked ahead in their third century as an independent nation, they were keenly aware of how the various minorities in their midst combined to make the United States a unique nation. The growth of the country began with the settlements at Jamestown and in New England a full century and a half before the colonies declared their independence in 1776. Yet America was still a relatively weak, agrarian society in that year, with fewer than three million Europeans and Africans settled along the Eastern seaboard and a smaller number of Indians scattered throughout the country. Although the foundations of American society were laid in the colonial era, the years of great growth and the transformation of the colonies into an urban and industrial society came much later.

In this process America experienced developments similar to those of European capitalist societies. Americans accumulated capital and invested it, constructed a transportation network, cleared and tilled the land, built cities, suburbs, and factories, invented and improved machinery and gadgets, organized large corporations, and reached out for foreign markets. Yet in some ways the American experience differed from that of the western European states. Largely a virgin land in the seventeenth century, America needed to import labor. The English colonies and later the new nation sought workers overseas. From Africa Americans brought black men in chains and from all over Europe they enticed strong laborers. In the nineteenth century they also welcomed, temporarily, immigrants from Asia; and in the twentieth century they looked to Mexico, South America, and Canada as well as Europe and Asia again.

The labor of these millions helped transform American society. But the mingling of so many peoples also had enormous consequences for the social history of the United States. While enslaved Africans and voluntary immigrants were prized for their strong backs and skillful hands, Indians were scorned because the white man believed they stood in the way of progress and economic growth. Since the Indians held the land, they bore the brunt of the white man's greed as he moved across the continent.

Because slaves and immigrants were desired for their economic contributions, it did not mean they experienced an easy time. These newcomers were different from the early Englishmen who set the tone for American society and culture. They were expected to conform to the Anglo-American customs and they were frequently abused when they did not. But many did change, and the gradual loss of an Old World heritage has been an integral part of American ethnic history. When they did not assimilate fast enough for some Americans, or were considered unassimilable by others, they encountered the wrath of nativism. Black men and women, slaves at first, suffered more than immigrants. No matter what they did, they were held to be different and inferior, a race apart.

Thus conflicts occurred in spite of the indispensable contributions the newcomers made to the building and shaping of modern society. Sometimes these conflicts were fierce and violent; at other times minorities experienced more subtle forms of discrimination and exclusion. It seems as if some ethnic struggles marked every age of American history. In recent years, the nation apparently has come to a public acceptance of ethnic differences and a growing toleration for all peoples. Certainly anti-Catholicism and anti-Semitism have abated and even white racism has lessened. This acceptance has also been accompanied by a new assertion of ethnic pride. Nevertheless, personal feelings and prejudices have not kept pace with the contemporary public and constitutional realities. Places of purely social recreation, such as country clubs, still show signs of "ethnic purity," and private comments to close friends and family often contain the most brutal kinds of racial and religious bigotry. Finally, individual perceptions of reality are significant. Children who attend integrated schools and people who live and work in integrated communities base their attitudes on what and whom they see about them. Although living and working with others often bring understanding, it does not always encourage greater acceptance and tolerance of different cultural values.

That the nation would eventually lay aside ethnic antagonism and seek a pluralistic society where all groups were accepted and treated with respect, even if they remained different, seemed more likely in the late 1980s than it did even a decade earlier. Although the growing toleration and legal and constitutional commitments to equality seem to point in a hopeful direction, the scars of conflict remain and the signs of inequality are still plentiful in contemporary America.

As the century enters its final decade most Americans do accept, to a certain extent, pluralism. And while there may not yet be full comprehension of the richness of ethnic contributions to the nation's cultural and economic development, it is important to recognize the changes in attitudes that have developed recently. And it is because of the changed attitudes that many individuals are less self-conscious about retaining those aspects of their heritage that allow them to harmonize their traditional ways with those of the dominant culture.

Selected Bibliography

For a brief survey of immigration see Leonard Dinnerstein and David M. Reimers, *Ethnic Americans,* 3rd ed. (New York: Harper and Row, 1988). Black history is covered comprehensively in John Hope Franklin and Alfred A. Moss, Jr. *From Slavery to Freedom,* 6th ed. (New York: Alfred A. Knopf, 1988), while Wilcomb E. Washburn, *The Indian in America* (New York: Harper and Row, 1975), and Roger L. Nichols, ed., *The American Indian,* 3rd ed. (New York: Alfred A. Knopf, 1986), provide good introductions to the study of Indians. Susan Searing, a University of Wisconsin (Madison) women's studies librarian, put together the as-yet-unpublished "Women, Race, and Ethnicity: A Bibliography in Progress" (June 1988), which is an absolute gem. More easily obtained surveys of the experiences of ethnic women are Cecyle S. Neidle, *America's Immigrant Women* (Boston: G. K. Hall, 1975), and Maxine Seller, *Immigrant Women* (Philadelphia: Temple University Press, 1981). Brief accounts of all minorities can be found in Stephan Thernstrom, ed., *Harvard Encyclopedia of American Ethnic Groups* (Cambridge: Harvard University Press, 1980). A survey of the urban immigrant may be found in John Bodnar's *The Transplanted: A History of Immigrants in Urban America* (Bloomington: Indiana University Press, 1985).

CHAPTER 1

For the relations among blacks, whites, and Indians consult Gary B. Nash, *Red, White and Black: The Peoples of Early America* (Englewood Cliffs, N.J.: Prentice-Hall, 1982). The development of slavery is treated in Edmund S. Morgan, *American Slavery, American Freedom: The Ordeal of Colonial Virginia* (New York: W. W. Norton, 1975); Peter Wood, *Black Majority: Negroes in Colonial South Carolina from 1670 through the Stono Rebellion* (New York: Alfred A. Knopf, 1974); and Gerald W. Mullin, *Flight and Rebellion: Slave Resistance in Eighteenth-Century Virginia* (New York: Oxford University Press, 1975). White racism is covered in Winthrop D. Jordan, *White over Black: American Attitudes Toward the Negro, 1550–1812* (Chapel Hill: University of North Carolina Press, 1968).

On the major white minorities in colonial America one might begin with Bernard Bailyn, *Voyagers to the West* (New York: Alfred A. Knopf, 1986), and then follow up with Albert B. Faust, *The German Element in the United States*, 2 vols. (Boston: Houghton Mifflin, 1909); Lucey Forney Bittinger, *The German in Colonial Times* (Philadelphia: J. B. Lippincott, 1901); James G. Leyburn, *The Scotch-Irish* (Chapel Hill: University of North Carolina Press, 1962); Ian Charles Cargill Graham, *Colonists from Scotland, Emigration to North America, 1707–1783* (Ithaca, N.Y.: Cornell University Press, 1956); and Jon Butler, *The Huguenots in America* (Cambridge: Harvard University Press, 1983). For convict labor, see A. Roger Ekrich, *Bound for America: The Transportation of British Convicts to the Colonies, 1718–1775* (New York: Oxford University Press, 1987).

The Indians in early America are treated in James Axtell, *The Invasion Within: The Contest of Cultures in Colonial North America* (New York: Oxford University Press, 1985); William Cronon, *Changes in the Land: Indians, Colonists, and the Ecology of New England* (New York: Hill and Wang, 1983); Neal Salisbury, *Manitou and Providence: Indians, Europeans, and the Making of New England, 1500–1643* (New York: Oxford University Press, 1982); and J. Leitch Wright, Jr., *The Only Land They Knew: The Tragic Story of the American Indians in the Old South* (New York: Free Press, 1981). Among the many histories of individual tribes during the colonial era, two good ones are Anthony F. C. Wallace, *The Death and Rebirth of the Seneca* (New York: Alfred A. Knopf, 1970), and Charles M. Hudson, *The Catawba Nation* (Athens: University of Georgia Press, 1970).

CHAPTER 2

For a general view of the South see Monroe Lee Billington, *The American South* (New York: Charles Scribner's Sons, 1971), and Francis Butler Simkins and Charles Pierce Roland, *A History of the Old South*, 4th ed. (New York: Alfred A. Knopf, 1972). An interesting book on the influence of the Celts on the South is Grady McWhiney, *Cracker Culture* (University: University of Alabama Press, 1988).

For the free black in the South see Ira Berlin, *Slaves Without Masters: The Free Negro in the Antebellum South* (New York: Pantheon, 1974). The literature on slavery is large; good analyses can be found in Kenneth Stampp, *The Peculiar Institution: Slavery in the Antebellum South* (New York: Alfred A. Knopf, 1956); Eugene Genovese, *Roll, Jordan, Roll: The World the Slaves Made* (New York: Pantheon, 1974); John Blassingame, *The Slave Community: Plantation Life in the Antebellum South* (New York: Oxford University Press, 1972); Herbert G. Gutman, *The Black Family in Slavery and Freedom, 1750–1925* (New York: Pantheon, 1976); Leslie H. Owens, *This Species of Property: Slave Life and Culture in the Old South* (New York: Oxford University Press, 1976); and Lawrence W. Levine's *Black Culture and Black Consciousness: Afro-American Folk Thought from Slavery to Freedom* (New York: Oxford University Press, 1977). Two extremely revealing accounts are Linda Brent, *Incidents in the Life of a Slave Girl: Written by Herself*, edited by Lydia Marie Child (1861. Reprint. Cambridge: Harvard University Press, 1987), and Deborah Grey White, *Ar'nt I a Woman: Female Slaves in the Plantation South* (New York: Norton, 1985). An excellent work about slavery in one community is Charles Joyner, *Down by the Riverside: A South Carolina Slave Community* (Urbana: University of Illinois Press, 1984). For black and white women, see Elizabeth Fox-Genovese, *Within the Plantation Household: Black and White Women of the Old South* (Chapel Hill: University of North Carolina Press, 1988).

Many books and articles discuss the Southern Indian tribes. Among the most readable general accounts are Dale Van Every, *Disinherited: The Lost Birthright of the American Indian* (New York: William Morrow, 1966), and Francis P. Prucha, *American Indian Policy in the Formative Years: The Indian Trade and Intercourse Acts* (Cambridge: Harvard University Press, 1962). Two other books, Michael D. Green, *The Politics of Indian Removal: Creek Government and Society in Crisis* (Lincoln: University of

Nebraska Press, 1982), and William G. McLoughlin, *Cherokee Renascence in the New Republic* (Princeton: Princeton University Press, 1986), deal with more limited aspects of this issue.

CHAPTER 3

Three books should be included in connection with the brief discussion of Northern blacks: Leon Litwack, *North of Slavery: The Negro in the Free States, 1790–1860* (Chicago: University of Chicago Press, 1961), Benjamin Quarles, *Black Abolitionists* (New York: Oxford University Press, 1969), and Gary B. Nash, *Forging Freedom: The Formation of Philadelphia's Black Community, 1720–1840* (Cambridge: Harvard University Press, 1988).

Among the many good discussions of American settlement of the frontier are Richard A. Bartlett, *The New Country: A Social History of the American Frontier, 1776–1890* (New York: Oxford University Press, 1974), and Ray A. Billington, *Westward Expansion,* 5th ed. (New York: Macmillan, 1982). Richard C. Wade, *The Urban Frontier: The Rise of Western Cities, 1790–1830* (Cambridge: Harvard University Press, 1959), considers early Western city life. George Rogers Taylor, *The Transportation Revolution* (New York: Holt, Rinehart and Winston, 1951), relates transportation to national economic development. An excellent brief discussion of economic trends is Robert L. Heilbroner and Aaron Singer, *The Economic Transformation of America* (New York: Harcourt Brace Jovanovich, 1977).

Although studies of individual tribes abound, there are few good general works about Indians. In addition to previously mentioned books, see Reginald Horsman, *Expansion and American Indian Policy, 1783–1812* (East Lansing: Michigan State University Press, 1967), and two books by R. David Edmunds, *The Shawnee Prophet* (Lincoln: University of Nebraska Press, 1983), and *Tecumseh and the Quest for Indian Leadership* (Boston: Little, Brown, 1984).

CHAPTER 4

Economic development before the Civil War is considered by Robert W. Fogel, *Railroads and American Economic Growth* (Baltimore: Johns Hopkins University Press, 1964), and Nathan Rosenberg, *Technology and American Economic Growth* (New York: Harper and Row, 1972). The previously mentioned Robert

L. Heilbroner and Aaron Singer, *The Economic Transformation of America*, contains the best short discussion of this topic.

For the immigrants see Robert Ernst, *Immigrant Life in New York City, 1825–1863* (New York: King's Crown Press, 1949); Oscar Handlin, *Boston's Immigrants*, rev. ed. (New York: Atheneum, 1968); Kerby A. Miller, *Emigrants and Exiles: Ireland and the Irish Exodus to North America* (New York: Oxford University Press, 1985); Jay P. Dolan, *The Immigrant Church: New York's Irish and German Catholics, 1815–1865* (Baltimore: Johns Hopkins University Press, 1975); John A. Hawgood, *The Tragedy of German-America* (New York: G. P. Putnam's Sons, 1940); Kathleen Neils Conzen, *Immigrant Milwaukee, 1836–1860: Accommodation and Community in a Frontier City* (Cambridge: Harvard University Press, 1976); and Jon Gjerde, *From Peasants to Farmers: The Migration from Balestrand, Norway, to the Upper Middle West* (Cambridge: Cambridge University Press, 1985). The standard work on pre–Civil War nativism is Ray Billington, *The Protestant Crusade 1800–1860* (Chicago: Quadrangle Books, 1964). An illuminating monograph is Michael Feldberg, *The Philadelphia Riots of 1844: A Study in Ethnic Conflict* (Westport, Conn.: Greenwood Press, 1975). For blacks during the Civil War see Benjamin Quarles, *The Negro and the Civil War* (Boston: Little, Brown, 1953).

Four good accounts of minority women are Hasia R. Diner, *Erin's Daughter's in America: Irish Immigrant Women in the Nineteenth Century* (Baltimore: Johns Hopkins University Press, 1983); Dorothy Sterling, ed., *We Are Your Sisters: Black Women in the Nineteenth Century* (New York: W. W. Norton, 1984); *Foreign and Female: Immigrant Women in America, 1840–1930* (New York: Schocken, 1987); and Jacqueline Jones, *Labor of Love, Labor of Sorrow: Black Women, Work, and the Family from Slavery to the Present* (New York: Basic Books, 1985).

CHAPTER 5

For the economic expansion of the United States after the Civil War consult E. C. Kirkland, *Industry Comes of Age: Business, Labor, and Public Policy 1860–1897* (New York: Holt, Rinehart and Winston, 1961), and for urbanization, Sam Bass Warner, Jr., *The Urban Wilderness: A History of the American City* (New York: Harper and Row, 1972). The background of European immigration is thoroughly treated in Philip Taylor, *The Distant Magnet* (New York: Harper and Row, 1971).

On Italians consult Richard Gambino, *Blood of My Blood* (Garden City, N.Y.: Doubleday, 1974), and Alexander De Conde, *Half Bitter, Half Sweet* (New York: Charles Scribner's Sons, 1971). For the Greeks, Theodore Saloutos, *The Greeks in the United States* (Cambridge: Harvard University Press, 1964); for Jews, Nathan Glazer, *American Judaism*, 2nd ed. (Chicago: University of Chicago Press, 1972). For French Canadians, Gerard J. Brault, *The French-Canadian Heritage in New England* (Hanover, N.H.: University Press of New England, 1986). The best book on any aspect of Slavic history in the United States is Ewa Morawska, *For Bread with Butter: Life-Worlds of East Central Europeans in Johnstown, Pennsylvania* (Cambridge: Cambridge University Press, 1985). Gregory Orfalea traveled to more than twenty American cities while preparing *Before the Flames: A Quest for the History of Arab Americans* (Austin: University of Texas Press, 1988).

An extraordinary work dealing with blacks during the Reconstruction era is Eric Foner, *Reconstruction: America's Unfinished Revolution, 1863–1877* (New York: Harper and Row, 1988). Black migration north is treated in Florette Henri, *Black Migration: Movement North, 1900–1920* (Garden City, N.Y.: Doubleday, 1976); Gilbert Osofsky, *Harlem: The Making of a Ghetto, Negro New York, 1890–1920* (New York: Harper and Row, 1966); and Allan H. Spear, *Black Chicago: The Making of a Negro Ghetto, 1890–1920* (Chicago: University of Chicago Press, 1967).

CHAPTER 6

Most of the works cited in Chapters 4 and 5 have considerable information on the process of adjustment. For social mobility see Stephan Thernstrom, *The Other Bostonians: Poverty and Progress in the American Metropolis 1880–1970* (Cambridge: Harvard University Press, 1975), and Thomas Kessner, *The Golden Door: Italian and Jewish Immigrant Mobility in New York City 1880–1915* (New York: Oxford University Press, 1977). Informative studies of different ethnic groups include Humbert S. Nelli, *From Immigrants to Ethnics: The Italian American* (New York: Oxford University Press, 1983); Marie Hall Ets, *Rosa: The Life of an Italian Immigrant* (Minneapolis: University of Minnesota Press, 1970); Elizabeth Ewen, *Immigrant Women in the Land of Dollars: Life and Culture on the Lower East Side, 1890–1925* (New York: Monthly

Review Press, 1985); Gary Ross Mormino and George E. Pozetta, *The Immigrant World of Ybor City: Italians and their Latin Neighbors in Tampa, 1885–1985* (Urbana: University of Illinois Press, 1987); and Gary Mormino, *Immigrants on the Hill: Italian Americans in St. Louis, 1882–1985* (Urbana: University of Illinois Press, 1986). For the Jews see Irving Howe, *World of Our Fathers* (New York: Harcourt Brace Jovanovich, 1976), and Sydney S. Weinberg, *World of Our Mothers* (Chapel Hill: University of North Carolina Press, 1988).

CHAPTER 7

Much of the early development of the American West depended on improving transportation and communications facilities. Among the many books dealing with these subjects, Oscar O. Winther, *The Transportation Frontier: Trans-Mississippi West, 1865–1890* (New York: Holt, Rinehart and Winston, 1964), and LeRoy Hafen, *The Overland Trail, 1849–1869* (Cleveland: Arthur H. Clark, 1923), are the best.

The mining rushes are carefully treated in Rodman W. Paul, *Mining Frontiers of the Far West, 1848–1880* (New York: Holt, Rinehart and Winston, 1963), and William S. Greever, *The Bonanza West: The Story of Western Mining Rushes, 1848–1900* (Norman: University of Oklahoma Pres, 1963). The story of one ethnic group is told in Arthur C. Todd, *The Cornish Miner in America* (Glendale, Calif.: Arthur H. Clark, 1967). James B. Allen considers the growth of *The Company Town in the American West* (Norman: University of Oklahoma Press, 1966); Duane Smith, *Rocky Mountain Mining Camps* (Bloomington: Indiana University Press, 1967), treats social problems and aspects of demography in earlier mining communities.

The literature dealing with Western Indians is both varied and voluminous. The most complete account of United States government–Indian relations is Francis P. Prucha, *The Great Father: The United States Government and the American Indians*, 2 vols. (Lincoln: University of Nebraska Press, 1984). Richard N. Ellis, ed., *The Western American Indians: Case Studies in Tribal History* (Lincoln: University of Nebraska Press, 1972), includes good brief discussions on significant problems that the Indians faced during the last half of the nineteenth century. Other works worth examining include Francis P. Prucha, *The Churches and the Indian Schools, 1888–1912* (Lincoln: University of Nebraska Press, 1979);

Peter Iverson, *The Navajo Nation* (Westport, Conn.: Greenwood Press, 1981); Jane B. Katz, ed., *I Am the Fire of Time: Voices of Native American Women* (New York: E. P. Dutton, 1977); and Gretchen M. Batille and Kathleen Mullen Sands, *American Indian Women: Telling Their Lives* (Lincoln: University of Nebraska Press, 1984).

Two works that cover a number of different minority women are Joan M. Jensen, *With These Hands: Women Working on the Land* (New York: Feminist Press, 1981), and Cathy Luchetti and Carol Olwell, *Women of the West* (St. George, Utah: Antelope Press, 1984).

Additional coverage of a variety of Western peoples can be found in Nels Anderson, *Desert Saints: The Mormon Frontier in Utah* (Chicago: University of Chicago Press, 1942); William H. Leckie, *The Buffalo Soldiers: A Narrative of the Negro Cavalry* (Norman: University of Oklahoma Press, 1967); Philip Durham and Everett L. Jones, *The Negro Cowboy* (New York: Dodd, Mead, 1965); Roger Daniels, *The Politics of Prejudice: The Anti-Japanese Movement in California and the Struggle for Japanese Exclusion* (Berkeley: University of California Press, 1962); and Andrew F. Rolle, *The Immigrant Upraised: Italian Adventures and Colonists in an Expanding America* (Norman: University of Oklahoma Press, 1968). The definitive work on the Basques is William A. Douglass and Jon Bilbao, *Amerikanuak* (Reno: University of Nevada Press, 1975). Next to the Indians, the Chinese and the Mexicans are perhaps the most written about ethnic minorities in the West. Gunthar Barth, *Bitter Strength: A History of the Chinese in the United States, 1850–1870* (Cambridge: Harvard University Press, 1964); Stuart Creighton Miller, *The Unwelcome Immigrant: The American Image of the Chinese, 1785–1882* (Berkeley: University of California Press, 1969); and Stanford M. Lyman, *Chinese Americans* (New York: Random House, 1974), are among the top works about the Chinese. A comprehensive account is presented in Roger Daniels, *Asian America: Chinese and Japanese in the United States since 1850* (Seattle: University of Washington Press, 1988). The best history of Mexicans is Carey McWilliams, *North from Mexico*, rpt. (New York: Greenwood Press, 1968), while Wayne Moquin's *A Documentary History of the Mexican Americans* (New York: Praeger, 1971), has the fullest collection of articles. Rodolfo Acuña, *Occupied America: A History of Chicanos*, 3rd ed. (New York: Harper and Row, 1988), has an enormous amount of information.

CHAPTER 8

In addition to the works on blacks already noted, George Frederickson, *The Black Image in the White Mind: The Debate on Afro-American Character and Destiny, 1817–1914* (New York: Harper and Row, 1972), deals with white racism. See also Rayford Logan, *The Negro in American Life and Thought: The Nadir, 1877–1901* (New York: Dial Press, 1954), and C. Vann Woodward, *The Strange Career of Jim Crow*, 3rd ed. (New York: Oxford University Press, 1974). Insightful coverage of blacks in the New Deal era is also provided in Nancy Weiss, *Farewell to the Party of Lincoln* (Princeton: Princeton University Press, 1983), while Joel Williamson reexamines prejudice and bigotry in *The Crucible of Race* (New York: Oxford University Press, 1984).

On attitudes toward the Indians see Robert F. Berkhofer, Jr., *The White Man's Indian: Images of the American Indian from Columbus to the Present* (New York: Alfred A. Knopf, 1978), and Brian W. Dippie, *The Vanishing American: White Attitudes and U.S. Indian Policy* (Middletown, Conn.: Wesleyan University Press, 1982).

Hostility toward a variety of minorities as well as interethnic conflict can be found in the general treatment in most of the works already mentioned. In addition, Ronald H. Bayor, *Neighbors in Conflict: The Irish, Germans, Jews, and Italians of New York City, 1929–1941* (Urbana: University of Illinois Press, 1988), has the fullest account of those groups' interactions during the depression decade. Anti-Japanese attitudes can be garnered from Roger Daniels, *Concentration Camps USA: Japanese Americans and World War II* (New York: Holt, Rinehart and Winston, 1972); Jeanne Wakotsuki Houston and James D. Houston, *Farewell to Manzanar* (Boston: Houghton Mifflin, 1973); and Yoshika Uchida, *Desert Exile: The Uprooting of a Japanese American Family* (Seattle: University of Washington Press, 1982). Ellie Berthiaume Shukert and Barbara Scibetta examine what happened to a number of different ethnic women in *War Brides of World War II* (Novato, Calif.: Presidio Press, 1988). An excellent comparative analysis is Joan M. Jensen, *Passage from India: Asian Indian Immigrants in North America* (New Haven: Yale University Press, 1988).

The standard work on nativism and immigration restriction is John Higham, *Strangers in the Land: Patterns of American Nativism 1860–1925* (New York: Atheneum, 1968). See also Barbara Solomon, *Ancestors and Immigrants* (New York: John Wiley,

1964); Marion T. Bennett, *American Immigration Policies: A History* (Washington, D.C.: Public Affairs Press, 1963); and Seymour Martin Lipset and Earl Rabb, *The Politics of Unreason: Right-Wing Extremism in America 1790–1970* (New York: Harper and Row, 1970). Kenneth T. Jackson's *The Ku Klux Klan in the City, 1915–1930* (New York: Oxford University Press, 1967), is an eye-opener. A recent account is presented in David H. Bennett, *The Party of Fear: From Nativist Movements to the New Right in American History* (Chapel Hill: University of North Carolina Press, 1988).

CHAPTER 9

Scholarly analyses of some of the newer arrivals to the United States are not yet plentiful, but the standard work is David M. Reimers, *Still the Golden Door* (New York: Columbia University Press, 1985). Interested readers would also gain some insights from Parmatma Saran and Edwin Eames, eds., *The New Ethnics: Asian Indians in the United States* (New York: Praeger, 1980); H. Brett Melandy, *Asians in America: Filipinos, Koreans, and East Indians* (Boston: Twayne Publishers, 1977); Bong-yuon Choy, *Koreans in America* (Chicago: Nelson-Hall, 1979); Rita J. Simon, ed., *New Lives: The Adjustment of Soviet Jewish Immigrants in the United States and Israel* (Lexington, Mass.: D. C. Heath, 1985); and Thomas Kessner and Betty Boyd Caroli, *Today's Immigrants: Their Stories* (New York: Oxford University Press, 1981).

Another valuable account on ethnicity in New York City is Nathan Glazer and Daniel Patrick Moynihan, *Beyond the Melting Pot*, 2nd ed. (Cambridge: M.I.T. Press, 1970). Also informative on that subject is Andrew Greeley, *Ethnicity in the United States: A Preliminary Reconnissance* (New York: John Wiley, 1974).

Worthwhile studies on Hispanics include Lester D. Langley, *Mex America: Two Countries, One Future* (New York: Crown Publishers, 1988) and Matt S. Meir and Feliciano Rivera, *The Chicanos: A History of Mexican Americans* (New York: Hill and Wang, 1972). On the Cubans see Richard R. Fagan, Richard Brody, and Thomas J. O'Leary, *Cubans in Exile: Disaffection and the Revolution* (Stanford: Stanford University Press, 1968). A recent survey of Puerto Ricans is Joseph P. Fitzpatrick, *Puerto Rican Americans*, 2nd ed. (Englewood Cliffs, N.J.: Prentice-Hall, 1987), while an older but still useful work is Paulette Cooper, ed., *Growing Up Puerto Rican* (New York: Arbor House, 1972).

CHAPTER 10

On urban blacks the *Report of the National Advisory Commission on Civil Disorders* (New York: Bantam Books, 1968) is informative. Also useful are Robert Conot, *American Odyssey* (New York: William Morrow, 1974); Kenneth Clark, *Dark Ghetto: Dilemmas of Social Power* (New York: Harper and Row, 1965); Sar Levitan, William Johnston, and Robert Taggert, *Still a Dream: The Changing Status of Blacks since 1960* (Cambridge: Harvard University Press, 1975); Harvard Sifkoff, *The Struggle for Black Equality 1954–1980* (New York: Hill and Wang, 1981); William J. Wilson, *The Declining Significance of Race* (Chicago: University of Chicago Press, 1978); and William J. Wilson, *The Truly Disadvantaged: The Innner City, the Underclass, and Public Policy* (Chicago: University of Chicago Press, 1987).

The historic struggles of blacks for equality have been treated in John Hope Franklin, *Racial Equality in America* (Chicago: University of Chicago Press, 1976); Anne Moody, *Coming of Age in Mississippi* (New York: Dell, 1976); Mary King, *Freedom Song: A Personal Story of the 1960s Civil Rights Movement* (New York: William Morrow, 1987); and Douglas J. McAdam, *Freedom Summer* (New York: Oxford University Press, 1988). Also useful are Benjamin Muse, *The American Negro Revolution: From Non-Violence to Black Power, 1963–1967* (Bloomington: Indiana University Press, 1968), and especially Richard Kluger, *Simple Justice: The History of Brown v. Board of Education and Black Americans' Struggle for Equality* (New York: Alfred A. Knopf, 1976). A moving book is Taylor Branch, *Parting the Waters: America in the King Years, 1954–1963* (New York: Simon and Schuster, 1988). On black nationalism see C. Eric Lincoln, *The Black Muslims in America* (Boston: Beacon Press, 1961). A contemporary analysis of black women's history is Paula Giddings, *When and Where I Enter: The Impact of Black Women on Race and Sex in America* (New York: William Morrow, 1984).

For Mexican Americans the following are helpful: Nan Elsasser, Kyle Mackenzie, and Yvonne Tixlery y Vigil, *Las Mujeres: Conversations from a Hispanic Community* (New York: Feminist Press, 1980), and Joan London and Henry Anderson, *So Shall Ye Reap: The Story of César Chávez and the Farm Workers Movement* (New York: Praeger, 1972).

For a brief discussion of Indians on the eve of World War II see Lawrence C. Kelly, *The Assault on Assimilation: John Collier and the Origins of Indian Policy Reform* (Albuquerque: University of New Mexico Press, 1983), and Donald L. Fixico, *Termination and Relocation: Federal Indian Policy, 1945–1960* (Albuquerque: University of New Mexico Press, 1986). A clear analysis of the pan-Indian movement is found in Hazel W. Hertzberg, *The Search for an American Indian Identity: Modern Pan-Indian Movements* (Syracuse, N.Y.: Syracuse University Press, 1971). The most comprehensive of recent studies on Indian civil and political rights are Stephen L. Pevar, *The Rights of Indians and Tribes* (New York: Bantam Books, 1983), and Charles F. Wilkinson, *American Indians, Time, and the Law* (New Haven: Yale University Press, 1987). The Indian viewpoint has been forcefully presented in Stan Steiner, *The New Indians* (New York: Harper and Row, 1968), and in Vine Deloria, Jr., *Behind the Trail of Broken Treaties: An Indian Declaration of Independence* (New York: Delacorte Press, 1974).

Index